THREE GENERATIONS OF BALLINGERS, 1914

EARTHBOUND

EARTHBOUND

———

RAYMOND EVANS BALLINGER
with
BABETTE BALLINGER

Frog Hill Press Edition, First Edition

Printed in the United States of America
ISBN-10: 0615749828
ISBN-13: 9780615749822

Frog Hill Press
2203 Parker Lane
Yorktown Heights, NY 10598

Book Design by Robin Hoffmann

www.Earthboundbook.com

To Thomas, Jason, Rebecca, Noah, and Gavin

For making it all worthwhile

MEMORY

———

To remember or be remembered is
always a thing past.
The memory is like a fine filament
of the past,
Burning itself out with a banishing
heat of the present.
And the future is like a blue-winged fly
buzzing itself around
That shimmering hot filament.
But it never lands
Until its time for present life has come.

–Raymond Evans Ballinger, 1964

TABLE *of* CONTENTS

———

INTRODUCTION

————

Babette Ballinger

My husband, Raymond Evans Ballinger, was a man of many contradictions. Raymond was born in Mount Holly, New Jersey in 1938, shortly before World War II broke out in Europe, and spent his early childhood on his family's farm. The Ballingers were truck farmers who supplied Campbell's Soup and farmed with teams of horses and migrant labor. They bought their first tractor in 1931 but continued to use horses to work the farm until well after the end of the war.

I believe that during each of our lives there is one event or one series of events that directly or indirectly shape the direction of our lives. For Raymond that event was when his mother, Clara, left her husband, Raymond (my late husband's father), and two young sons, ages seven and ten, and their nine-year-old sister and one-year-old asthmatic infant while pregnant with her fifth child. My husband, affectionately called Raymie to distinguish him from his father, was the baby of the older brood, the seven-year-old who never understood how his mother could have abandoned him, her favorite son.

His life became a journey of search and exploration while attempting to understand what there was about him that would allow his mother to leave him. It was complicated by his deep seated love of a childhood on the Homestead that was rich and harmonious. He had an obsessive need to understand why his mother could have hated that life so much that she decided to abandon it as well as her children.

Raymond's journey took him from the Homestead in New Jersey to New York City where he worked as a soap opera and stage actor, teacher, cabdriver, printer and more. He left the city to farm in upstate New York and built his own video studio. He also worked as a rehab counselor, bred horses, married, divorced, and fathered two sons before returning to New York City.

I met him in 1980. Our life together mirrored his earlier one. He worked as an actor and taught acting classes. We bought a small farm in Rhinebeck in upstate New York and raised horses and planted a disproportionately large garden. He worked in his darkroom, and built and ran a summer theatre, taught acting and directed. We had a daughter and we shared his sons.

With Raymond there was always an underlying current of unrest and a need for personal resolution. Ten years prior to his death in July of 2005, he began researching and writing *Earthbound*.

Laughingly, we called it the white man's *Roots* since he started with one of his earliest progenitors, Henry Ballinger, a Quaker, who sailed up the Delaware River to help establish a colony in Burlington County around 1678. Nine generations of Evans and Ballingers farmed the Indian Springs Homestead until development and subsequent taxation consumed farmland in western New Jersey. The original family Homestead was swallowed by suburbia. The green spot left is Indian Springs Country Club and Golf Course. Today the urban sprawl of Philadelphia and Camden, New Jersey is a short trip by car, but in the early 1900's it was a healthy distance from the Homestead by horse and wagon. The world of the Ballingers was centered in the town of Marlton where the Homestead was located and the small towns nearby - Haddon Heights, Barrington, Pine Grove, Medford, Mount Holly, and Mount Laurel, all within a ten- mile radius east of the Delaware River.

The tree of a family with its New Jersey roots dating back to the seventeenth century has a great many branches. This book is principally concerned with four generations of the Ballinger family—Raymie (the author, Raymond Evans Ballinger) his father, (Dad, Raymond Ballinger), Raymie's grandfather, (Pop) and Raymie's great grandfather, David T. The ramifications of the family tree are somewhat complicated by the complex web of relationships with the Evans (Evens) family through multi-generational intermarriage.

Earthbound is also the journey of a man trying to connect the child his mother left with the man he became. It is the story of a man living with the burden of feeling unsuccessful, unlovable and uncreative and his journey to validate the life his mother abandoned. I had heard these stories multiple times, but in editing this book, I was stunned by the commonality of the stories. *Earthbound* is the history of our American families throughout the twentieth century. It mirrors the changes in values and morality of this country. It is especially poignant as we struggle to understand where we have come from and where we are going. It mirrors our need to renew the qualities that have made America strong and to rebuild our nation and its families.

Babette Ballinger

PROLOGUE

———————

Raymie, Raymond Evans Ballinger

Raymond Ballinger, my father, was a very capable farmer. When he took over the family Homestead pressures from the outside world meant that he had to leave the Homestead in order to survive. With taxes steadily increasing, the Homestead had become too small for "modern" farming.

By 1951 New Jersey was no longer a predominantly agricultural state, and people no longer wanted to work on a farm. Dad sold the Homestead and moved to Milford Neck, Delaware. On the road to "success" Dad bought, fixed up and sold farms every few years, calling it growth, insight and creativity. The moves were triggered by personal discontent. When a son seemed deceiving or hurtful, he moved, hoping the move would just "fix it."

It was not so important to Dad where he came from or where he was going as the pleasure of the shared journey. When he could no longer share the journey with his sons, he quit. All of his decisions traumatically affected his children, yet they had no say in these matters.

His personal past and his unresolved relationships with his sons haunted him. He carried out his life with consistency. He raised nine of his ten children successfully, and owned his own land. He had decided when he was young, that all he wanted to have when he grew up was a herd of dairy cows and a pack of fox hounds. That's exactly what he ended up with.

While this is a personal history of my family, in it every reader can see pieces of his or her family and perhaps renew the strength of character that is within us all.

In 1984, when I began *Earthbound,* I was forty-six years old and I felt I was in my prime. That summer I had opened the Rhinebeck Summer Theatre with William Inge's *Picnic* taking actors from my classes in New York and fulfilling the enormous challenge of converting our farm's antiquated Dutch barns into a summer theatre. For the first time this integrated the feelings of paradise that I had had on the Homestead as a child with my passion for acting. The actors and my sons worked with me. It was one of the most fruitful years that I ever had.

I had remarried in 1982. Babette was the partner that I had always wanted. Now there was nothing to keep me from succeeding at anything I wanted to do, from my successful studio with acting classes in New York City to my own summer theatre in Rhinebeck. Both of my sons were living with me. Babette was pregnant with our child. I felt surrounded by a loving family for the first time in my life.

While producing and acting at my theatre in the play, *Equus* and as a method actor playing Dysart, the psychiatrist, I used pictures of my brother Larry and my Dad to recall emotional memory. Dysart's mid-life crisis started my reflection on my life. The sixth play, *The Dark at the Top of the Stairs* by William Inge, was the last of the season. Rueben Flood, the father and central figure in the play was a man who was lost in his past, and couldn't find a space for himself in the present or the future. As with Dysart, the people of his town rejected his old fashioned values.

As for me, the actor playing Dysart and Inge's Rueben, I was still searching for my place in this world. Just as I was closing the theatre for the winter, I received a phone call from Babette that we were going to lose our baby. Quickly driving back to the city, I attended to all the things that had to be done and then, without thinking, I packed my suitcase and told Babette that I was heading to Delaware to see my father and to begin my journey and my search for my roots. I had not seen Dad since 1975. It took me about five hours to drive. It seemed like one of the longest trips I had ever taken, for in my mind the wheels were turning so fast and the car was going so slow. I had to return to confront and rectify all of these things that I had been feeling.

Upon arrival, I parked the car near the carriage barn that my father had built. You could recognize his buildings anywhere. They were painted red and overbuilt, very straight and strong, and you knew they would last throughout his and my lifetime. My heart was pounding.

"Hey there, boy," he said. "Well, it's about time."

I left my bags in the car. Dad walked toward the kennel where he kept his fox hounds. Following him I noticed that he had really aged and he was no longer the agile Matt Dillon of "Gunsmoke". Nevertheless, he walked with the same confidence and easy, solid long strides of knowing exactly where he was going. He had been building a set of loading gates for his hounds. We talked for a moment about incidental, trivial things, as he hammered small staples into the chicken wire of the gate.

Dad, in his seventies, was also questioning the measurement and validity of his life. As we talked I saw that he was full of so much pain and anger about all his sons, but especially us first born, Larry, Leslie, and me. He felt that we had all done him an injustice and that he had failed to raise us properly.

During our conversations I took him back to his childhood and then, while he was telling me about his childhood, I told him about my childhood as though he was not my father and he hadn't been there.

Together we drove to the old Homestead in Evesham.

Earthbound is based on oral history compiled from interviews with multiple family members, primarily my father, Raymond Ballinger, my stepmother, Jean Shuster Ballinger, my Aunts, Ruth Ballinger Dickinson, Lois Ballinger Mikell, and Virginia Ballinger Davenport, and my brothers Larry Ballinger and Leslie Ballinger, and my sister, Sandra Wilkins.

Each person I talked with was remarkable to me. Each journey was made with strength, passion, romance, gentleness, and dreams, even if the end result was not always perfect.

If our family were still farming, would it have changed the world in any way? We would have remained *Earthbound*.

I let Dad talk.

-Raymond Evans Ballinger.

Dad, *RAYMOND EVANS BALLINGER Sr.* GENEOLOGY

1914	Birth	Born in Mount Holly, Burlington Co., New Jersey
1920	Age 6	Residence: Evesham Township, Marlton, Burlington Co., New Jersey
1930	Age 16	Residence: Evesham Township, Marlton, Burlington Co., New Jersey
1935	Age 21	Marriage to Clara Virginia Williams
1940	Age 26	Residence: Pine Grove, Burlington Co., New Jersey
1944	Age 30	Residence: Barrington, Camden Co., New Jersey
1946	Age 32	Divorce from Clara Virginia Williams
1946	Age 32	Marriage to Jean Shuster
1993	Age 79	Died in Georgetown, Sussex Co., Delaware

Dad's Grandparents
> David Thomas *(David T)* Ballinger 1851 – 1917
> Sarah Burroughs *(Sally B)* Evans (Evens) 1852 – 1938
> Nathan Stokes Evans 1859 – 1923
> Lottie M Ross 1871 – 1958

Dad's Parents
> Raymond Lippincott *(Pop/Grandpop)* Ballinger 1891 – 1952
> Alice Rebecca Evans *(Mom, Grandmom)* 1892 – 1959

Dad's Siblings
> Ruth Elizabeth Ballinger Dickinson 1918 – 2011
> Lois Anne Ballinger Mikell 1926 –
> Virginia *(Ginny)* Ballinger Moore Davenport 1931 –

Dad's First Wife & Children
> **Clara Virginia Williams 1915 – 1981**
> Lawrence *(Larry)* Ballinger 1935 –
> Judith Ann *(Sissy)* Ballinger 1936 –
> Raymond Evans Ballinger, Author, *(Raymie)* 1938 – 2005
> Leslie Allen Ballinger b. 1944
> Sandra Wilkins b. 1946

Dad's Second Wife & Children
> **Jean Shuster 1923 –**
> Marjorie Ellen Ballinger 1946 –
> Dale *(Skippy)* Stokes Ballinger 1949 –
> Nancy Lee Ballinger 1952 –
> Jean Elizabeth Ballinger 1956 –
> Richard Ashley Ballinger 1961 –

Some members of the family have spelled their last names Evens or Evens at different points in time. To avoid confusion, Evans is used throughout with the exception of Clayt Evens.

PART I

The Homestead: 1876-1930

SUNDAY DINNER AT THE HOMESTEAD, 1914

Dad's Story, Raymond Ballinger Sr.

THE STORM HIT HARD. The next day, after the funeral, David T. realized he couldn't make it home with the horse and buggy. His baby, Ethelind, was sick with dysentery, and he needed to get home. He left his horse and started walking nine miles through the worst part of the blizzard, across farmland and over four foot rail fencing. In some places the snow had drifted

as high as fifteen feet and he couldn't tell if the fences were even there. The wind was up to forty miles an hour.

I forget how many hours they said it took him, walking from Moorestown to the Homestead in Marlton. The storm lasted three and one-half more days leaving snow six to seven feet deep. They said this was the worst blizzard in memory. People died of exposure, pneumonia, and influenza and most of the telegraph lines fell.

Poor little baby Ethelind died during the snowstorm. Grandma couldn't get the doctor there in time. Uncle Herm was eleven years old and she died in his arms. He told me he dreamt about her for years.

In 1888, life for children was harsh. My grandfather, David T., had hitched up his buggy and headed to the funeral of his sister in Moorestown, nine

3

miles away. He left his wife, my Grandmother Sally B., at the Homestead with his boys because of the upcoming storm.

My grandfather, David T., like all the Ballinger men, was tall and broad-shouldered with a square face and pale copper tone curly hair and piercing blue eyes. Grandmother had the darker Welsh Evans' coloring with softer features.

When David T. and Sally B. married in 1876 they bought the original large brick William Evans house on the Homestead with some of the acreage that was part of the original Evans plantation from Sally's aunt and uncle, Thomas and Abigal Evans, uniting the Ballinger and Evans families under one roof.

David T. had owned twelve to fourteen head of cattle and would grow a patch of tomatoes with other patches of cantaloupes, watermelon, sweet corn and a few potatoes. He raised a lot of chickens and he sold pigs and vegetables. The pigpen was too close to the house and would smell in the hot summer, but our family liked pork, so no one complained. He fed his family from the farm.

My five uncles were all raised on the Evens-Ballinger Homestead and they worked the farm together. They were educated in a one room Quaker school house in Pine Grove not far from the Homestead, just a fifteen-minute walk through Cousin Clayt Evens' fields. My oldest uncle, Herm, was born in 1877 and the youngest, my father Raymond, was born in 1892. In between were Harry, Dave, Anna, and Evans.

During the haying season of 1895, Granddad, his sons, and his father in law, Samuel Burroughs Evens, mowed, raked, cured, and hauled some fine timothy and clover. Dave, having just learned how to read was quoting the Farmer's Almanac predicting "destructive thunderstorms throughout the Northeast." My father, the first Raymond, was four years old.

Sally had cooked her usual big breakfast for the seven men. The horses were restless. The wind was coming up and everything was dry. David T. had promised to take Sally into town to buy a new dress for daughter, Anna. They reached the end of the lane when a large crack of thunder bolted through the sky, followed by two streaks of lightning. Within seconds, all three barns were burning and quickly went up in flames.

Afterwards, Granddad decided to get the finest hemlock he could buy and build one large barn to replace the three small ones. Through the help of barn raising neighbors, this was completed in less than a month. The problem was that it set David T. back financially to where it almost broke him. His grand new barn was admired throughout Burlington County. It stood about fifty feet high and sixty feet wide, and one hundred twenty feet long, and provided enough space for at least eighteen to twenty cow stanchions, two birthing box stalls, and a bullpen. At the east end was a twelve-stall barn for horses. Next to the big barn was a wagon barn connected to a long machinery shed with corncribs on each end. This is the barn that I grew up with.

Uncle Herm stayed and worked the farm. He was dependable and easy going and never got rattled. He wasn't hot-headed like my father and Harry. When Herm left the Homestead he became a herdsman for the Ephraim Gill Dairy and worked his way up to manager. Ephraim Gill's farm was right in the middle of Haddonfield until it was sold for development. Herm lived in back of the school in Haddonfield and eventually ran the Haddonfield waterworks.

Harry was born in 1879 and went into the candy business. Harry was clever and shrewd and could socialize with anyone. He started out going house to house with his horse and wagon. What he was really selling was stories, not candy. Children came to him to listen to his tales about the early Ballingers, the Lenape Indians, and the other local families who settled here. Harry had a big garage right up there in back of his house on Church Street in Moorestown, which he turned into a warehouse.

All of the kids loved his special peanut brittle. Harry would always bring it to the Homestead and give it to us kids in a can, with wax paper in the middle, and we would eat until one of us got sick - it was so sweet. He whole-saled and distributed candy from Shrafft's, Hershey's and Taffy. Dave also helped by driving his two Dodge candy trucks.

Dave became a secretary and bookkeeper to the president of DeCou Ironworks in Philadelphia. He was a quiet mild mannered man who never got upset about too much of anything. He kind of just rolled with the punches and never had a cross word to say. After the Ironworks folded during the depression, Dave drove a milk wagon. He loved to listen and a lot of the women on the routes would like to talk. We kids would often go with him but we could never get him to move fast enough to get home early.

Evens was a tall and strong man and his grip was powerful. He could kill a rat with one hand or lift a three-quarter ton beam to his chest. Evens married Anna Kirby of Kirby Brothers Feed Mill in Medford and worked at the feed mill for six years. They lived in the big brick house that belonged to the mill. Evens and his brother-in-law bought another grist mill that eventually failed when the mills became obsolete.

Instead of buying feed locally, you could buy cheaper from co-operatives like the GLF (Grange League Federation) and the Eastern States Farmers Exchange which shipped in feed from out west already ground up and put in feed bags. There were only a few small stores that would buy and sell feed from Evens and Kirby Mill, but soon grain stopped coming in from local farms. From 1920 to 1941 Evans worked at the Kirby mill and part-time in his brother's candy business until he became a policeman and then the police chief of Medford for nine years. Uncle Evens would take his grandkids out of a scary movie in his police car until the movie was over, and then he'd take them trout fishing.

He was an amazing man to us, and very interesting. Despite his size, he was a gentle, caring man. He was also very stern, determined to do his job and do it well. His sons thought he was a hard man, but Uncle Evens had a softer side and used to bake pies. He would fall asleep in church holding his Bible. He passed away when he had a heart attack carrying a basket of tomatoes from the garden to the garage.

Their sister, Anna, never married and lived on the other side of the Homestead until her Mother's death at the age of eighty-six.

Pop, the first of the Raymonds in the family, was the youngest son. He was just under six feet and the shortest of the boys with fine features and the best looking. He also had fair copper hair and blue eyes, just like my son, Raymie.

The last family member was Jake, George Naylor, who was a "taken" child. His family couldn't support him and the Ballinger family "took" him in. Often children who were abandoned were either sent to farms, or put onto orphan trains that went across the country. People took children off of them to work on their farms or to care for their children.

Pop hadn't quite turned 18 when he left home. That last summer he helped his father, David T., bring in the vegetable crops before he left in September after graduating from high school. He took a train into Camden and he got a job working for Barber and Perkins wholesale grocers. In a year he had worked his way up to becoming a buyer. Of course he knew vegetables from working at the Homestead all those years. At nights he took a business course in management. Pop was a lot better in school than I was. He was educated in that one room Quaker school house right there in Pine Grove. Later on he went to school in Moorestown, some nine miles away. He walked from the farm to the train station at Hog Pond Road where we dropped off the milk.

The Marlton School, built in the 1870's, was three miles away but that was a little bit out of his reach. The Quaker school was right there off the Marlton Pike, a fifteen minutes walk. Both schools only went to the eighth grade.

My father met his future wife, my mother Alice Evans, at a social one night in Camden at a Quaker Fellowship. Soon they were getting pretty serious. In 1913 his father, David T. went to see him in Philadelphia and persuaded him to quit Barber and Perkins. It was the beginning of the planting season. Grandfather David T. knew his health was deteriorating. He wasn't doing any of the physical work at the time, but he was getting weaker. He was almost sixty-two.

Grandfather was barely able to explain to Herm what to do and how to do it and he panicked. Uncle Herm, the eldest son, had always depended upon his father to make all his decisions. David T. realized that when he died if Herm still ran the farm, they would lose it. Though my Pop was the youngest son, he was an ambitious man and a go-getter like his father. Things had to be done just right by him, and of course the other brothers were no longer living at home. My mother Alice was the type of woman who would make the Homestead work, unlike the other sons' wives.

POP WASN'T ABLE TO MOVE to the Homestead until June and during that time he asked Mom to marry him. He drove over to Fellowship that Friday after work with his horse, a Standardbred named Gamwood, hooked to the courting carriage. Alice knew something was up. Pop explained to Alice that he didn't have much time but that she was the woman he wanted

to marry. Three days later Pop and his Alice came drivin' into the Homestead with his Standardbred hooked to one of the Barber and Perkins market wagons containing everything that they owned. Pop was nineteen years old when he left the farm, and twenty-two years old when he returned. I came along in 1914 - the second Raymond in the Ballinger family.

Herm realized that it wasn't him but his younger brother, Raymond, who would take over the farm. He was okay with it but his wife Mary wasn't. She was a bitch. Pop farmed for twelve years on shares and gave his mother half of the profits.

When Granddad decided to sell the farm to my father, all the children came to the house to meet and sign the deed. They waited for Mary. Uncle Herm didn't have the gumption enough to get up and say she wouldn't come.

Uncle Harry was quick and asked, "Herm, when's Mary coming?"

"To be truthful, she said she wouldn't come."

She had come to Moorestown from Haddonfield, but she wouldn't come to the meeting. She was holed up at her brother's place.

So by God, Harry went right to her brother's house and he told her, "Now, you're going to come."

Mary Ellis refused to sign away what she thought belonged to her children.

"Well" Herm told her, "What makes you think your children are any better than any of our children? Mary, if you don't sign it, none of our children will be getting anything out of it. We want to keep it in the family, and we want Raymond to have it. There's nothing to be left." Reluctantly she signed. Nobody could get along with her.

Pop made a home in half of the house for Grandma, Granddad, and Aunt Anna. All the sons and their wives came to visit on Friday and Saturday evenings. They ate and partied and hunted there. Pop and Mom entertained and when Granddad died all the sons gave Sally B. and Aunt Anna ten dollars apiece every month. That was enough for the two of them to live on and have a little spending money. There was no social security in those days.

During Mom and Pop's second year they added a complete kitchen attached to the west end of the large house.

Granddad David T. used to take me everywhere he went. I rode with him on the buckboard. Granddad loved to hook up to the no-top delivery wagon with me on his knee. We'd take the milk over to the Elmwood Road railroad station and then we'd go and herd the cows down the back lane.

The first horse I had was the Standardbred, the one that Pop courted Mom with, Gamwood. The gelding had been in an accident. The man who owned him, Mr. Wilson, had raced him all over the country. Gamwood was right in his prime. Wilson had told Granddad he was the fastest harness horse he had ever owned, especially on the take off. They had had an accident when they were racing him out at the old track in Philadelphia. Gamwood was pulling ahead from the inside and another horse came up on him and threw him against the fence and run a splinter up from the fence into his fetlock and it crippled him. They didn't think he'd ever be able to race again. They had to drag him off the track.

Josiah, David T.'s youngest brother, was at the track that day and was friends with the vet and the owner. The vet had decided that since Gamwood was a gelding it would be best if they put him down, but the owner resisted. Josiah suggested calling his brother, David T, and said that if anyone could heal him he could.

That afternoon, they hoisted Gamwood into a freight car. Josiah rode with him to the Evesham stop off the Marlton Pike. My grandfather and Pop met them. Granddad was reluctant to take on such a fine horse, but the owner convinced him to. Granddad agreed to take him with no guarantees, and said that he assumed that they wouldn't want the horse back.

Now Granddad was awfully good with horses, he just had a very special way with them which I guess I inherited, and so did Raymie. Granddad devised a beech wood splint which he put screws in so that it could be loosened or tightened. He made a high boot out of sheepskin that he mounted over the top. Sally B. mixed liniment for Gamwood. Gamwood was kept in close quarters for about six to eight weeks.

Pop groomed and cared for him and applied the liniment regularly. His father told him that if the horse could make it he would be his. A race horse is a powerful incentive for a twelve year old boy and that's the way the story went. It wasn't long before Pop was riding him and driving him with the buckboard. Gamwood was the only horse he used for the courting carriage. Occasionally Harry and Pop would take him down to the Tabernacle Quaker meeting.

Now Harry's horse was also a Standardbred, but he couldn't move like Gamwood. Gamwood just couldn't stand a horse in front of him, and one Sunday, when they were heading down past the Methodist church in Pine Grove, Harry pulled out alongside of Gamwood and yelled over to pop.

"Is that all your horse can do?"

Pop let up a little bit on the lines. My God! That horse took that carriage right off the ground. By the time pop got to the meetinghouse, he had left Harry in the dust.

Before my father got his car he used to go grocery shopping with Gamwood hooked to that little buckboard. When I started riding him he was already twenty-five years old. He was a bay color, with a little white spot right on his forehead, and he had that white spot on his back leg where that sharp piece of wood had gone through. I rode him for herding cows, chasing chickens, and riding with my buddies, Herb Schimmel and the Foster boys. They all had horses, and they tried their damndest to beat Gamwood. Old man Schimmel would go to Philadelphia, to the bazaar, just to buy a horse for his boy to try and beat me, but he never did it to this day.

When I started rodeoing, I used to calf rope with him. He was like a lot of these quarter horses. He might pretty near jump and snap your neck if you weren't watching him. He was the fastest horse I've ever seen. Now you've got to realize he was already thirty-five years old by then, and by God !, when that calf came out of the gate, you'd better be ready. Gamwood lived to be forty-one years old. That's almost a record for a horse's life.

The railroad was built in Marlton around 1871. In 1931 they tore the tracks out and used the railroad bed to build Route 70. By then there was another big station out on Hog Pond Road with a platform. A special milk train stopped there.

We'd hitch up to the no-top and load the cans from the milk house. Granddad, in Quaker fashion, would give a yell, "Buddy, if thee wants to go with me, thee'd better climb aboard."

The next day the train dropped off the empty milk cans. They had to be picked up through all seasons, whether it rained or snowed. Granddad did this up until the day before he died. The milk was taken on the train to Supplee Wills and Jones dairy in Camden and also to Philadelphia.

Businesses did all their deliveries with horses. They would sharpen the shoes on one side in the winter time, so the horses wouldn't slip on the icy streets. Often, some of the horses would get sore from being on the streets too long, so a farmer could go over there to Camden and buy a nice team of horses for a pretty good price. You'd take them home, yank those shoes off, and they'd straighten right out, so you'd have a real nice team of horses.

We were coming back in the buckboard from taking milk to the station. We hadn't quite got to the old Marlton Pike when Teddy stopped, balked, and wouldn't go any further. Granddad got the whip out, and laid it on him a little bit, but he still wouldn't move. He just shook his head. The next

11

thing you knew, we heard something coming. It was a car, coming down the Marlton Pike. Poor old Teddy knew that car was coming. He wouldn't move. The minute that car was gone he went right on as though nothing had happened. He was a balky son of a gun, but a great big horse. Seemed like Pop used to beat that horse unmercifully.

Granddad was a proud man. Everybody said they could tell David T. Ballinger's teams from the way they went down the road. They were high stepping. He had matched horses, and shiny harness rings and tassels on them. Everything had to be matched perfectly.

The graders that scraped the gravel roads throughout Evesham Township were pulled by teams of horses. Joe and Orville Evens were on the Township Committee and decided to employ their own teams. People got tired of the outrageous fees they were charging so they persuaded Pop to run for mayor of Evesham. They knew Pop's character and what he had succeeded in doing on the Homestead. He had paid off all the debt his father had incurred putting up the new barn after the fire. That man could work and everybody knew it.

The first election Pop ran against Orville Evens. I think pop got between a thousand to thirteen hundred votes. Orville didn't even get a hundred. Pop had taken the job only on the condition that he would get the town out of debt, but he wasn't going to make a political career out of it. The first year he had his teams on the scrapers he didn't do any farming at all.

He remained in office three terms, two years each. After the first election, the Township Committee agreed to buy a new mechanized road grader and do away with keeping those bums on the payroll to scrape the roads with teams. Some folks disagreed with spending all that money but Pop told them to pipe down. That grader would be paid for in a year and a half. After that, it would cost less than one third of Joe and Orville's excessive expenses.

The second time he ran against Joe Evens he won that election by a landslide.

Pop was pretty straight with things, no monkey business. Pop would have voted for anybody before he'd vote for a Republican. His mother's first cousin, Clayt Evens, was a stiff Republican. Clayt would come over and he and Pop would get right into it. Clayt always subscribed to the *Philadelphia*

Enquirer, a Republican paper. Pop took the *Philadelphia Record*, a Democratic paper. Folks took politics seriously back then. They felt their votes counted. I remember going to a Democratic political rally once, right there in Marlton. The politicians stood up on a wagon with torches and spoke. No lights, no electricity, just torches and talking straight to the people. I was just a little kid and I stood there proudly with Pop.

Old Jake, who was pretty much family, lived on the farm his whole life. He worked for three generations of Ballingers, for Granddad and my Dad and me before he finally left and retired. He had to quit. He was getting unsafe to have around machinery.

There was also another guy, Mike Donnegan. He worked for Pop for a while after I got married. He had a big handle bar mustache and big blue eyes. Mike was rummy but a sweet man who made dolls carved from wooden spools for my sister Ginny. He'd dress them up in burlap and paint little faces on them. Pop had had three or four other workers from town.

We had Italians from Pine Grove. Down by the big bridge there was quite a settlement of them. Pop also had some Spaniards from over to Crow Foot. After I went to work in the shipyard the last immigrants I remember were all Mexicans. A lot of them worked in the cannery, at Fredericksburg, Maryland.

I learned most of my farming at home, doing it myself. It just came natural to me. Mom used to say, every time I put my hand to the ground it grew. Pop would never explain anything. He was always too busy to take the time to tell me how to do this or that or the other thing. I learned a lot more from old Jake than I did from my dad. But, I think it was just born in me, and I was a great one to read. I got my education from reading.

I quit high school in the tenth grade. Pop's health was bad then. He had had double pneumonia and almost died. I told him and Mom "I'd do more good here. I'm not learning a thing in high school. You need me here."

I knew what I wanted from the time I was four years old and I never swayed.

I never got paid a nickel. What I made selling my pigeons was where I got my money, and from that I bought my first car and my clothes. From the time I was nine years old, pop never spent a nickel on me. It made me a better man, I think.

I did mind it at the time. I thought he was hard. Other kids belonged to the YMCA, and they could go to ball games and movies. I never got to see a movie till I was eighteen. By then I had my own car and went myself. The only entertainment we had was when we went to Sunday school picnics in Pine Grove once a year. That was the only outing from the time school stopped till it started. Otherwise, I went to the field and the barn and that was it.

My mother went to Sunday school when she was young, but after she got married none of them went. Grandmother Sally B. was more religious than any of them, and so was Uncle Evens. He went to Quaker Meetings. Sally B. was a good woman. David T. was too, straight as a string. Whenever he told you something, it had to be done a certain way at a certain time. He was big enough to see that it was done.

When he fixed the house for Pop and Mom to come back and live, they dug a cistern under the back kitchen. Before that you had to use the hand pump to get water for washing clothes. The cistern collected soft rain water off the roof. David T. went after some parts and lumber and when he left he told the worker how he wanted the cistern done. When he come back it wasn't done that way, David T. picked the man right up by the coat, and right in his face, he said,

"If you want to work here another minute, get your tail in there and do that like I told you I want it done." Pity you can't do that anymore.

I didn't have a team of my own horses until I was around twelve and then I kept them until I was twenty.

We had no electricity, and no well or hand pump in the house. I had to carry water from the milk house in the barn. That was my job from the time I could walk. Pop had aluminum buckets, one of the first aluminum buckets I'd ever seen. Every meal and in between, I was the keeper of the water from that well in the milk house. There was an old hand pump in the milk house at Marlton. That pump was still there when we moved out.

Not too long after Pop bought the Homestead, we put in an artesian well for the house. Digging that trench across that yard for the pipe was almost impossible. After two hundred years the ground was just as hard as cement. Pop decided to hook a team to the plow to open it up. The plow wouldn't even make a mark on that hard gravel, so I wound up digging the whole thing by hand, at fourteen years old. We didn't have electricity until 1928. We used kerosene lamps and lanterns in the barn and kerosene lamps in the house and heated with wood stoves.

In those days, up to around 1925, everybody had wood lots. If folks didn't have them on the farm, they'd go up into the woods. People would have sales and they'd lay off wood lots and survey them off. Someone might own a thousand acres of timber, way up in the woods, red oak, mostly, and white oak and people would go up there and buy these wood lots. They weren't buying the land, just the wood off of them. Then, in the winter time when the work was a little slack, Jake and I would take the team of horses and a bolster wagon - four wheels with a bolster and a pit over each axle with little stubs with rings on them, and we would go up to the wood lots and cut and chop all day. We'd take blankets to cover the horses. Some of the logs would be so huge the two of us couldn't lift them. Later, we'd have somebody come in who had a table saw mounted on an old Model A or Model T. chassis, and could run the saw with an engine out of that old car. Those wood cutters would go around house to house and when they'd arrive the neighbors would come around and we'd go to sawing wood. We'd pile it up as high as the house.

We never would cut until winter. We used last winter's wood so we always had dry wood to cook with and corn cobs to start a fire. There was a wood box with a lid on it in the kitchen. My job was keeping that wood box filled. Every night I had to get the corn cobs and pack them in there, so I'd have enough for the morning. Then I would carry them in with the split wood.

Pop had a puppy somebody gave him, and they told him it was a collie. 'Course, he took it, and it grew up to be a German shepherd and collie mix, a mongrel. I called him Dandy, because he was always grooming himself. The son of a gun stood about two and a half feet high, a great big dog, and he weighed about seventy-five pounds.

I got into Pop's old harness cabinet and took a breeching from it... that's the part that goes around the horse's back legs to hook to the shafts so they can back up. I made a piece to go over Dandy's back and I rigged up a harness and put it on that dog and broke him to pull my express wagon. I'd load that up with wood, and that son of a gun pulled it right to the back door.

Course, Dandy was a big strong dog anyhow, part husky. I spent more time fooling with that dog than I would have filling the wood box.

SALLY B. HAD THE SAME STOVE she started her married life with in 1876. She was married for forty-seven years, and a widow for twenty-one and she was still cooking on the same stove, sixty-five years later.

Mom used to make soap. She had a large boiling vat that she kept in the cellar for storage. She'd keep all the chips from the used soap, and she would take cans of tallow fat, and melt it down and dump those chips right in. She would bring the vat up into the kitchen. For the bathing soap she wouldn't use the lye ash. Instead, she would use some lemon balm, verbena, or sweet smelling oils, and she'd let that boil. To get the potash she used a barrel at the end of the small back porch where the rose arbor grew and the wrens used to nest. She would let the rain water drip through the barrel of white ash to a crock at the bottom with a slate over the top and a little valve coming out into the crock. It looked like a tap from a maple sugar tree, and the rain water sifted through the ash and came out the bottom through that tap and into the crock. That was what she put into the soap barrel. She used about six or seven pounds of tallow or cans of lard from the cellar, and some kind of rosin that she used from a red can and she'd add about four or five gallons of water, counting the potash water.

She'd boil that for about five or six hours, stirring it off and on with a big wooden paddle, the same one that Granddad smacked the back of my chair with the one time I didn't eat my breakfast.

After all of the ingredients boiled she would pour it into flat trays, about as deep as a piece of soap. Then she let it sit over night, and the next morning we would cut it into bar sizes. It was still somewhat soft and then she had this hard wooden seal with a bird carved in it which we would press into the soap. That was the part that I liked to do.

After it dried she'd break pieces from the roll of meat packing paper and wrap each bar individually. For the body soap she also used salt and sometimes a bit of dye, just to make various colors, separating out the work soap, dish soap, and the body soap. The oils that she put in it varied. I don't know whether she got them from the fields, or from a store, but it all varied depending on what the soap was used for.

I used to like going down with Granddad to the smoke house where he kept the pickle barrels. I liked to watch him inject the hams with a big metal syringe full of spiced and flavored brine, and then he would put them into these barrels and let them pickle and soak for a period of time. Then he'd hang them until they dried out and put them up in the attic. It wasn't just ham. I know he did it with lamb and probably with beef. It sure was good! There was nothing like it.

Pop liked a lot of pork; that's why he kept all those pigs.

Grandmom used to pit grapes to make raisins. She'd sit there on the larger back porch where the wisteria was, and she and I would eat more than we'd pit. While she was pitting she would ask me all kinds of questions and tell me things that she thought were important. They were nice moments. She would say to me, "I want to be proud of my Raymonds."

I was probably about sixteen or seventeen when Pop got that first tractor, in 1931. We still used the team of horses, but then we did most of the plowing and disking with the John Deere to save the horses.

I was very sick when I was four. Grandmother Sally B. got the blame for it. She and Aunt Anna always baked bread for the week as well as pies and cakes every Saturday in that old wood stove. They had a long dough tray that was bigger than a dining table. Grandmom made a lot of apple sauce cake in a flat pan with white icing and raisins. Anybody who came over had to have a piece of pie or cake. Cousin Clayt would come over two or three times a week just to have some.

There was a little porch on the side of the house, and I played out there. Every time I'd come around Grandmom would come to the door and ask "Buddy?" she called me Buddy, "Does he want a piece of cake?"

I ate some cake that had been sitting around and it got moldy and poisoned me. My temperature was near one hundred and five and there was a blizzard on at the time. Uncle Harry and Aunt Ida come over and he took one look at me and said, "My God, Raym! You've got to have a doctor to that boy. He's going to die."

They only had one doctor, Doc Brick, in Marlton. Pop called him and he said he couldn't come. He was so busy, he couldn't get away.

"By God, I'll get him." That was Uncle Harry for you. He took off, and he got that doctor out here. If it hadn't been for Harry, I guess I'd have died.

I was too small to handle the ice taken from the pond, but I was right there watching when they filled the ice house, with those thick walls. We had our team of horses, and took an old shoveling hay wagon. They used ice saws, a big saw with a grip on one end, and a piece that stuck up like the old two man saws. The men pulled out large square blocks of ice weighing sixty to seventy pounds with the ice tongs and slid them across the ice to the bank where they loaded them in the wagons. Neighbors would all come around and work together in those days. There'd be five or six teams. You would start cutting a hole out in the middle of the pond and cut toward the shore. The ice would be thick. Damn right you had to be careful, 'cause pulling that ice out of that water, it was as slippery as glass. The ice would sometimes float. The men grabbed it with the tongs and pulled the large blocks out on top of the ice. A lot of the men wore spiked shoes.

You could take one of those blocks of ice and sling it, and of course, men were men in those days, and they could shoot it clear across the ice to the shore. There'd be a couple of men there to grab it and throw it up in the wagon, and other men on the wagons loaded it. It took a dozen men. You couldn't just go out with horses and a sled. You'd wind up in the millpond. There'd be at least four wagons. It wasn't far, two miles, probably, but that was a good little jaunt with a team of horses in the freezing cold.

The men would then pack the ice house with a layer of ice and a layer of sawdust, then another layer of ice and layer of sawdust. They had as much sawdust as ice. The ice would be about eight to ten inches thick with five or six inches of sawdust in between. In the summer, we'd have enough ice to last for the milk house and the main house. We'd dig around in the sawdust with our ice picks and cut one of them in half or quarters, and then pull it out, and cover the ice back up right away. We'd dig in there and get a piece out, and then keep coming down with the boards till we worked our way in. Eventually you had to crawl up and get a chunk out. Nothing else but that sawdust was ever put on. Of course the walls of the icehouse were solid, no windows or nothing. It's unbelievable how the ice would keep in sawdust all through the summer.

Every winter in Marlton we'd go ice skating. The ice on the pond would be ten inches thick. You'd build yourself a big bonfire out on a little island, or on the bank where you'd come in and get warm, and then you'd take the girls out ice skating and swing them around.

Grandpop Evans, my mother's father, who lived down in Woodstown, had a nice herd of cows. He gave me a heifer calf when I was just four years old. She was white with little speckles on her ears and on her neck, out of one of his good cows. Pop went down there and got it for me.

I raised that heifer, and when she had a calf for the first time Pop said, "Well, she's your cow, but I've raised her." I took care of her, but he had furnished the feed.

Before that I'd been milking at night, sitting on a little peach basket, with an eight quart bucket, but he didn't make me milk in the morning, not when I was that young. I didn't even come up to a cow's udder, even sitting on a basket.

"When she calves, you take care of her. You're to milk her. I'm going to feed her and I'll keep the milk. You can have the money you get for her calf."

I got a calf once a year and sold it for around six dollars. Pop got all the milk. That's when I started milking, I was between six and seven years old, and I milked morning and night for the rest of my life. Every day, I got up, milked, fed and watered my pigeons, ate my breakfast, changed my clothes, and walked a mile to the bus. The school bus would be out there at 7:00.

That was my life.

Just before my fourth birthday, on December 21, 1917, Granddad David T. passed away. My sister Ruth had just been born.

MY MOM, ALICE ROSS EVANS grew up in Moorestown, off Fellowship Road where her father, Nathan Stokes Evans had his farm. She was the oldest girl in her family born in 1893. Aunt Charlotte, the youngest, was born in 1898. They moved to Woodstown before I was born, after Mom and Pop got married.

Pop used to take the *American Agriculturist* and the *Pennsylvania Farmer* magazines. When I found pictures of nice cows, I'd cut 'em out and paste 'em on cardboard, and make cows out of them. I used to have a little ten-cent Mack dump truck. I would go outside and play under the roots of that big elm tree in the driveway circle. I'd have my dairy farm all laid out with roads, fencing, barns…. everything. Then I'd add all my cows that I cut out and pasted on cardboard.

I'd play in the kitchen with corn cobs that we used to keep in the wood box to start fires and make them into cows. Grandmother Lottie, my mother's mother, would stand there cooking by the stove and she'd ask me,

"What's he doin', sonny?"

I'd reply, "Grandmom, I'm puttin' my cows in, getting ready to milk."

She kind of thought a minute, and said, "What's he want to do when he grows up?"

I'd answer, "I want a herd of Holstein cows and a pack of long-eared fox hounds."

I don't think I'd ever heard the word fox hound in my life. I was only about three or four years old then.

Grandmother Lottie had come to take care of Mom and cook for Pop when Ruth was born. I believe she was also their midwife. That's the way they used to do it then. Grandmother Lottie's maiden name was Ross.

When I was a young boy I took the *National Sportsman*. It was a little hunting magazine out of Connecticut that I used to order with my pigeon money or my trappin' money that cost twenty-five cents a year. I loved to read fox hunting stories and that's what got me started. When most children grow up they don't know what they want to do. I knew exactly what I wanted to do from the time I was born, fox hunt and dairy.

Nathan, her father, was a big powerful man with black hair and a dark complexion and a big mustache. I don't know how he met his wife, Lottie. In those days with horses and carriages Moorestown was far away. There were three girls, my mother Alice, and her sisters Ruth and Charlotte who were said to be the prettiest Quaker girls around. Their brother Horace never left home. Being the only boy, he took over the farm after his father died. Horace and his father kept mules. Their tails were clipped. They had these fancy harnesses and equipment for them. Horace liked to fox hunt. He married Aunt Bessie from Moorestown and her brothers used to fox hunt on their farm.

Most farmers could not afford a large threshing machine, so when it came time to thrash their wheat, they'd hire a man who owned a threshing machine. That was his business. You would arrange for him to come when it was time to harvest and he would go around from farm to farm. Now when he drove this machine onto your property, it was a real exciting thing for kids. He needed two or three teams of horses to pull that big machine.

We'd greet him and follow him into the driveway, through the gate of the farm. Once he got it into the compound he'd unhook the teams and stabilize the thrasher by jacking it up and blocking the wheels. On the back of the thrasher was a great big diesel engine which would give power to the thrasher with two pulleys and a large belt. Later on, when they had trucks, they would mount the belt to the rim of the back wheel.

Once everything was set up we had to bring down the shocks of wheat, barley, oats, or whatever we were threshing from the hay barn, untie them, and feed them into this big machine. This would separate the seed from the bellows and the straw stalks. The seeds would shuffle into burlap bags and the shafts, or straw if you like, were blown into a pile where the cattle bedded around it and fed off it the whole winter.

Great Granddad Ross had an old drivin' horse with some age to her. I think it was a mare, just turned out with the cows. One day after the harvest she was just standing there eatin' some straw off the stack and Great Granddad Ross was walking around and looking stern. He slapped the mare on the rump, and by God! She jumped up and kicked him with both feet. One caught him on the head and face, and the other one nailed him right in the chest, and I'll be damned if it didn't kill him. He died the next day. He was around fifty at the time. I was about eight.

Grandfather Stokes-Evans died of an appendix operation in 1931 at the age of sixty. He had had gotten pretty fat in his old age. They had one Jersey cow and brought her fresh milk into the house and he'd drink glasses of rich milk, six percent, and he got fat. By the time they got him to the Hahnemann Hospital in Philadelphia, the appendix had burst open. They operated on him, but peritonitis had set in and killed him.

Grandfather Evans had a beautiful herd of Holsteins. That's where I got all my dairying ideas from. We would visit them two to three times a year. It was thirty-two miles away from Marlton to Woodstown! We'd usually visit at Christmas time and I'd never want to come home! I loved going out in that barn, smelling the silage, seeing those cows all standing there with straw underneath them, all combed out, their bags and their tails clipped. Then I had to come home and look at Pop's cows!

When Grandfather Nathan Stokes died and Horace took over, his mother Lottie lived with them. Uncle Horace died of a heart attack when he was forty. He ran after the cows before eating a lot of ice cream. The cows had gotten out and he ran down after them. I guess he got over-heated, sweatin', and pantin' and what-not. He came up, sat down and ate a whole mess of cold fresh ice cream. It gave him a heart attack and in two weeks he was dead. He left a wife and four little children.

The youngest sister, Charlotte, never married until she was about forty. Married a bum. He was no damn good at all. Charlotte waited all those years for a good husband and could've had most anybody. It made no sense.

Lord sakes, we were the last ones to get rid of horses on the farm. Everyone else was using trucks, and Pop, he wouldn't go to a truck. He wouldn't buy a truck. Tight. Yes, sir.

Most of the time we had eight teams of horses. Of course Pop didn't do any of the work in the field. Old Jake and I did. I had a team and Jake had a team. I was planting corn when I was twelve years old. Pop never planted. He'd lived on a farm all his life and never planted a hill of corn with a corn planter. Old Jake was always there to do that kind of stuff.

Pop helped set the plants out. He'd grow the plants in the garden and help with milking and with the chickens, but he never really did the work. Pop picked tomatoes and helped cut cabbage and sweet corn, but the planting, I never knew him to do it.

You have to know this about Pop, to understand how he wound up with his health like it was. He worked himself right to death. When he agreed to give Grandma and Aunt Anna the proceeds of the first fifty acres and to save enough money to buy the other half from his father and still support his family from that half, he worked himself right into the ground, and everybody around him. He worked me hard. It used to make my Mom so mad.

From the time I was twelve years old, I worked right in the field, and hauled manure and hay with a man opposite me. I guess I'm lucky that I got out without being any the worse than what I am. I was six years old when I started milking. Bare footed! Damned cow stepped on my big toe one night, and I cussed him. Pop give me the devil. He wasn't worried about my toe! I mashed it. The nail turned all purple and black.

Pop caught me before I got over the fence. He said, "I better not hear any more of that cussing. You'll get your mouth washed out with soap."

He'd a done it, too. Pop would take a lot, but when he did cut loose, he didn't have any sense. My Dad was like myself. I always felt he loved me, but he didn't show it much. I always loved my children. I wasn't the kind to show it much. The older I get, I think the worse I got. I knew I loved my kids. I thought they all realized it.

Pop was about thirty-five and I was around twelve when his severe asthma was setting in. Pop went to the University of Pennsylvania hospital in New Bolton every week, once a week, for years. They would take all kinds of blood samples trying to find out what was giving him asthma. They never did find out.

His bone deterioration came at the same time. The vertebrae in his back turned solid and fused together. His backbone was one solid piece. He couldn't bend his back at all, and had to bend from the hips. He couldn't even turn his head. If anybody had cracked him under his chin it would have broken his entire back or his neck. Pop suffered tremendously. He used to wear a corset and brace that came up under his arms and was padded steel which came around the front. He would button himself up tight and go out and pick tomatoes all day on his knees. Pop had a lot of guts.

He couldn't sleep at nights with the asthma, so he would sit and burn powder in a little pan. I see people nowadays and I wonder could they have to put up with what he had to put up with? Today they'd be on disability and welfare and have insurance and everything else. In those days you never even thought about something like that. There wasn't anything. Pop worked that way for years. When I was twelve years old and big enough I worked alongside the men loading manure and loading hay, and everything else.

I didn't think it at the time but it was a little too much. Of course I felt big by doing it. Mom used to tell him "You're going to break the boy down before he grows up."

WHEN WORLD WAR I BROKE OUT I was only four years old. I remember sitting there on the front porch and seeing the caravans of horses and covered wagons loaded with guns going along the Marlton Pike. Sometimes they'd run for about two or three hours, one right behind the other. They had big guns, mounted on caissons pulled by horses with two teams hooked to them. The cavalry played a big part in the beginning of World War I. It was still a time of horses.

There were some cars and some trucks, but automobiles didn't boom until after the war was over.

Prohibition came after World War I. That's when the gangsters took over. There was Al Capone, and Pretty Boy Floyd and all those guys. Prohibition was where they made their millions, in bootleg whiskey in Chicago. Old man Joe Kennedy was a bootlegger. He had a franchise on a great deal of the Scotch whisky that came into this country. They had a port here in Prime Hook Neck off the Delaware. Their motor launches came in at night from ships anchored out to sea, and these launches brought the liquor in. There was a place to unload their trucks back in the marsh and they backed the trucks right in there, by Mr. Roche's place. They'd be up and loaded and gone before daylight.

Mr. Roche could see them working at night. We used to fox hunt together and he told me just where it was, that old man Kennedy's operation. One night they had a little bigger load on a truck and broke through a country bridge. The boys had to get help and get that truck out and unload it... The whole back end broke through the bridge. Somehow they got it out and replaced the planks on the bridge. By daylight the next morning they were gone. Mr. Roche said they had men standing right there with machine guns. If anybody had come to stop them they'd have mowed them right down. The young boys would slip out on the marshes and crawl up and watch them unload in the moonlight.

The Depression didn't affect us too much, because Pop had paid for the farm by that time. He didn't owe anybody any money. He had worked and saved enough by working on shares with Grandmom. Pop paid cash for the farm. I was about twelve.

From the time I was old enough to remember, Pop had a Model T. I bought my first car, a Model A, when I was seventeen. It was a four door black sedan with green wire wheels. Later I got another Model A with a rumble seat that was a '27.

I was going through Mount Holly one day and I was coming down a hill and the guy in front of me slammed on his brakes. He had a big black Cadillac with a red light sticking out. He stopped so fast that I rammed into him with that curled steel bumper from the Model A. It tore the hell out of his fenders and broke all his lights. Boy was I hot! I stopped right in the middle of that hill and got out of that car and grabbed the guy. I thought I was going to kill him. He got out and looked at his car, all smashed up. My Model A wasn't even scratched. He looked up and apologized to me profusely for smashing up his car!

My father hadn't much of a dairy farm. He had sixteen to eighteen head. We only had eighteen stanchions in the barn then. Pop farmed from 1913 to 1946. That's thirty-three years. Pop farmed just like his father, David T. They would grow a patch of tomatoes, patches of cantaloupe, water melon, sweet corn and a few potatoes. They raised a lot of chickens and kept several sows and sold pigs. Pop had some nice pigs and he used to let the grandkids help him feed them. He'd take milk and leftovers from the house, make a swill, and pour it in the pig's troughs.

Pop didn't make the dairy a priority. My dad would run a little short of feed or hay and he'd stretch out what he had. He fed that old meadow hay that the hogs wouldn't even eat, and a little quart can of cob meal ground up.

If one of Pop's cows gave eight quarts of milk a day when she was fresh, he thought he had a cow. That was my dad!! You can't dairy like that.

He made money by growing tomatoes for Campbell's Soup Company on contract. I worked for nothing, and Jake worked for practically nothing all his life.

Pop used to sell hay to the big stables in Philadelphia. Everything was horse-drawn. The milk trucks had teams. They had two to three hundred horses at the Supplee Milk Company, for deliveries, that they kept in stables in a double-deck barn. The bakeries, laundries, and everything that has delivery trucks now were all horse-drawn then. It took a lot of feed for all those horses. Sharpening the shoes so the horses wouldn't slip on the icy streets was hard on the horses. That's how I got Silver who had been a bakery horse. Supplee was all milk, Supplee, Wills, and Jones. I think Kraft bought them. My grandfather and my father shipped to Supplee. They took their good hay to Philadelphia for money, and fed the cows and their horses the poor stuff. It was all loose then. Pop never baled a bale of hay in his life.

Jake would drive loads of hay to Philadelphia. He had ratchets on the hay shovel, and put two big hay ropes over. A seat fit on the front of the shovel so that the driver was almost outright over the top of the team. No shelter or nothing. The hay would be as high as you could get away with it.

For grain we'd plant grass seed, timothy and clover. After you got the grain off, you cut it for stubble hay. Then the next year that would be prime hay. That's what they all wanted for horses, only clover and timothy. We'd put that in the mows right along the driveway, where the wagons come in, so it would be handy to pitch off there on the wagon. What he ought to have been doing was feeding the quality hay to his cows. Then he'd have gotten more out of the milk than he would have hauling that hay clear down to Philadelphia.

One day we saw a couple of kids come along and toss a match into a load of hay in the cart, burning the wagon and everything else. They were lucky to get the horses off.

Pop never had extra money to put out for help, and he never gave me a dime for all that work. I never got one penny of anything from him until I was twenty-two and married! Not one penny!

To get myself some spending money, I caught pigeons in the barn. The men would come up and put their teams up, and feed the horses at noon, while they ate dinner. The horses would eat their corn, and they would slop a little bit over the manger into the entry way. The pigeons would go in and eat the corn.

I got smart and closed off all the doors and caught them, 'cause they couldn't go anywhere. I took them and put them in a wooden brooder. I was barely six years old. 'Course they never missed me at the dinner table. I'd take them and put them in by the hen house. I'd walk right by Pop. He never paid that much attention. I shouldn't have done it, because some of those pigeons had squabs. I didn't know enough to realize anything like that. Ruth told Pop, and Pop went out and dropped the lid, and every darn one of them flew out of there, but two.

He said, "You can keep those two."

They mated after a bit. One of them was a squab, and the other one was a racing homer with a band on it. It was a red checker and the other one was a blue bar. They mated and that's when I started selling squabs. I saved up money, and I got some more squabs out at the barn. The nests were Uncle Harry's. Uncle Harry used to have wild pigeons, when he was home.

Then I got the big birds. They were French Mondains that I got from a man in Haddonfield. After I married and moved away from home, I built pigeon pens in the end of the garage, right back of the house.

My mother showed me how to keep records. I'd started school when I was six. She got those little notebooks in the five and ten for five cents. She'd lined them and wrote down everything. Each one of the pairs of birds had bands on them, with a number. The cock bird was on the right leg and the hen was on the left leg. I had the numbers and I wrote down for twelve months out of the year, how many squabs I had each month.

Pop told me "I don't want to see you in my corn crib. If you don't make them pigeons pay, they are gonna leave here." He was hard. He would have done it, too. Pop didn't have patience with nothing or nobody, Pop and I were just as different as could be.

We had a car when I first went to school. It was a model T Ford, Tin Lizzie. Boy, I cranked that thing until…I wonder that I didn't have an arm broken. Pop never cranked it. He'd sit there and pull the choke and the magneto and I cranked it. Those cold mornings, well you didn't have any antifreeze. You had to drain the water out every night and put fresh water in the next day. If you went somewhere and stayed for a while, you had to cover it up. If you stayed too long, you had to drain the water again and fill it before you went home. We would put cardboard up in front of the radiator to keep it from freezing while we drove along. Pop kept the son of a gun running till there was no running left in it, like he did everything.

There was a gas house in Marlton. It was piped into the houses of the village and to the streets for gas lamps. This particular one had a big pit with something that looked like lime in it. It was on that back street by the school. They were always warning us kids not to get near it. I guess that liquid could eat right through you. Electricity didn't come in till the twenties and thirties to replace the gas.

The only butcher I remember was Fowler Brothers' slaughter house right across the road, on the back street from the school. We used to watch 'em bring cattle and pigs in there. They had a big chain in the concrete floor. They'd chain 'em and shoot 'em, cut their throats and then bleed 'em. Of course, us kids, we'd watch that.

George Cline's barbershop was in the parlor of his house. Cliney was an old rough kind of a feller, baldheaded. He always wore one of these plastic bill sun visors with a rim over his eyes. He had a big potbellied stove with benches down the whole side. You'd go in and that place'd be right full. They had two or three barbers besides Cliney. There were spittoons for those that chewed tobacco. The men would sit and spit for six to eight feet and hit that basket every time. Once in a while somebody'd shoot one right in the stove when it was open, it would pshhhht!! I used to get scared. I'd never been around anybody that chewed. It was something different.

George Cline's wife was a lot younger, about half his age. George never married until he was an older man. She wore her hair in a knot like they all did. She'd come in and talk to some of the men while he was barbering.

When I was twelve years old I started to do a man's work on the farm. Now if a fence rail broke on one of the fences, Pop would take out about a dozen nails, and Pop'd drive them damn nails in every which way, and when he got done it wasn't a bit better than it was before. Soon as somebody put a foot on it to climb over, boom! There went the fence.

Me, I'd take the rail off and put another one on, and fix it right. He'd bitch at me because it took too long, but it was okay if he took the time to fool with those nails for nothing.

It was the same way with that lane when I finally convinced him to put a path across from the back of the barnyard to the back lane. I'd tried for years to get him to do that. He'd run the cows around through the yard, right in front of the kitchen window, and through the gutter where the water used to run out from the sink. They'd track great big wide holes and shit all over the yard. You'd go walking out there to hang up clothes and there's cow manure all over the yard.

He done that for years and he wouldn't do any different. By the barnyard there was another ditch from the milk house that they had to walk over. Well, every summer they'd have a place as wide as it was long, but pop just wouldn't change it. When I got older, Mom and I worked together on him, and finally he agreed to do it. After he done it, he said,

"I don't know why I didn't do these years ago."

My mother saw the things that her husband lacked.

Pop was a truck farmer. We hauled a lot of tomatoes to Campbell's Soup. We had three wagons, three teams of draft horses, and two carriage driving horses. The wagons would hold from one hundred and twenty to one hundred and forty bushel baskets, depending upon how full the baskets were and how ripe the tomatoes were. We hauled those wagons with just one team, but we rotated the teams with each new load.

There were no brakes and only the breeching on the horses could hold them back.

It was fourteen miles to Campbell's Soup from the Homestead. We'd send Jake out at daylight. He'd go clear down there, get weighed with a full load, unload, get the empty baskets on, get weighed again, and then drive back anywhere from noon to three o'clock in the afternoon, depending upon the traffic. As soon as he got back we'd have another load of produce, sugar corn, cantaloupe or cabbage, depending on the season and the harvest, loaded with a fresh team of horses and ready to go.

Jake'd take this load to the Caley Hill Market in Philadelphia that night. That's going up and down hills and on and off those ferry boats with no wheel brakes on the wagons. Pop didn't realize what kind of a mess he could have gotten into.

There was a lantern hanging along the back between the wheels. That's all the light they had. Caley Hill was a big open market with stalls. Pop shipped to J.C. Cook, produce merchants, just the same as Granddad done. They'd sell it for a commission. Caley hill was on the Philadelphia side of the River and Campbell's was on the Jersey side.

The next morning we'd load him right up n' send Jake back to Campbell Soup again. He'd sleep on the road. That's the way they used to do it.

Occasionally Uncle Horace would take the load to Philadelphia. The teams were getting worked every day so that would make a lot of difference between a horse that is not worked, and a horse that is. Eventually Jake got so feeble and so careless that people kept telling Pop that he was going to have an accident and kill somebody. Pop was the last man that I ever knew that used a team of horses. It was about 1930.

Finally Grandma and Mom persuaded him to get a truck and he bought a used '29 half ton Chevrolet truck. It was a stick body and I cut the stakes off. We hauled dirt and everything with it. You could even chop stalks by jacking up one wheel, and putting a blade saw on it, and using the belt to grind stalks. That's the only truck he ever had.

When I first started farming in Barrington I bought an old dump truck for $100. Some boys had an uncle who was a banker, and he died and left each one of them boys $30,000. They come out and bought that farm and went into the dairy business, and lost everything they had. They didn't know a thing about it and nobody could tell them. They had one of them W-D forty-five tractors, and they'd go out plowing about eight miles an hour throwing the dirt clear halfway across the field. They were foreclosed on and they sold me that truck for 100 bucks.

CLAYT EVENS HAD A COW PONY, Twilight, who he brought back from Denver. He lived across the road by himself, and he looked like Lincoln. Clayt would go to the opera. He had seen Edwin Booth play Hamlet on Broadway. He was a college educated man, but you'd never know it. He could have talked with the best of them. He'd come over a lot to see his cousin, Grandmother Sally.

This old man, Joe Jones, worked for Clayt and his father. Jones went out West and joined the cavalry in 1886, as an Indian fighter. Joe came back when he got out of the cavalry and Clayt took him in. Joe was a heavy drinking man. He would lay there on that old couch in the kitchen back of the cook stove and nip that bottle about every ten minutes. His hair was snow white and he had a goatee like Buffalo Bill used to wear and a mustache. Joe had also been a Texas Ranger.

Boy, I used to get over there, and get him to talking about Indian fighting. You'd better believe what he could tell you. He had his old rifle and bayonet and his McClellan saddle, his boots and spurs. I was right in for that kind of stuff. He could talk for hours.

He boasted he could drink a quart of whiskey after supper and never get drunk. I believed he could do it. Clayt kept him right there with him until he died. Clayt thought a lot of him.

When Clayt got older, his brother's son, George, Old Hog Nose as we called him, that son-of-a-gun took the farm away from him. I don't know how he done it, some crooked bit of work. He got one of them shyster lawyers.

George Cooper, Clayt's nephew, was a plumber and a good one. He put the heating system in that big house on the Homestead for Pop, right in the middle of the Depression. Pop bought all of the material from a plumbing house there in Camden. He gave George $1,000 for him to put it in. Cooper had a truck. Instead of George Cooper written on the door, his truck had his wife Nelly's name on the door. George had gone bankrupt so he had put everything in her name.

William and George were brothers. They lived over there on Hog Pond road. George and Clayt were just neighbors, that's all. George got that property away from old Clayt.

George had been living at Clayt's since Clayt was only using two rooms. Course, Clayt had let the buildings fall down so he let George have the house for nothing. George claimed that he fixed the one barn and tore the other one down and the property now belonged to him. He wound up getting away with it. They declared Clayt incompetent.

Clayt didn't come out with anything in his old age and he went around in rags. He didn't have a place to go and he had no relatives close by. He finally took a caretaking job in Pennsylvania with two women.

That George Cooper was a common waste of a man. We never had any trouble with neighbors until that son of a gun moved there. He'd come out with his mules, and work them hard all day. Then he'd come home and takes the harnesses off of them and turn them right loose. I've seen them go out across that field on a run, and you'd see tomatoes flying everywhere. The mules would get right down there and roll right in the tomato patch.

"Well, Raymond," George said to Pop."They don't hurt too much."

Pop was getting mad and madder.

One day, George had a mule he called Jack. Jack come over here, and he went through that gate down the back lane. He laid his chest on that gate and smashed it right to the ground. George drove over and he had his wife Nelly with him, and Pop walked out and stopped him.

"Now, that's far enough. You see that?"

"Well, Raymond, a couple of patches will fix that up."

Pop reached in the car door and grabbed him by the front of the shirt, and throwed him right up to the window, and rubbed his fist right in his eyes. George was scared to death. He was a coward.

Clayt was driving his mule team for him and they were setting out tomatoes. One day they left the planter sitting up there and took the wagon and barrels back. He got Clayt to stay and count how many more plants they'd need. My corn was already high. George took a wheel and run right down a whole row of my corn, mashed it right into the ground. He had a nice road, with ten feet to spare, but he drove clean out on that row of corn.

Well, about that time, I see Cooper coming across from the barn. I turned away from Clayt, and walked right out there, and put my face right in his.

"You are the commonest son-of-a-bitch I think I ever seen!"

"You know damn well, what I'm talking about, that row of corn! If you were half a man you'd stand up to me." Clayt got between us. So I turned off home.

That night he came over after his milk. Pop gave him milk, two quarts a day, for two years and he never took one earthly nickel. Pop came out from milking the cows and George asked, "What's got into young Raym? He's crying the blues about the corn."

Pop said, "You common bastard. You know what I told the boy? I told him to go up there and run down a row of your tomatoes. I'll take care of the boy, but who's going to take care of you?"

Cooper never said another word. He picked up his milk jug and he went home. He kept coming back for milk too! He'd send his son over. One night the boy come over crying, with his hand up on his face, and blood running right down his elbow. His old man had taken a mule bridle and had hit him over the head with it. The bit cut part of his face right to the bone and then he sent him over with the empty milk bottles. He was a big boy and he was crying. Pop was mad. He said, "If I had my hands on him right now, I'd half kill him."

They had had money at one time, and they went right through every bit of it. They had had a farm given to each of the brothers, and livestock to run it, and thirty thousand in cash. Every damn one of them lost it.

William and his wife had bought the Grand Atlantic Hotel, in Atlantic City, with his share. They had a couple of rainy summers, and they went bankrupt. They moved out and took all the silverware with them. Then they come back up here to the farm. When they used to come to a Sunday School Picnic, they'd bring their silverware and there was Grand Atlantic Hotel, written right on the silver.

IN HIGH SCHOOL Ernest Seton Thompson came to speak. He was a great outdoor writer and sportsmen and big game hunter. He'd been like Zane Grey, a government trapper. He brought slides and gave quite a talk about this wolf out West. The wolf had killed a lot of cattle, and the government sent out trappers, but nobody could catch him. He had a white mate. Thompson had caught her and he cut her legs off, and took her feet and made tracks and left her scent. That's the way he finally caught him.

About a week after that, the teacher said we all had to find a subject

and get up in front of the class and make a speech on it. We had to talk at least one full minute and I got up there and made a speech without any script or notes or anything. I just started in on that film and talk of his and I talked for seven minutes. I got the first prize. The teacher said she never heard anything like that in her life. It was something I was interested in, something I understood. On any other subject I couldn't have got up in front of that class, and talked like that. I never faltered once. It just rolled right out of me.

We made our own entertainment. I was in the woods most of the time. When I got a little bigger I got to go out riding horseback. I didn't have much time, so I went sometimes at eleven o'clock at night.

We rode, swam, and played baseball. Pop had a lawn tennis court in the side yard. We played quoits and croquet. This was in my time off, which wasn't very much. I never could belong to the YMCA or the Boy Scouts. I couldn't go out for any sports.

I never saw a movie until I was old enough to have my own car. I went to my first movie with Dave and Albert in Haddonfield. It was a comedy, Laurel and Hardy.

I went to see all of Zane Grey's pictures, and soon Pop got to going with me. He liked Zane Grey. George O'Brien played in them, *Riders in the Purple Sage*, and Robber's *Roost*. That's what got me started with horses, seeing all those Western movies. There wasn't any radio. We didn't have electricity.

We ice skated on the Marl Pond. Uncle Dave was always building something. He built an ice boat that we sailed on the big Centennial Lake that was a mile and a half long. It would take your breath away. Uncle Dave and Uncle Even could get up to sixty miles an hour. It had two skates mounted on the wide end, and on the narrow end a single skate mounted to the rudder like a lever with a pole tied to her. Whoever guided the boat worked that lever back and forth to turn the boat. The mast was mounted at the center from the bottom of the hull through a support cross beam the same level as the seats. It took three to four men to handle it. We kept it up at the top of the wagon shed there where the big sleigh was at the Homestead

Eventually the seasons got so much warmer, and we couldn't even ice-skate toward the end. It got so that it didn't even freeze in the winter time.

All the small towns had to go to Moorestown High School because that was the only high school. I took agricultural class with a lot of the fellows from Marlton, Mount Laurel and Indian Mills.

When I was fourteen years old, right by myself, I killed my first deer. I had to go get the old colored man, and the horse and buckboard to get the deer. He helped me gut it and take it and hang it up in the corn crib. Pop had driven up twenty miles into the woods and, as usual, he never saw or heard a thing. He came back home, and old Bill and I was milking.

Pop came in the barn, and he said, "I don't see any deer hanging around."

Bill was down there laughing so hard, that he could hardly hold his bucket between his knees. I kept right on milking too.

Pop asked, "You boys do anything?"

I think his whole club had killed one deer that day. He went on talking.

I said, "I believe I've done a little bit better than you did. Go out and look in the first corn crib." I had hung the deer up in there on purpose.

He went out and boy, when he come back, I heard him just a hitting the floor. Pop was stepping ten feet high.

"My God! Boy. Where did you get that buck?"

I told him all about it. I got one almost every year. I killed seventeen all together after that. I was in the woods all the time, riding horseback and fox hunting. That's the reason they made me the leader of the club over there, when Mr. Foster died.

Around this time they built the bridge from Camden to Philadelphia. Before the bridge they had ferry boats going across the Delaware. My sister Ruth's husband, Bob Dickinson, was captain of one of those ferries.

The bridge was built during the big Depression around 1926. They had an awful time because they had to tear down a lot of houses for the bridge construction and the highway, and of course there were court battles. They took away whole blocks of homes and properties. They did the same thing on the other side of the river in Philadelphia but it wasn't as contentious because there were already a lot of warehouses along the river.

The real estate brokers and some developers come out and they tried to buy up all the farms along the Marlton Pike. They bought Clayt Evens' farm, but then he had to take it back because they didn't need his space. The developers also tried to buy the Homestead, but Pop wouldn't sell. Of course Doc Haines wouldn't sell, but up around Pine Grove where all the Italian settlements were, those farms were all sold. Most of that land was where Grandmother Sally Burroughs Evans was raised. This was when the bunga-lows along the Marlton Pike started being built.

There were a lot of homes built on that original thousand acre Evans tract. That's where the Italian settlement was. The Italian immigrants were coal miners out of Pennsylvania. You take a thousand acres, that's a lot of ter-ritory. Thomas Evans had first built and lived in Doc Haines' house.

The first bungalow on the corner of Elmwood Road and the Marlton Pike was built by Mr. Lake. Lake was the manager of Haddon Press in Camden and he had left his wife in order to take up with his secretary and they bought that little place. His secretary was a beautiful woman. Lake was a tall fellow and a smooth talker who looked a little bit Indian. He had some pigeons of his own and he bought some off me. He had acquired a lot of white pine crates that had been used for shipping and he used them to build his chicken, pigeon, and rabbit houses.

Lake sold the bungalow to Mr. Schill from Yonkers. There was another German from Yonkers called Werner who lived next to Schill. Werner started in the pigeon business and bought off me as well. The last house had the German shepherds.

The man that owned the Savitch farm was president of Strawbridge & Clothier department store in Philadelphia and when he bought the house he put a man in there who managed his herd of brown Swiss cows. We used to talk over the fence.

When I first got married, I rented a bungalow for $25 a month. Larry and Judy were born there. It had a closed-in screened front sun porch.

The bungalow that I later bought was Clarence Foster's place. Clarence was an automobile mechanic, born in Marlton and Pop's age. My boys tried to buy a part of an old wash machine he had to use for a steering column for a tractor they were making. Clarence told us it cost $20 so we left it. As we were leaving he handed us the steering column and said:

"Here, your boys can have this, but I want a partnership in that tractor!"

From the time I was twelve years old and big enough I worked alongside the men loading manure and hay and doing almost everything else.

When I was in high school Walker Gordon Farms milked up to a thousand cows. They had a hundred cows and a manager in each barn and they all milked by hand. They had certified milk for babies that was sold in New York City. Bangs Disease got in there and they lost most of their herd. Bangs disease causes contagious abortion in cows.

Ben Cooper wanted to buy some of the cows. That shows how much brains he had. Pop finally convinced him not to. Bangs will spread right through your herd. The cows have to be slaughtered. The milk can become infected and this can cause undulant fever. That's what Granddad had, undulant fever. He was in the hospital for quite a while. It went through the country like wildfire.

Granddad bought very few cows from the Greenbergs. Pop went down to Woodstown, to see Dick Bartington, a cattle dealer dealing in Canadian cows. Old man Stony Harris, the one that used to have the Harris Cowtown Rodeo and auctions, was his father.

Pop bought ten Holstein Canadian heifers and we had to have them tested for TB, and we lost seven out of the ten. One of them was my heifer. Some of the farmers lost their whole herd. The Federal Government and the State reimbursed us for each cow. We had to drive them to the railroad in Medford. They had stock pens next to the Kirby Brother's feed store. Ben Cooper lost his whole herd from tuberculosis.

The State had never tested for TB before 1930. We had about sixteen cows and we had lost half our herd. We drove them the back way through the woods to the Hoot Owl farm and put them in the stock pens at the railroad. They shipped them up to Jersey City and slaughtered them there. They ate them with the TB. It wasn't too bad according to where it was. The remains went to dog food, I imagine. Then they claimed that people couldn't get TB from the meat. Some of them were just barely infected and didn't show any lesions on their lungs. Others were bad.

Nobody farms one hundred acres anymore and makes a living out of it. When I was a boy there were farms with twenty and thirty acres, and a man and a woman raised eight or ten kids on it. People worked then. Now they don't want to do it.

Pop grew tomatoes for the Campbell's Soup Company. He contracted with them and got about ten dollars a ton, for number ones, eight dollars a ton for twos, and so on. They inspected them when you picked them, and you took them into the plant. They wanted them red-ripe. You'd let them sit all night in a basket with pressure on them, and you can imagine what they were like the next morning. By the time they got to you, they'd want to turn you down, and send you home with the whole load.

We used to plow the ground, disk it, and work it with a Darnell Marker. That was a sled guide with iron runners on it with a ridge down the center to keep the disks from moving to the sides. We hooked two horses to it and a man rode on it. First, you would go across the field and then we'd take the marker and the disks off, and you would go the opposite way. Then we'd take a two-horse wagon and a load of fertilizer in one hundred sixty-seven pound burlap bags.

After we'd set the tomatoes, we'd go out again with that same wagon with a whole mess of barrels of water for the tomato plants. Aunt Anna would drop them down and I would set them out. Somebody else would water them, and another person would close them up. That's the way we set out twenty acres of tomatoes.

The tomatoes didn't get out much before the first of May. Most of the time we had a frost and it would kill those Southern plants. We plowed anywhere from March on. We used to plant the corn right around the tenth of May. With the cabbage it didn't make much difference.

When they first got fertilizer we had this dog that used to sleep on the fertilizer bags, and the buzzards would come circling around. They'd look at that sleeping on the bag and they'd smell that fertilizer and think that the dog was dead. Once a buzzard came right down on top of that dog and took a bite out of him. The dog took the buzzard and killed him.

Pop wasn't inventive in any way. Because Granddad had done it that way, he did it that way. He went on for years, slopping and messing all over the yard, and the gutters and everything. I had a heck of a time getting Pop to agree to any change. I was always thinking about a way to do things easier.

I was the first one that planted rye in the early fall for spring oats. It came in and it got high and just as thick as hair on a dog's back. I fertilized it with a little nitrogen. I pastured that stuff, and talk about cows, a 'milking!

Pop farmed all his life, and I never knew him to own a grain drill.

He'd plant by broadcasting. Pop could do it right down to a tee. I never could do it like he could.

When I was a boy, we would have to thrash the grain. We used a flail, with a long handle and a club on the end of it. During the winter, we laid the sheaves on the barn floor, on the planks. Then we would go along with a flail, and beat it out of the straw. Then you had to run it through a chaff and bellow and a fan, maybe twice. Somebody had to stand and crank that win-now machine by hand. Ohhh… Man!!

It's the same way with corn. I had to shell all that corn. Pop would stand there and shove the ears in, and I had to turn the sheller. Hour after hour, I turned that sheller to get maybe sixty baskets of corn out of the corn crib.

Pop always sold milk. We never made butter or cheese. The milk was too good an income. Down in Tennessee and those places where milk wouldn't bring anything, that's where they make cheese and butter.

We always had our own meat. I never knew Pop to kill for beef. I was raised on pork, that's the reason I like pork now. Pop would go to the Philadelphia Stock Yard in the spring, and get eight or ten Virginia Lambs, very thin. He'd get them for five dollars apiece. He'd bring them back and turn them out in the back lane, down by that apple orchard. In the winter, he put them up and feed them a little corn.

We killed the pigs and the sheep. We shot the pigs. That was my job too, when I got to be about ten years old. I shot them with that old twenty-two pistol. I got so I'd drop them every crack. There'd be a man standing there with a knife, to stick them, so they'd bleed good. Then we had those hog hooks. They would hook it right in their lower jaw and drag them. A great big hog weighs three to four hundred pounds. It got so they wanted them a little smaller. Then we took them to the scalder. You would get up at two o'clock in the morning and start a fire under that hog scalder.

First we would get the milking done, and then feed the horses. You couldn't get the horses to come out of the barn to drink with the smell of the hogs and smoke. They'd kick and rear, and carry on. The smell of blood especially bothered them.

After breakfast we'd want to start killing hogs not long after daylight. All the other work had to be done. Sometimes we'd kill twelve or fourteen. I've seen those great big poles in that high part of the shed, next to the horse stable hanging right full of hogs.

The scalder looked like a casket with a chain and a rack in the bottom. That's where you built the fire. It had a little lid that leaned up where you put the fire in. The bottom rack had a chain lift on each end. You cranked a hog right up, after he was scalded, take him out of the water, and turn him over, and scald one side and test him with a shovel, to see if the hair was loosening up. Then you would put them saw horses down, and lay some oak planks or boards and roll them hogs on there. They would shave that hair off around their eyes and nose and everything else and then Pop did most all the gutting, taking the big dishpan and cutting the hog open. The guts, they'd fall right out in the dishpan. They'd hang up on another pole the liver and the lungs.

The women folk would get the sweet breads and melt. That was good eating. Then the women took the small intestines and scraped them, and washed them to case the sausage and fill them with sausage.

I've seen my Grandmother Sally B. sit there in a little chair with a tub of water between her feet, and a sack for shingles stuck in the water. She'd take the small intestines and wrap them around her finger and scrape them to get them clean. Then she would turn them inside out and scrape them some more and keep wrapping them around her finger and scraping on that shingle, and wrapping them once again. When she got done, it looked just like cellophane. She would stretch it out again and put the sausage in it.

After she cleaned the sets, they were put in a wooden tub, with salt, and soaked overnight, or for a day or two, to further clean them.

They'd take off the sweet breads and melt. Delicious eating that is. Sweetbreads were just like the roe in a shad. They would dip it in bread crumbs, and fry it. God Almighty! It was delicious. That's what the women folks did, besides getting us a great big dinner, when they killed a hog. We'd have that big table which was eleven to twelve feet long when all the leaves were in it in the big dining room. I've seen times when there'd be sixteen men around it. It would be a great big meal, all kinds of vegetables, and pies when you had done, and of course coffee.

We'd all sit around the table for a little while. After everything was cleaned up, we'd wash those planks off and take them under the shed, and bring the hogs down. We'd have the liver fried with onions.

There was a big wooden ham tub in the old smoke house. Many a time Pop would mix up brown sugar, and molasses, to a consistency that would float a potato, the size of an egg. It had to be a certain thickness and then it was right for curing the hams and shoulders and bacon, and the jowls. He would pack them in there, and put salt on them for around three weeks. The only thing wasted on a hog was his squeal.

Souse is pig's feet. You ain't lived, until you have eaten souse and hog tongue. I liked it crisp, and put a few drops of vinegar on it. And of course, there was the scrapple. We'd get the jowls out, and whatever else we wanted to put it in and add the cornmeal and the seasoning, sage, and salt and pepper and what not, and put it in the great big iron pot and cook it. We had a big wooden paddle, what Pop called the blisterer. I would stand there, and keep stirring it or it would stick and you'd ruin the whole batch, a whole great iron pot full. When that got cooked to a certain consistency, they'd dip it out, and put it in these little pans, and take it down to the cellar to put in the Safe. That was just a little square thing with a wall around it, so no bugs could get in.

They didn't have refrigerators then. When they got it done, they'd put a little lard on top and that would seal it. It would keep all winter. We had the hams and the shoulders and the bacon. After they were cured we'd wrap it all up. The sausage meat was just odds and ends.

After the meat came out of the brine, it was cured. We'd hang it up, and smoke it. Of course the hams had the rind left on one side. We'd take a knife and make a hole, and put a piece of string in there. We had nails all up and down the rafters of the smoke house. We'd take the big iron pot, turn it upside down, on some bricks, and build a fire, mostly either hickory or apple tree green wood. That's what we smoked with. The smoke would damn near strangle you. The floor was cement. You'd put the wood right underneath a big iron pot on bricks. It would burn and it smoldered. That's where we got more smoke to penetrate the meat and help cure it.

We'd take the hams and shoulders and the bacon down, and wrap it in meat paper we'd get from the butcher. None of that gauze, that's Virginia commercial. Then we hung them up in the attic all summer.

Whenever we would run out of ham, Pop would send me up in the attic to bring down some ham, or a piece of bacon. Sometimes if it was there too long, it would get a little moldy. We'd take that big butcher knife and trim the mold off.

We canned the vegetables, beets and carrots and parsnips. In the fall, before freezing, we had boxes full of dirt down in the cellar and up on the planks. We'd bury the parsnips in that sandy dirt. They'd keep for quite a while. Apples were the same. Of course it was cool and damp. We could make apple pies, and apple sauce. Everything went in the cellar. There were great big jar closets that Mom had and she would put them in the pie cupboards.

Granddad had a lot of those old shoe irons. You used to have to sole your own shoes and then put heels on them. Course in those days, they nailed the soles on.

Pop bought cedar shingles. Pop never made them, that was long before our time, but I did see him make them for patchwork, because the bundles were too expensive for just patching. We got cedar from our cedar forest. I didn't make split rails but Pop and David T. did. That fence in back was done before my day. Those rails lasted all up until my time. I suspect some of them fences were a hundred years old.

Pop had left the meadows to grow up for pasture. When I started getting more cows I turned them to pasture, and they'd scratch their tits on them Blackberry Briars. I tried my best to get Pop to mow that. He never had time.

"I'll mow it."

"No. It'll tear the mower up and break the Pitman Bar on them stumps."

That was an excuse you couldn't even shake a stick at. Finally, when I got older, I just went ahead and did things, whether he liked it or not. I took my team down there, and I bet I worked for two weeks. Those meadows hadn't been mowed in forty years. They were full of hassocks tough as wire.

Yes sir. I mowed them, and after I got it done, in a year or two, the grass came right back and there was a pasture. Afterwards he'd admit that I did a good job. Course I'd kind of dropped a few hints and he could hardly help it. It was like pulling hen's teeth to get him to do it.

Mom backed me up all the time. She could see it, but Pop wasn't that way.

When I was going to high school, after I got up some size, Jake got so he couldn't milk, and Pop got so he couldn't get around. He finally bought himself some Surge Milkers.

Pop would get a lot of milk in the spring, when the cows were turned out on grass. The rest of the time, he got nothing. He bred them whenever they came into heat. He always kept bulls, of course, and there wasn't any artificial insemination. The bull would run right with the cows all the time, and when a cow came into heat, he'd breed her.

We had a blacksmith in Marlton. When we got ready to start hauling to Campbell's Soup, we'd take the teams up to get them shod. When we kept them off road, we pulled the shoes.

I was always grasping for new things and different ways of saving labor. I'd got tired of working my brains out for nothing. Pop, I couldn't change him. That's all there was to it. But if I could do a job in one-half the time, with half the work, then I would take a week to fix something that would help me to do it that way.

In order to have an efficient dairy farm, the first thing you would want to do is get your feed established, your hay and pasture. That's where Larry failed. Larry bought his cows without his feed, and then he wound up behind the eight-ball.

Living with this your entire life, it's natural to you. Now I don't know half this stuff, and nobody else does. It's becoming a lost vocabulary. I tell all the kids, if you want to know anything, find it out while I'm still here to show you. There's nobody in my family that knows. Larry might know, but there is a lot Larry doesn't know. He was too young.

PART II

Raymond and Clara

RAYMOND (21) AND CLARA (20), 1935

Dad, Raymond Ballinger

I MET CLARA AT A PARTY in Mount Holly when I was twenty years old. Clara was making eyes at me. She was going with my cousin Dave, Uncle Evens' boy, for quite a while. Of course, I had never really been out with girls to amount to anything. Just kids stuff, school stuff. At these parties they would spin the bottle. Clara was trying to get with me. I don't think that we really had any love. I think it was more or less just hero worship and sex appeal. She just let it be known that she wanted me.

Clara came with Dave to visit me out at the farm. She went with me to see the horses in the barn, and that's when she started to have those wild feelings. Her friend Ruth told me that "Clara had fallen for me real bad." Poor old Dave, he didn't have a chance.

Clara quit going out with Dave but I never asked her out.

One night I was just driving around Mount Holly. Clara and her older sister, Grace, were working in the five and ten cent store. I went in and she came right up to me in the store. I said "I just stopped in to see if you'd like to go to the movies when you get off work." Clara was a woman. I really didn't know or understand her because she was a city woman.

And that's the way it started.

The second time I took Clara out, when I brought her home, she asked me if I loved her and she told me she loved me. Well, that wasn't love, infatuation maybe, but not real love. I wasn't the first man she had ever been with as far as that's concerned.

I always had the feeling that the very reason for her getting pregnant was to sway me into marrying her. I was paralyzed when she became pregnant. My mother said I had to do the right thing and marry her. That ended my dreams of going out west. I felt I was trapped by my naivety. Clara had her first child and she kept having children. She named Larry for T.E. Lawrence, the romantic hero of the time, Lawrence of Arabia.

We had gone out about one year before we married, in February of thirty-five. Her minister married us in the church in Mount Holly. We just went home that night and went to bed. Pop hollered up the next morning at daylight for me to get out and milk. That's the kind of honeymoon I had. They couldn't spare me.

In my mother's opinion, nobody was ever good enough for me. Mom had a mind of her own. If I had a particular friend in school, and they came home to see me and their manners or speech wasn't just quite right, she wouldn't like them. I get a lot of that from her. I'm a little bit that way. My parents didn't get along too well with Clara.

I had a book about the Ballingers that a cousin, Edna Wirth, had written and it went back three hundred years. Edna said the main characteristic of the Ballingers was they thought they were pretty much the chosen people, proud people. I can relate to that. My folks didn't think that Clara was one of those chosen people.

I was twenty-one, married, and still living at home. Shortly afterward I rented my first bungalow, a nice new home, for one-and-a-half years for $20 a month. Pop said the most he could pay me was $18 a week. Before that he'd never paid me and I worked there all my life just like a man, from the time I was twelve years old. He had never paid me a nickel's worth of wages. I had to earn money on my own and I bought my own clothes from the time I was nine years old. I was a cheap kid. I never cost him nothing.

Pop let me keep my pigeons. I made a little money on them and went over to a neighbor's who had a lot of guinea hens. He gave some eggs to me. I took them home and set them under a hen, and that's where I started with guineas. I raised about two hundred guineas every year for extra money, the grey pearls. Then the man who bought my chickens asked me to try the white guineas. He said they'd bring a little more money, since they're not as dark-skinned. The old pearl guineas when they're plucked and ready to cook are black across their back. A lot of people who don't know look at them and think they're half spoiled. The white guineas are yellow and more like chickens.

Two years later we moved into the Pine Grove bungalow that I owned for five years, until I sold it and we moved to my first farm in Barrington. I had paid $2,100 for it. It was built in 1929 and had four acres and a big garage and two chicken houses. Larry was born at home, but Judy was born in the hospital. Raymie was born in that old green '34 Chevy. He couldn't wait.

It wasn't because I didn't want to take Clara to the hospital. Grandma had had a stroke in the back yard that morning at the Homestead and I was the one who carried her from the back yard and laid her in her bed till the doctor came.

Clara had called to tell me she was having contractions, but Mom and Pop were so upset they forgot to tell me. By the time I got home, she was running real close. I hadn't driven more than five or six miles toward Mount Holly when she yelled that the baby was coming.

I stopped the car and let her lay down in the back seat, and she had our second son while I was driving the rest of the way to Mount Holly Hospital. All we had was some newspaper in the car, so Clara wrapped Raymie in that. We pulled up to the hospital and I ran in and got the doctor. They came out to the car with a stretcher, a doctor, and two nurses. Soon as a nurse rewrapped the baby and picked him up, he started screaming like the devil, and Raymie hasn't stopped since! God! I can see that like it was yesterday. Carrot red hair he had. Clara said that he was the ugliest baby she had ever seen. He was long, skinny, and bloody, and slipped right out!

I rented additional acreage at the bungalow in Pine Grove that was grown up in trees, some of them twenty feet high. I grubbed all winter in my spare time. I cut those trees by hooking my team to them with a log chain and pulling them out and burning them. Altogether I had seven or eight acres that I cleaned off. I worked like a sucker, and the first time I plowed it, of course I had to be a little careful 'cause of roots and stuff, you know...but I owned that little bungalow with four acres.

I used the teams of horses most of the time, but I had this one big stump right in the middle of the lot and I just couldn't get it out with the team. I went over and got Pop's John Deere, and when I pulled the stump gave way on one side and made the stress uneven, and the right wheel kept on turning, while the left wheel came off the ground. The tractor went over with me on it. I almost killed myself. Then, like a fool, I had to go over and get a team of horses to pull the tractor back on to its wheels.

I decided to put tomatoes in there and send them along with Pop's for some extra money. With the tomatoes, the sugar corn, and my pigeons, it made a nice little extra income. I kept my paint horse at the Homestead. I used the buckboard to drive back and forth and I would take the boys with me. We lived in that bungalow until I went to farming at Barrington.

Dad, Raymond Ballinger Sr.

CLARA AND I STARTED OUT not getting along. She wanted things her way and that would have meant our kids would have been raised in a city. She didn't care what I wanted. She just thought that I should be working in some damned nine to five factory job like her father and her brother-in-law. Clara didn't know any better. She had no idea how to make a man happy.

We moved from our little rented bungalow to Pine Grove where I bought our first house and we lived there for five years. By that time we had three children and Pop was paying me only $18 a week. There wasn't any way I could get along and make the payments on that place. I was working Sundays and nights with a team of horses clearing land, farming, growing tomatoes, managing laying hens, and selling squabs. I did everything I could to make do. During World War II prices got so high for everything, so I went to Pop and asked him for more but he refused. Damn it to hell! He was making money but he just didn't think he could pay me more or he just didn't want to.

Clara wasn't satisfied. There wasn't enough money for her. With Clara, things just went from bad to worse, and that was it. She liked the party life and I didn't, never did. I tried that party scene with Dave and Albert before I met her, dancing and drinking and smoking. 'Course I didn't smoke and didn't drink and I just didn't care for those party games. I don't like small talk, I never did. Clara got me in a little deeper into those speakeasies than I wanted to be. I finally just came right out and told her I wasn't going to go any more.

She stopped complaining for a while, till I got to working in the shipyard, then she wanted to go out again. It was almost as if she had to go. When I went down to the New York Shipyard in Camden, I got a job right away. I went to school and I wound up a first-class ship fitter and I made good money, but it didn't do me any good. Clara spent it just as fast as I made it. She wanted to be social and go out smoking cigarettes, playing cards, dancing and partying with her friends. She couldn't drive but Edith, her younger sister, would always come by and pick her up.

Her other friend, Ruth Hickinbotham, would take her to the Baptist Church or to the Grange and all the other gatherings where she said she was doing volunteer work. My younger sister Ginny would be left watching the kids.

Clara went down to Edith's in Merchantville most of the time. I'd take Clara to her sister's, and leave her off and go to work and I'd pick her up on the way back. They were able to have their parties and drink and smoke and God knows what else while I was gone, and that was it. Clara's brother-in-law Alex was also working at the shipyard.

I don't know where she went. Her mother wouldn't have any part of it. Mrs. Williams thought a lot of me. She said, "If it hadn't been Raymond, it would have been somebody else. Clara would have had just as hard a time making a go of it."

I was a hard worker, and I was trying. If she had tried to help me I might have been a little bit kinder to her.

By this time we'd gotten so deep into the marriage with our three children. I just felt that it was too late to get out. I didn't know how to go forward and neither did she.

I wasn't satisfied. I worked in that shipyard for three years working my way up from a third-class helper to a first-class ship fitter. I had some real responsibility. I put all the bomb elevators on heavy cruisers. They converted them to airplane carriers and they had to be perfect. There were Navy inspectors on your back every minute. I had my own tackers and burners and welders and chippers.

I was okay there, but that wasn't where my heart was. I loved dairy farming. Initially it was bad enough at the shipyard but then they brought women in there, and, my God Almighty! They gave me a tacker who was a young farm girl and just as hot in the ass as she could be. If you wanted a tacker in a hurry you were in trouble. There'd be an empty line in her bucket, and she'd be gone somewhere, running after some man or something. It got so I'd just take the torch and do the tacking myself. Of course, if the union had caught me I'd been in trouble. I got fed up with that mess.

One time I was about to enter a trunk that went clean up to the flight deck. I had put my tools out and started to stick my head through the hatch to go up the ladder and some simple bastard up there dropped one of the heavy cables, about as big around as your thumb. It was rolled up with a heavy block with metal clubs on the end of it right down to the bottom and it just took the hat right off my head. Talk about cussing! If I'd been two inches further, he'd have hit me right in the head and broken my neck, and killed me. I sat in that hole, and I said, "I'm done with it."

I come home and a feller that I was riding with from Marlton told me he knew where I could rent a farm, but it wasn't set up for cows. I didn't care. I knew I could do that myself.

I'd take anything on in those days. I wanted to get away from that shipyard. I went to see the farm in Barrington and I looked it over and I rented it that winter of 1943. I told Clara that I quit the shipyard and rented a farm. I wasn't happy being away from farming and never had been. I went to Camden to please her and it didn't put us any farther along than we were when I was farming.

Clara said she wasn't going with me, and I told her that I would go by myself and she could starve or finish with me. She wouldn't give in, and I wouldn't either. I went ahead and remodeled the house and the lawn. The house had been abandoned for awhile. I had it all papered and painted.

When Clara and I sold the bungalow that just capped it off. Clara was angry, I mean bitter. Clara just didn't want to be on a farm. She wanted to be able to go to those parties down there at Edith's, have her beer and smoke her cigarettes. She was a city woman. She knew enough about what it would be like from seeing how hard our family worked at the Homestead and wanted no part of it. Even though Clara finally moved to Barrington she was never happy. It just went on from bad to worse until she left.

We didn't really belong together from the very beginning, and the more I kept going the angrier I got. Except for my children, they were wasted years.

During the winter of 1943-44, the boys and I rebuilt those Barrington barns in the evenings and on week-ends while I was still working at the shipyard. We tore out all the wooden planks in the cow stable and put in cement floors and gutters and mangers. It was so damn cold that Larry would chase Raymie around the barn just to keep him warm. Raymie kept complaining about being cold so I gave Larry my belt to keep him moving. We managed to pour a whole barn floor of cement with just a little cement mixer, and bolt in forty stanchions. I was still working at the shipyard in the daytime. At ten or eleven o'clock at night I was hauling gravel. I paid for everything except for some second hand lumber I used to build the milk house. I fenced the whole farm and cleared the meadow. It was all full of briars and junk. I was twenty-nine years old with three kids and a reluctant wife.

We lived in Barrington for just under three years. We moved in in March. Clara didn't want to move until I fixed up the house for her. She refused to come there for two whole weeks and I lived there with the kids and without her. She hated it and I did everything I could to make it work. When she moved in, she got pregnant with Leslie.

I bought my first cows for the Barrington farm from Herb Tallman, and then three or four from another fellow in Medford. They were first-class heifers. I also bought a pair of bay horses from Johnny Wilkins.

Johnny Wilkins had quite a reputation around there. Johnny's wife was a schoolteacher and I guess her youngest sister was living with them. The rumor was that the younger sister went riding on the tractor with Johnny and the first thing you know they were going at it hot and heavy. It wasn't long before his wife found out, so she left him. After they divorced, Johnny married the sister. His wife was a right nice looking woman, but her sister had her teeth stuck right out in the front. She was as homely as blue mud but she was built well. His first wife was heavy, but she was better looking.

I come in from hauling stalks one day and my smaller gelding, Doc, jumped in the barn door and headed for the wrong stall. I went to get him out and he reared up as he was backing out and hit his head on the beam and cracked his skull. After that happened I was lacking a horse, so I went to a sale near Swedesboro and bought additional purebred cows, and the Delaval milkers. I also bought an old gray horse for six dollars. He had the heaves, so we put him down and skinned him and put him out for the dogs. I sold Major to Buck and bought the two iron grays, Molly and Dolly. I needed a strong team to work in the fields and spread manure. They were a fine pair of Percherons, Molly and Dolly. Larry used to get up on one of those tall bushel baskets to harnesses them.

When I first moved there I didn't have a milk box. I shipped my milk to Abbotts' Dairies. The Inspector helped me find one. In the meantime I was milking about four cans a day. I was milking around thirty-six cans when I sold the farm.

I cooled the milk in an old bathtub with ice, so I had to get my ice from that ice plant in Haddonfield. They used to have a man, old Schwarzenkruger, a guy that was deaf and dumb, bring ice. Finally, the Milk Inspector bought me a six can box from a farm sale and I set it up in the milk house. I used ice in it for a little while until I got the electric run in there. Pappy Shuster, Jean's father, hooked it up for me.

I knew nothing except farming and that's all I ever wanted to do from the day I was born. Clara just wasn't comfortable in that way of life and didn't know anything about it, wasn't about to learn, and always thought her way was right. Mom tried to talk to her and teach her how to can but she remained a city girl. Her sisters were just like her. If I hadn't been so damned naive about women at the time, I would never have married her. Now that's the truth of the matter. She just didn't know how to compromise or to share a life with a man.

Clara just didn't want to be on a farm, didn't want to be tied down. Of course she couldn't drive at the time. She couldn't go anywhere unless I took her, and I mean I was just tied up. There was a mess of work there. I got her friend Ruth to come in from Marlton. She papered the whole house. I tore the old paper off and painted the woodwork and I sanded some of the floors. I had always tried to have a decent home for Clara. It still wasn't enough. I worked day and night and I guess that I should have taken more time for her and the kids, but then I could never have gotten done what I had to do.

I just felt I could make it, and there wasn't a thing could keep me from making it, including Clara. I knew that I had to keep driving, driving. If I let up one little bit, just one half hour, I would slip back through. That's what kept driving me.

You take a farm that size, one hundred fifty acres, all tillable and you have to harvest hay and grain and plant and cultivate corn and milk the cows. I was doing almost all of it with a team of Percheron horses and two young boys, a mess of work. With all the friction in the marriage, I tended to either blow up or shut up. I'd just go right back out in the field and go to work, just to get away from the tension. The honest truth is that neither one of us really tried, I don't think, to save anything.

PART III

Raymond Evans Ballinger: 1938-1952

RAYMIE ON DOMINO (4), 1942

Raymie, Raymond Evans Ballinger

I WAS BORN at 11:30 the morning of May 5, 1938, in Mount Holly, New Jersey in the back seat of a '34 Chevy, going from our bungalow in Pine Grove to Mount Holly Hospital. I don't know what my father was actually doing at that moment, but I've been told two things as fact. Sally B., my great-grandmother, had had a stroke, and my Dad was over at the Homestead. My mother, Clara, had called the Homestead, but my Grandmother Alice was too upset and forgot to tell my Dad that his wife had to go to the hospital, quite an oversight. By the time they remembered, her contractions were less than five minutes apart and she was already in an advanced stage of labor.

I was born in our car on the White Horse Pike while my Dad was driving toward the hospital. I made it to the hospital, wrapped in newspaper. My mother told me that I was the ugliest and bloodiest child she had ever seen, very long and skinny with carrot red hair. She couldn't believe that she'd brought this ugly baby into the world by herself. Maybe that was why she named me after my father.

In later years when I had returned from the Navy and was living with her, my mother also told me that I was one of the most charming little boys that she could have wished for. She said I was probably the best baby out of all the children that she'd ever had, including her two other children from her second husband. I didn't fuss, I didn't complain, and I didn't fight. Then, when I got big enough to walk around, I was into everything. I could be the most monstrous child. I still have those dual qualities inside of me.

As a child I continually asked my grandfather to tell me stories about the past. My family felt I was obsessed with this and I needed to stop and not be encouraged. I continued to ask and he told them "The boy is looking for his identity. He's searching. All I can do is help him."

This journey of searching for my roots went on through my lifetime until my father's death in 1993. Through this process I learned that our journey begins from birth with the anatomy of the soul, and only death is the end of the journey. Maybe the soul transcends life, lifting itself from the body and traveling through space and time.

The search for our identity and for our roots is, I think, the most important task in life for all of us.

WHILE MY GREAT-GRANDMOTHER SALLY B. WAS ALIVE and my Grandmother Alice and Grandfather Raymond (Pop) farmed the Homestead, there were large family dinners at least once or twice a month on Friday or Saturday nights. This custom continued until after Sally B. died.

Uncle Harry and Aunt Ida were always there with boxes of candy and accompanied by their daughter Sarah. Uncle Evens came with his five children and later his grandchildren. Uncle Herm would come, but without his wife Mary. Uncle Dave brought young Dave and, of course, our farmhand Jake and my Aunt Anna was there, since they lived at the Homestead.

We called him Jake, but his real name was George Naylor. He was a "taken" child. When a family could not afford to raise a child, he or she would be "taken" by another family who could raise the child and needed them to work on their farm, household or in their businesses. Jake had been adopted and raised by David T. and Sally B. and he became one of the brothers, the sixth brother. Jake was the Ballinger Teamster. He drove hundreds of wagon loads of tomatoes, two trips a day, to the Campbell Soup Company in Camden New Jersey, approximately seventeen miles. He would go in the early morning and he'd come back late at night with an empty wagon, in the dark, with lanterns under the wheels.

Jake married a woman later in his life. She was a foundling as well, a found child. Jake and she had no children of their own. They would have been too old. They were very quiet, introverted, and kind people.

Jake was a very important person in my young life. He gave me the title of Master Raymie, Master of the Horses, when I was four and it seemed to stick. He had a handle-bar mustache and he could spit tobacco juice eight feet away.

The house, during these gatherings of the extended family, would be full and buzzing with conversation and laughter. Sometimes there were arguments about politics, agricultural techniques, herbs, gardens, etiquette, and discussions about the best wool and the best linen. I loved the smell of the pipes and cigars and the women's perfume along with their dresses whispering against the floor.

The men usually ended up in the den embarking upon what they no doubt thought were earthshaking and enlightening conversations. The women would gravitate to the large parlor to escape the smoke and loud voices. Their conversations were just as informative for me as the men's. I never differentiated between them. It was all a learning experience for me.

In the white picket-fenced yard, a dozen children ran around after dusk catching fireflies and playing some hide-n-seek game or Ghost in the Graveyard. It seemed to me as though the festivities went on through most of the night. I never wanted it to end.

In the dimness of the evening light, after the romping in the yard or an early baseball game on the huge orange gravel driveway, the ancient elm acted as a centerpiece embracing and witnessing all. This went on until the evening came to a close, leaving only the tree frogs and the chirpers. Inside the old Homestead, lights still burned brightly in rooms filled with murmuring conversations, arguments and agreements. Women's gowns shuffled along the floor. Aroma from men's pipes and cigars floated from the den to the living room. One season was over, and a new one was beginning.

My aunts, Lois and Ginny, were up in their room, at the top of the stairs, giggling, and posing in the mirror of the chiffonier, exercising the possibilities of becoming women. I loved the idea of looking through the keyhole and witnessing their secrets. These young girls were transforming their youthful years into womanhood. They were our aunts, but they were too young to be called aunts. They were just our father's younger sisters, growing up.

Judy, my six year old sister, Sissy I called her, and I loved to go into their bedrooms.

"Can I come in?" I asked as I pushed open the door.

"Get out of here, you little brat!"

The femininity was rampant. The girls were attempting to feel every experience of womanhood. From the perfumed sprays to the hairpins, everything was in its place. The jewelry boxes, the tortoiseshell comb and brush sets, were waiting to prepare them, to present them to the world. I tried the perfumes, one by one, and ran my hands through Lois's platinum hair, awed by her beauty. I tried to sit in her lap. Her young maternal instinct held me for a moment. Then I dashed off to take a look at Ginny's grand horse painting, a sorrel stallion standing on a mound, mane and tail blowing in the wind, so apropos of their romantic views.

"I want you out of here," Ginny screamed, "Both of you."

Sticking my tongue out at her, Judy and I left the room, as a stern voice came from the bottom of the stairs."

"Yes, Daddy, we're fine," Judy reassured him. "I saw Lois kissing her boy friend last night, Raymie" she whispered.

"I did too. They were down in the parlor. I was behind the couch."

"What did they kiss like?" Judy asked.

"Like the pigeons do." I said. "Yuck!"

"What did she do?"

"Nothing, she liked it. Yuck!"

ROCKING CHAIR LOVE, comforted, being petted with maternal kindness. There was my mother Clara, with her auburn hair. Sissy, my sister Judy, Cousin Kate and Aunt Ginny -- they all loved me voraciously.

And the esteem with which I paid them back was limitless.

With utmost cordiality and affection I worked for them.

I'd chase my Aunt Ginny through the hollyhocks, and pick buttercups in the far meadow, and then I would tell her she was beautiful when she was downright ugly.

There were the late evenings in the boundless picket-fence yard where I would capture at least a quarter of a million fireflies and imprison them in this huge pickle jar to make Sissy her very own lantern.

And big Cousin Sarah who suffered from elephantiasis almost her whole life sweated something awful. She used the wicker rocker on our front porch and she'd rock and rock and chew Chiclets, swat flies, and watch the passersby until dusk. She'd give me the chewing gum right out of her mouth and then pat me on the head and tell me to go play.

Most of all I remember my mother, Clara. I would sit with her in the hot afternoon. I would hold her hand and walk through the meadows while she chanted sad love songs to me. Near the edge of the meadow there was a huge buttonwood tree with a swing tied to it, and she would swing with me, clutching me to her bosom. We would tower above the small trees, up to the fragrance of honeysuckle and down again to where my father stood waiting to scold her for acting so childishly.

All five of my grandparents' sons and their daughter, Anna, wanted to maintain their close family relationship after marriage, and to help care for their parents when they reached old age. The only one who did not feel disposed to fulfill family obligations was Herm's wife, Mary Ellis. She felt her husband had been short-changed. Herm was the oldest son and did not inherit the Homestead. He had come to terms with this, but his wife never did. Herm faithfully came by himself to every reunion, sharing and enjoying.

My grandfather, Pop, would sit at the end of the table, and cut and serve the meat. He sharpened his knives and served the food that he had raised, butchered, smoked and pickled. His vegetables were grown at the Homestead so each meal was a personal gift. If anyone didn't respect him, they heard about it fast. It was all part of the Saturday ritual.

At the end of those evenings, Pop and Grandmom stood at the door and graciously kissed everyone goodnight and wished them well for the next week. Sallie B's children also made sure that she had money; each child would contribute something so she could buy flour and other things that she might need for the following week. It was the understood responsibility of all the sons and daughters to take care of their mother because her husband was dead. Sally B. lived in the small side of the house with her daughter Anna, but she still had her responsibilities. She would bake all day long giving the breads, pies and cookies to my grandmother for those dinners. When my grandparents moved into town, the brothers and their families did not appear as often. When they did come, it was not for the grand gatherings, but instead for individual family visits.

My grandfather was such a happy man. He would say to me in the morning, "Master Raymie, the sun is shining," or "God, look at that sun come up. Come on with Granddad, we're gonna shuck corn today." We would go out with the horses and my grandfather would talk to them. "Pull up there Silver. On to the next shuck. Are you sleeping?" The horse would snort and kind of turn his head and pull up. Granddad was communicating with the world. He was so into life. He had no time to follow anybody else. He was in touch with the Earth.

In the cold part of the fall, when the crisp moist air and the frost was on the ground and you could freeze the tips of your fingers, my grandfather would be taking those ears of corn, shucking them out and putting them into a box carted by the horse. I'd see him out there with the wind blowing his hat off across the field. He'd get his hat and he'd come back and I'd hear him singing or whistling or talking to the horse or to himself.

Folks would ask, "What makes him so happy? Why is he so happy just about the sun coming up in the morning?"

Grandpop would tell me, "That is the first gracious moment among the happenings in a day of all of our lives. Even the rain, snow or wind bites the day with happiness. Today might give me some rain or wind. The day's going to give me snowstorm or frost. My fingers are tingly. You feel the tingle, Raymie?"

My grandfather opened the doors of the spiritual world of nature for me. My father did that as well in the woods of the swamp at Taunton Lake.

We had a clock in the den of the Homestead called a Regulator. It had a pendulum, and you could see it through the prism glass as it swayed back and forth and measured time. My grandmother, Alice, reminded me of that clock. She was a child of the Gibson Girl period. Like her contemporaries, I am sure she wore a girdle most of the time, and she kept her hair rolled up, often with a net on it. She wasn't religious like Sally B. or her own mother, Lottie. She was a bit rebellious where religion was concerned.

She dressed in a very refined manor, always appearing somewhat formal even in cotton work dresses. She had many aprons and her dark hair sprinkled with grey was always done up well. She wore black shoes with a little thicker, raised heel. Alice always wore her cotton stockings going up to her knees.

When my father went out West in 1946, I went to live at the Homestead with my grandparents. I felt alone and cried all the time. My mother had left and Dad had gone and I would cry. I couldn't sleep at nights by myself, so I'd sleep with Grandma. She slept in the middle room in the hall. She'd take me in with her and she would hold me close until I slept, talking to me and comforting me. My grandfather slept in his own bed, an old Victorian in the southwest room. He had asthma and with his back problem he had to sit up all the time. She would go to his room when he asked her to, leaving her bed with me alone in it.

At night she would let her hair down. That was the first time I was in a woman's room. On her bureau were the tortoise shell brushes and beautiful large combs, a mirror, her perfumes, and other feminine things. I felt the room was surrounded with feminine qualities, delicateness.

She worked very hard, making soap, and candles, and cleaning the chimneys of the oil lamps. We had an old washing machine with the gyrator in the bottom and the wooden paddle up front that she had to pound, and the wringer that she had to crank before she could hang the clothing out on the line. When she was working in the garden picking the vegetables or harvesting and canning she'd be perspiring. A piece of hair would fall down, or she'd wear a hair net and after she was finished she'd wash her hands.

She had an inner balance. She would cook, and lay out the tablecloths, always linen, under the two chandeliers that hung above the twelve-foot-long table. The smaller table would be ten feet long if it was only the two of them for lunch. My Grandfather would sit at one end of the table and she would sit at the other end.

I remember Grandmother Alice rubbing her hands across the linen and feeling it, as if she'd woven it. Her fingers knew her linen, china and the silver and the cooking. She was in command of that whole room. When she laid out the dishes of food, she would look at the faces of the people to see how they felt about the food, and she would be satisfied if they liked it. She didn't serve you. She allowed you to eat there and you felt honored to sit at her table.

Her pies, covered with the towels, would be on an antique wooden table with fine legs in the kitchen area, left of the entrance. Alice had her tea towels hanging out on a little porch off the back kitchen, where the rose bush was and the little chickadees used to keep a nest. She'd talk to the chickadees all the time.

I'd get up on the green antique bench and look at a chickadee sitting on its eggs or feeding its babies. I could watch one for hours. When the rose bush was in bloom, it would climb around the whole side of the little porch onto the lattice trim where the porch overlooked the fields. The little chickadees were always in that rosebush, and Alice would hang her tea towels out there, keeping time with the day.

When Granddad came in from the fields, it was as though they were meeting on their first date, and they never stopped looking forward to these noonday meetings.

Alice felt her own presence in the morning heat, the sound of the locusts, the harvest, and the accomplishment of her duties. She was leisurely and relaxed, living her life and doing her duties with both satisfaction and command. She supervised her children, the herb garden, the canning, the making of soap and oil, the dairy, the cheeses, and the men that came to be fed. She kept an eye on the help and on their women.

Alice didn't clean a house. She put a house in order, but it was her order. None of her duties were ever insulting to her, belittling or beneath her. She saw them as an extension of herself. Her fulfillment in life was within her marriage and being harnessed to the Homestead with Granddad. He was pulled out into the field and she was pulled into the house, the garden and the dairy. They could be a quarter mile apart and yet they still had the same harmony, the same steps, the same motion, and the same rhythm in the seasons they lived.

My grandparents were very quiet at the table. I don't remember them talking very much, unlike my father. Grandmother's table was almost a prayer, not before the meal, but during the meal. It seemed very spiritual, and you could hear the china and the spoons touch as our hands went across the tablecloth.

We picked up the crumbs with a little silver dustpan. When the dishes were taken away the girls would come into the kitchen and wash them. This became a party, with their talk about schools, boyfriends and activities, filled with music, singing, dancing and laughing. The men would sometimes come into the kitchen and sit on stools and watch the women. Other times the men would sit in the den and talk about farming, different cultivators, and their teams of horses, ploughs, seed and corn. The conversation would center on whatever they were dealing with seasonally, like cutting ice and smoking meat.

Alice's daughters would get angry about her ease and her peacefulness and fullness with her life. She was coming out of the nineteenth century, but they were coming into more modern times. They resented her, as I think my father resented his father, for being at peace with her life.

FOG WOULD OVERLAY THE BACKFIELD in Pine Grove behind the bungalow. I would hear my father stirring in the bedroom, going into the kitchen and putting on his shoes. The laces on his work shoes went around hooks instead of through eyelets. Once I heard him stirring I would get up. I would scurry about and throw on my things. Often in my rush, I would put on my shoes without socks. By the time I got dressed and got out, usually grabbing something from the refrigerator as I passed by, bread, or anything else that was in the kitchen. I'd be running and he'd be harnessing Silver up to the buckboard wagon. I wasn't in school yet.

"Oh, so you made it. Well, come on up here."

I'd climb up on the wheel, to the rim and then I'd climb up on to the wood part of the seat. The wagon had a spring seat in the front, kind of a bluish green with red on it. The spokes of the wheels were yellow. Dad would lift the lines up, and I would sit on his lap or I would sit on the side of the seat, and we would go along.

I would wrap my hand around his leg, and I'd be looking over through his knees, to his arms on the reins. It was as if I was looking through to another world, through him and the horse and the reins, which framed off the view. I would look at the high Indian grass and the fescue and the rye grass, and we'd ride through the field, past Coopers' and past the bungalows on to this half dirt, half grass road going along with the horse.

The horse would be waking up and farting, and snorting, and the wagon would bump a little bit on the ground, with a soft swampy texture. You could smell the earth, and you could feel the entrance into Nature. The mist would rise off the ground. Everything was silent except for the horse, the wagon wheels, the squeaking of the bolster, and a few of the bumps. Your body would hit on to the bolster and you could hear the horse's lungs setting in when he was pulling, and sometimes you could hear the chains from the swingle-trees.

My father didn't talk. We would just ride. We'd be going and listening to the music of the wagon. The mist would be rising and the horse's breath would smoke up from each nostril. When it was a little hotter, the sweat would come off the horse once we reached halfway. I would see the steam from the horse, the grass, and my father's breath and my breath, fused with the mist, and we would enter this mystical world.

We would cross over past Hognose's. Across Elmwood Road you'd hear the cadence of the hooves on the road. Finally we'd go down the orange gravel road to our Homestead.

By this time I could hear the lids of the milk cans being knocked off, and the men talking. My grandmother was in the house preparing breakfast and getting her daughters up and getting them going.

When we arrived my father would take his work jacket off and put on his milking jacket. As we would enter one of the milkers would come into the milk house with its cement floor and dump his fourteen quart stainless steel bucket of milk down through the strainer and into a milk can. The warm milk would steam as it was poured into the cold metal cans and for me that connected the horse's breath, and our breath, and the breath of the earth to the steam from the milk.

We would go into the barn entering along the lime covered floor, just past the gutters, and over the manger walk. If it were still a little bit dark, we would have lanterns. The milkers would take canes and slide the lanterns down on a wire. All the men would have three-legged stools tied to their behinds. They looked kind of funny, like hunch backed men, as they'd pulled their linen smock to their sides and sat down and turned their hats backwards, putting the tail of the cow between the stool's legs while wrapping it around the stool. Then they would put their head against the thigh of the cow, and begin milking again.

The men could milk twelve to fourteen quarts of milk in three to four minutes each. There'd be three to four men in line, going down through the barn, milking. Cats would be walking small velvet steps along the lime-covered walkway, wistfully winding their tails as they meowed to us, sitting in anticipation of having being given a squirt of warm milk from the cow into their mouths. As the milker would step alongside their cow, the cat would go and sit in his place, knowing that this was the next step toward getting more milk. Each milker would go to every odd numbered cow, so that the men wouldn't be back to back. The cows would be moving in their stanchions. You could hear the chains, and you could see them eating their silage and grain and barley.

Finally, the men would knock the lids back on to the cans with a rubber mallet, or a piece of pipe, and they would roll the cans out and put them into the icebox. They had to lift them down, not up, into the pit of the icebox, and then lift the lid up. There would be more steam coming from the icebox. Then they would roll the empty buckets, cans and strainers into the washroom where they'd have hot water and fill up the milk cans in the washroom. As the milkers finished, they would take off their jackets and hang them back on the hooks inside the door of the milk house, and then, as a reward, throw a forkful of timothy hay in front of the cows that had eaten all their grain.

Everyone would proceed into breakfast except Jake, who would go out to give the horses their ears of corn. He would tell me how many ears to put in each standing stall, and he'd carry the bushel basket with him full of corn. I'd pick the ears out of the basket, and if I were really concentrating, I would remember each horse, what they got. Then Jake would take the three-pronged hayforks, and throw a small amount of hay into the manger because the horses were going to go back out to work.

We would all go into breakfast. Breakfast was made for everybody. We sat in the dining room with the two chandeliers at the big long table covered with a linen tablecloth and ate. My grandfather sat at the end of the table and all the workers on the farm and the rest of the family sat on each side. Grandmom sat at the other end, and the old Regulator clock on the wall reminded us that the day had begun. We'd have breakfast, and even though I was this little four year old boy, I felt like I was one of the men. I was Master Raymie, sitting at the table with them and having my eggs and my bacon and toast, just like the men did. Everything that they would do, I would try to copy.

Jake would go back out to the horses. He'd leave a little earlier from the table. I'd get up with him and go out too and watch as he'd start watering the horses and harnessing them. I'd ride the working horses out. Afterwards, he'd take them back into their stall and I'd ride another one out sitting tall on that big horse. Sometimes he'd leave the horse with nothing but a halter on, drinking, and Jake would go back into the barn and harness another horse. The horse would turn around and go right back into the stall with me on him. I thought that was really exciting. Each horse knew me. I would sink into their flesh and slide into their hair and grab their mane in my fingers, and feel each horse and greet him personally. I was never afraid. I felt I was part of the horse, the barn, and the harvest. I was part of the work. I was part of the mist.

The rest of the men would come out. My grandmother would be standing on the back porch watching. We finished harnessing the teams and hooked them up to go down the long driveway. The men headed out into the fields and the women said goodbye from the porch.

Grandmom would go back into the house to complete her morning chores before she had to cook and set up for lunch. She fed so very many people each day. She relaxed with her darning and sewing. The girl children had house chores. They would clean the chimneys of the oil lamps, dump the chamber pots, make the beds, wash and change the linens and make soap and candles. They would also clean up the dairy after the men had gone.

At noon Grandmom would knock the triangular clapper and the men would come up for lunch. She would make hot meals, not sandwiches. She watched the teams go down the driveway, and Granddad would wave to her. Everybody who worked for us on the farm would call her "Mrs. Ballinger."

She did this daily while working harmoniously in her gardens, caring for the lawns and the flowers. There was a rhythm to her days. Life was an integral part of the physical universe. It was not disconnected. Life was harmonious with nature and living went on with a natural pace. The men working on the farm didn't hate their jobs. They didn't hate their day. Grandmom didn't hate cooking for them and she didn't hate her life. It was a complete way of living.

You could tell by the attentiveness of the horses that they knew what God was asking in order to recreate the servicing of the soul with the experience of the men picking the tomatoes in the sun drenched fields. This was a spiritual experience for me. I felt that God had spoken down to me as I had reached up and asked him for this gift of the seasons with the morning sun and the echo of the locusts. The smell of the sweet round tomatoes surrounded me. I had been given the task of taking a wagon with empty baskets and pulling off the baskets and putting them up and down the rows as the men started picking each morning. The sun was fresh up. I would walk down the row and start picking, and as I got deeper into the row, I was deeper into the spiritual experience. I was fused into the earth. We had been given a seasonal calling.

Moving into the rows the baskets got fuller and my eyes got heavier. The field lifted its carpet of heat onto my face. Then the noonday bell sounded telling me it was time for lunch. My grandmother stood on the back porch waving her dishtowel. The horses knew it was break time and they could feel the men, the earth, and the sun. The wagons pulled up under the buttonwood trees and the horses stood there and swatted the flies with their tails while the men went in to have their lunch. They waited with canvas feed buckets of oats tied to their bridle.

This spiritual conditioning carried through the whole lunch, until the teams and the horses reconnected as we came back up into the fields.

We were in a velvet cradle cuddled by nature into a hypnotic state. The smell of the tomatoes on the vine came right off onto your hands.

THE FOURTH OF JULY WAS AN ICE CREAM CELEBRATION. Granddad would get cream from the dairy and put it in this big churn surrounded by salt in order to keep the ice from melting. We'd take fresh strawberries from the garden and we'd have this huge Fourth of July celebration. Everyone would be in the yard, inside the big white picket fence under the elm trees and the old maple. Uncle Harry would bring some of his candy. He had invented this peanut brittle and he made a fortune out of that. He was our candy man. Charley Biddle would come over. He owned Biddle's, one of the largest hardware stores around the country at the time. It was as big as a Sears and Roebuck's. My father still has their knives that were so sharp that after thirty years you could still cut a piece of steak with them.

We would play baseball. There was a big section in the middle, probably half the size of a ball court, within the circle formed by the big barn, the wagon barns, the carriage barns and the house .We would hit the ball toward the elm tree in the center aisle where the carriages would drive around. We'd all play the outfield and we would pitch and hit. We had a particular kind of energy that comes from having twenty five or thirty people gathered who all grew up together.

My grandfather and his brothers knew each other intimately, and they were all part of my childhood. They knew my brothers and sisters and my mother, Clara, and later Jean, the woman who would marry my father. When we sat down at the big table everyone would wait for my grandfather to sit at one end and my grandmother at the other. Ginny and Lois would giggle and sometimes they would bring dates. Judy, Larry and I would scoot around the house trying to see everything. There was a unity of spirit sparked by shared experience.

The evenings were like holidays. You'd hear the music coming from the little cylinder record player. My grandfather loved opera. He had a beautiful baritone voice and he would sing along with Caruso. You'd smell the cigar smoke and sometimes even a pipe. Granddad would sit in his Morris chair, and sometimes he would burn incense for his asthma. That smell would permeate the room and the screen door would be open to the front porch and the glider. I loved the swing that sat on the porch. The walkways were all parquet brick from the yard down to the picket fence and out to the orange gravel road and the hundred foot high elm tree.

The sacred picket fence was mended yearly. I could hear the rap and the tap of my grandfather's hammer flowing across the slats as he walked the yard with me behind him. When the rap tap tap, became rap bang... I knew there was a weak slat, or maybe one that needed replacement. This same balance kept the old fence whole for over one hundred years. It was never totally replaced. The locust posts remained solid. The slats were occasionally replaced. The Fence, like the family, had a history. Children, like the slats, made up the new generations.

Dad rolled with the times, trying to keep up... which meant often times rolling over Larry and the rest of the family, trying to do what he thought needed to be done... pressuring himself beyond limits, off the scales of balance.

With Dad, if there was a rotten post or slat, he would tear down the whole side of the fence and rebuild it with much expense and effort, which added to his anxiety. Granddad would only replace one slat at a time as it was needed.

The hard lesson was that bigger and newer was not necessarily better.

WHEN I WAS FOUR I USED TO GO TO A BAPTIST CHURCH in Marlton with my mother. Downstairs, there was a little Sunday school class room where they gave out book markers for the days that you showed up to Bible school on time. Once you reached twelve book markers you got a Bible. I really wanted that Bible, because the Bible had tons of pictures in it, wonderful pictures, colored pictures, and pictures of Jesus with doves. I manipulated and worked my way around to everybody in the church trying to get them to give me their book markers. I had my Bible by the second week of school.

In return for their bookmarkers, I gave out numerous pigeon feathers from the farm and the other kids happily gave me their bookmarkers. When I got my Bible, I carefully studied the pictures of Jesus wearing a robe with the doves flying all around him, sitting on his shoulders and on his hands.

Afterwards I went into Dad's pigeon house with a blanket as my robe, and opened the Bible to make sure I was in the correct position. I had the pigeons come and fly around me the way they did with Jesus. I felt next to God.

My mother had canned a whole bunch of red cabbage. I wanted to take one jar to give to God. I insisted on taking the jar to church, so I hid it under my arm. When I saw that no one was around I put the jar on the shelf of the pulpit. I sat back on the seat on the left side of the church in the pews on the aisle and I watched and waited. I wanted to see God take my cabbage. Everybody had been talking about him and I figured he must be pretty big. He had a big house, and he's certainly was going to be hungry, so he had to eat and I had the cabbage offering.

I waited and waited and waited. I patiently watched the women singing. After the service, my mother told me, "You're a gentleman. Go and help girls on with their jackets."

I went to the end of the church where the people were leaving as they shook hands with the preacher, and I helped the women on with their coats. I was rushing everywhere and frantically putting jackets on everyone.

"You don't have to help everybody, just your friends and people you know."

"Well, I didn't know that. Nobody told me that." I was putting on everybody's jackets and making a fool out of myself.

Later that day I returned and quickly looked under the pulpit, and the cabbage was still there. I wasn't happy. I took my cabbage home, very disappointed.

The next Sunday I didn't want to go to church. I said, "There is no God, and he's not going to show. He's not going to ever be there. I don't want to go there anymore."

Dad had a clothesline where he used to kill and then hang the pigeon squabs he harvested for market.

The first time I went out and I saw them there must have been a hundred squabs hanging from it. He would cut their throats with a penknife. All I could see were all of my pigeons from the Bible, my doves, hanging on a clothesline. I kicked him and screamed, "You killed my pigeons. You killed my pigeons!" He tried to explain to me what he was doing.

I wouldn't listen to any explanation. He had killed my Bible pigeons. I couldn't put on my blanket robe and do my scene any more. It was horrible!

The lady at the Bible school tried to get me to understand, and started giving me new pictures and new bookmarkers, and stories with other pictures in them. They thought they had a new apostle. I just felt so much. I could have been a child evangelist when I was young. I just wanted to give my heart and soul.

The following spring, in the black secret of the night, I waited for Granddad to rouse me from my bed. I walked, sleepy but excited, to the barn feeling as if it was a Christmas morning. We climbed to the barn loft making ourselves known to its silence.

Standing at the edge of the loft to catch our breath we could hear the cooing from the wild pigeons under the eve planks as we lifted the trap board to their nest as we reached for the nearest squab with the black wings and the white body. Not yet having flown from her nest, she offered little resistance. Carefully we put her into our getaway brown burlap sack. She complained little about her new and unexplained life.

Granddad smiled at me acknowledging the accomplishment.

Moving down the line I pointed to the third nest where there was an all white bird with just a splash of gray on his wings and tail. Quickly, Granddad cradled him into his large hand brushing fingers though the new neck and head feathers.

"This is a fine bird Raymie, a good breeding mate for the black winged one."

"Thanks Granddad. He's strong."

"Yes," he smiled, shaking his head in agreement. "Strong and promising."

This solidified my lifelong love of pigeons.

In Marlton, at the Homestead, Larry and I always kept bantam chickens and we hatched chicks from them. We'd put them in coops every spring. Banties were always good setting on eggs. In twenty-one days, we'd end up with a nice bunch of colorful chicks. Larry and I looked forward to this every spring.

We probably got the idea from Granddad, because the coops that we used had been his. He had always raised a large number of meat chickens for market, primarily white rocks. Larry and I preferred the banties, because of their beautiful colors. I always looked forward to the morning, going down to the coops in back of the hen house where I would give out fountains of fresh water and a little growing mash in their feeders. No sooner than I had put the feed out, and pulled the sliding board from their coop, that the mother would hop out clucking away, as she called her young.

There was a little hole at the bottom of the coop through which the chicks would greet her. She would line them all up and talk to them. Skirting the ground with her wings, shuffling them all in line, she showed them how to peck the corn from the mash. She'd scold one if it were out of line, verbally and physically. When the chicks needed protection, she would covey them all together and hold them under her wings. Now, as a five-year-old child, I found their behavior patterns fascinating. I'd watch them for hours. I would just lie on the ground, on my elbows, chin tucked in my hands observing and watching their habits.

People always say that birds don't really have brains, but I've watched chickens train and treat their young better than a lot of humans do. I still raise chickens. I love breeding them and seeing how their unique colors keep appearing through generations, depending on the combinations of roosters and hens that you are mating.

For me my chickens were like Mendel and his peas. They taught me heredity and offered a key to evolution and life.

The first dogs that Dad owned were beagles. My grandfather was a great beagle person.

He rabbit hunted at the beagle club over at the old Ballinger Estate. When Teddy Roosevelt was

President he had had beagle hounds and he hunted there. It was a very popular sport at that time. They had great rabbit warrens and they would let out the rabbits and run the beagles for a few hours and then put them back in their pens and go home. It was a pretentious and lazy way to hunt.

Initially, my father took some beagles that he had and he went out with his friend Buck Pyle into the hills of West Jersey. Later he bought his first fox hounds, Whitey and Blackie, from the Italians in Pine Grove. That began his love of fox hunting.

Dad had taken the rumble seat out of the old model T and he put a dog box back there. He would go down into the Taunton Lake or to the nearby cranberry cogs where there were lowlands, swamp and dwarf pines. It was a very mossy and sandy soil.

He finally got Queenie, the perfect bitch, and then he found Plunder, a little white dog. Plunder stood square on all four legs, and he had a chest like a bulldog. He was almost snow white with a thick tail, and he had a big bell voice. When he yelped you could hear it through his whole body. He was a power house when Dad took him fox hunting. Queenie was very royal, and a leader in the pack. She had a very cold nose. She'd smell the track and straighten all the dogs out, and not fight with them.

Dad bred the dogs and he became known for his foxhounds.

My brother Larry was old enough to go into the woods, but since he was working the only time he could go was at night with Dad. Dad would pull up and turn the headlights off and listen to the crickets and the night chirpers, and the owls. He'd smell the forest and the pine in the barrens. Then you'd hear a note, and Plunder would jump out of the truck and go right onto a trail. He'd call the other hounds and then O-Woo-o-o-o-w. Queenie would answer."O-w-u-g-h-w-o-o-o-e"

Dad depended upon his hounds. He had a reputation and he had to keep it. He also made serious extra money from them because he'd breed and sell fifteen hounds a year for top dollar. He primarily kept the females but none of the males.

Larry would hunt with him. Naturally, I wanted to tag along. I was four or five. Dad told me to dress warmly and wear my rubber boots and a heavy sweater. I rode between him and Larry in the old Model T. The bushes would rub against the doors and the windows as you were bumping all over and turning and twisting in the sand. We would ride and then we'd stop in the dark. I would squeeze Larry's hand.

Dad opened the doors and they stepped out. Larry went around and pulled the pin out of the back of the little dog box and the hounds came jumping out. They just smelled the air finding the direction of the wind and the fox. Once Queenie found it, the dogs ran deep into the bogs.

"Raymie, you and Larry stay here by the box, and I'll go over and get the dogs and bring them back because this fox is closer to the car." My father had a stride on him that you couldn't keep up with. You had to literally run to walk with him.

I got scared. "Larry, what's that? I want to go with Daddy." I started sniffling a little bit.

"Cut it out, Raymie, just be quiet," Larry said.

Then Larry heard Plunder going in the other direction. "I'd better go over and get him. You don't want to come with me?" he asked. "Then stay here."

Larry left me alone in the woods. I was wet and crying and terrified and angry. Larry didn't know any better. He was only eight years old. He'd already been hunting with my father for three years.

Within minutes I stopped screaming. I sat there and watched a bird come down and heard an owl screech. A deer broke some branches down the path, and I saw an opossum on a limb and a raccoon at the roots of a tree. I just started laughing, and I would make sounds back to the owl, to the grouse, and to all the other birds.

I could feel the grass in my hand, and the moisture of the earth. I could hear the sounds of birds and animals and smell the marshland and the moss. By the time Dad came back, I had been initiated into the wilderness and to the hunt. The woods have been part of me ever since.

I had heard my Dad call, and he came back to where I was standing. He had an inner compass.

"What the hell are you doing here alone boy?"

I said "Larry left me."

He said, "That wasn't very nice, was it? Let's go back to the truck."

When I was about five years old in the fall of 1943, I went fox hunting again with my Dad in the cranberry bogs. One of his other hunting friends had a hound that was running deer. I heard the hound going from barking to yelping like he was being beaten. When I asked my Dad what happened he said,

"The damn dog was running deer. We can't have that."

That next Sunday when we went out in the afternoon, the sun was still shining. It was a fall day and the leaves were turning. In the cool you could hear the breeze from the leaves of the trees in the woods. There were wild turkeys, grouse, and pheasant.

Within twenty minutes Plunder ran off in the other direction. Dad took a piece of heavy stick and broke the tip off.

I got very frightened. My father could be extreme. He was not a cruel person, but if this dog did something bad, he would whip him.

The dog came right out with an eight point buck. Dad jumped on top of Plunder, grabbed him by the collar, took the stick, and beat the living shit out of him, and beat him, and beat him, and beat him. And he cried, my father cried. He had just beaten his favorite dog almost to death. My father held him up in his arms and cried like a baby,

I'd never seen my father cry before in his life. And he said "Plunder, boy, why? Why would you do a thing like this? What has gotten into you?" He had lost total faith in his dog.

He laid him against the side of the hill. The blood mixed with the sand. I went over. I peed in my pants and I said, "Daddy, don't hurt him. Don't hurt Plunder. I love Plunder. You love Plunder. Larry loves Plunder."

My father picked Plunder up like a baby, laid him in the truck and he took him home. He didn't hunt him for the longest time, because he was frightened by what might happen if he took Plunder into the wood and the dog ran a deer.

Plunder stayed at the farm chained to one of the half-barrels that served as a kennel. He bred him to a couple of his bitches.

When the winter came and snow was on the ground, we had a few litters of pups. They were kept tied up to the half barrels on six-foot chains that shaved the snow off the top of the ground as the dogs moved around.

Dad went out and he walked through the barrels. He took all the male puppies and knocked their heads against the barrel. He held them on the outside of the barrel by the back of the legs like you do when you kill pigeons. He just had them all together almost like on a string. He'd go through all the barrels and killed almost all the male puppies.

When I saw the blood on the snow it was the most terrifying experience in my life. To this day I can still remember it vividly. It was even worse than when he killed all my baby squabs for meat, and sold them to the big markets in Camden.

When I was a child I didn't understand why my father did that. Later I understood that if there were too many pups, some would starve. He kept the best of the litter, most of which were females.

Larry said Dad had killed the puppies because they were males and they had enough. Well I was an extra boy, and this really scared me. I was very frightened of Dad for a long time after that.

He used to put me on his knee all the time, and talk to me, and hold me. I wouldn't get on his knee any more. It was just very hard to handle.

I never saw my grandfather that way.

IN 1943, MY FATHER WAS a twenty-nine year old man with a wife and three children helping his father at the Homestead, and working at nights at the shipyard. While living in Pine Gove the beginning of the end of our childhood years came when Dad rented an abandoned farm to build his dream. That spring he sold our comfortable small bungalow in Pine Grove and decided to bring his wife, our mother Clara, and us three kids to the new farm on

 the edge of Barrington, New Jersey, not that far from the Homestead and Pine Grove. Clara refused to move into a raw house on a raw farm. All she could see was a house with no heat, bare bones electricity, chicken shit everywhere and only a sink in the kitchen, not to mention a privy in the backyard. This was not her vision of home life in 1944, war or not.

Dad and we children thought the place seemed reasonable. Clara saw nothing except one used kerosene stove. Dad had the floors refinished and promised a furnace and indoor plumbing. After Mom's friend Ruth Hickinbotham and a man from Haddon Heights came in and did all the refurbishing she consented to moving in. A week later our mother still had reservations but she was there. With his first milk check, Dad fixed the electricity and put in a furnace. The toilet still was a wooden privy in the back yard. In Pine Grove we had had a brand new modern house.

When we first lived in Barrington we had no tubs. Clara had to go out and pump water up to the back porch with a hand pump and then heat it in a big bucket on the stove. She poured warm water from the stove into the basins, and she'd stand us up on top of the kitchen table and wash us all over. She always kept us and our clothing clean and ironed. Many times on Sunday mornings, when Mom wanted us all to go to church, she'd wash us at seven o'clock in the morning on that cold table. The water wasn't warm enough to not be frigid. She'd wash us and rinse us off and we'd have break-fast and put on our good clothing and go to church with her. Dad would be in the barn milking. Larry would stay with him and milk and she'd take Judy and me.

We had a wood stove on one end of the kitchen, and the kerosene stove was at the other. Judy was responsible for filling the kerosene stove. My mother and my father were starting to fight again. Judy went out and she mixed up the gas can with the kerosene can. Dad was coming

in for lunch to have soup. Clara lit the match and Dad smelled gas and stopped her just in time. We'd have blown ourselves up and the whole place with us. He found Judy and he whipped her with his hand. She should never have had that responsibility.

Initially in Barrington, we had an old big round privy and we played in there. We used it for a long time. We had little chamber pots and I had to dump those. We had no electricity and gas. We had oil lamps..... and this was a time when there was electricity. I thought my mother was happy. I thought my father was happy.

She was so beautiful, with her copper blond hair and sea green eyes. Sometimes she would wash out the milk cans and the dairy. I would hear them making love. Larry was busy and content with his new school. Judy was doing well. I felt like I was somehow left out. I probably wasn't, but I was a dreamer and I was dreaming a lot. I kept going inside of myself and into nature.

I missed my Granddad and my Grandma a lot, and the teams of horses. We only had two teams and there were six at the Homestead. I felt that something was not quite right.

Mom and Dad had been fighting when they first moved in. After we got the furnace, running water, and a bathroom inside, it seemed better. We raised chickens and we had a cherry orchard. We had a big garden in the back and the cows were milking well.

That first spring and summer that we lived at Barrington, it seemed like things were going to work. Clara was starting to adjust. Dad put in the garden with vegetables and flowers for her. That summer we all picked cherries and Clara made cherry pies and canned the rest.

We planted corn. Sometimes I would dig it up to see how it was growing. I would look carefully and then plant it back in the ground. When the baby chicks would be hatching I would take them out of their shell and then put them back. I always wanted to know how things worked and what happened to them inside themselves.

Leslie was conceived that spring. As children we did not realize how fragile our lives were going to become. We all seemed to be filled with seasonal joy and happiness. That November Leslie was born.

We had this bull that was very mean, and I would tease him in the field and dare him to chase me. I confused stupidity with courage. The bull weighed a half a ton. He came at me one day and hit the door with his head and pushed the whole big double pine door through the barn. My father had to take a pitchfork and put it through his nose which was the only way to stop him. He backed him all the way around the barn.

I was just turning six and in the first grade. I had ended up staying out of school a lot that winter helping Dad. He usually took Larry with him and Larry got so far behind in school. When we moved to Barrington they had put me back in the first grade.

Before we moved in, we ripped out all the wooden planks in the old dairy barn, and we put in cement floors and gutters and mangers. I was so cold working in that barn that Larry would chase me around with Dad's belt just to help me keep warm and stop complaining about being cold. Dad cleaned it out on weekends and at night with lanterns and then he managed to pour a whole barn floor of cement with just an old cement mixer that had a gasoline engine to turn it, and he bolted in forty stanchions while still working in the shipyard. He would put in cement and lime and sand and then mix and fill it.

He did all the masonry work, and put in the stanchions and the gutters, the mangers and the aisles all by hand that winter with only Larry helping him. He tore all the planks out and made the barn into a dairy. When he had it ready to move in by the following spring, he ploughed. He didn't bring the cattle in there right away. He had some cows that were at Granddad's place, that he'd bred. When we finally moved in he brought some more cows.

He took telephone ties that were free. He had gotten them from town and he cut them up and made corner posts from them and put them in the ground by hand, with one of those shovels that make post holes. He put up acres and acres and more acres of fence by himself.

He'd go out with a light on the old truck, or tractor, and put fence poles in at night time and cut the excess post off. The next morning he'd run wire. He would hook it to the back of the Model T with a spool and he'd run barbed wire and staple it all round the fields.

My father was a power house, a work horse, and he worked hard. When he finally had his dairy and he brought cows in, he had no milk-house. He built a little cinder block milk-house, but he couldn't find a milkman.

They said "You can't keep shipping milk without a milk house."

There was a deaf and dumb man who drove an ice wagon and he would bring us these big blocks of ice. Dad chopped up the ice and put it in two big old bath-tubs. He kept his cans of milk in that thing for months, because he couldn't afford a big refrigerator. The milk man finally found a used milk box for Dad. Pappy Shuster came and hooked it up.

Then he found a big wooden forty footer silo with vertical boards on it. Larry and I went with Dad to take down all the tongue and groove boards in order to move it and we loaded them on the trucks, and brought it to Barrington. The silo stood up by the barn. The place was becoming our own new Paradise. It was really quite wonderful.

At first Clara seemed content, but soon Dad was fighting with my mother and then he was angry all the time. She was just so tired of all the work and the stress. She didn't want to do anything anymore.

Clara was an attractive twenty-eight year old who wanted a pay check every week, and who didn't care that her husband had to work in a shipyard to get it. She was very happy rolling up his sleeves at three o'clock each afternoon, before he left. Wanting to have some fun in her life and to be social and smoke cigarettes, play cards, and dance and party with her friends was enough for her. She had thought she finally had Dad where she wanted him, living in a bungalow and working in a shipyard. He was no longer just making $18 a week on the Homestead. Spending his money and having parties while he was in the shipyard working, rather than trying to save money to rebuild the farm that he had just rented, made her happy.

Clara refused to come to Barrington the first two weeks we were there. When she finally succumbed to Dad's wishes she became pregnant with Leslie. That summer Dad hired someone to put a furnace in. This just happened to be Dwight Layman Moody Shuster [Pappy].

Barrington was also the place where Jean Shuster and her family solidified a relationship with my Dad. We children had no idea of the ultimate consequences of that relationship. I, unseen, saw Jean and Dad kissing in the loft while my mother was still living in Barrington. Then Dad bought Chief, his strawberry roan Tennessee Walking stallion, and his first team of Percherons, Molly and Dolly. Soon there were two palominos in the barn. Dad had gotten those palominos for Jean and for himself. Clara didn't ride. When he bought Chief, why did he buy those two palominos if he was so short of cash?

Struggling with three children and a new infant while her husband was out buying riding horses, assured for her that there was never enough money.

Clara became more isolated from us and stayed away from Dad and me. I saw more of the Shusters and less of my mother.

DAD DROVE US IN THE GREEN CHEVY to the outskirts of Haddonfield to Leonard Duffy's to look at a horse that someone had told him about. He bought Chief, our first Tennessee Walking Horse, that spring. The snow was barely off the ground.

He had just quit working in the shipyard. We drove east and Duffy's was on the right, cut down off the road. The stables were set in, parallel to the road. We parked the car at the circle. Duffy greeted us and continued walking along the front of the stables, explaining to my father that he had this older strawberry roan Tennessee Walking stallion. The proverbial Doctor had owned him and hardly ever ridden him. Chief might be a little bit stable sour because the last time the good Doctor rode him he reared up and threw him, so Chief was a rare bargain.

Duffy hemmed and hawed a little bit. "Now I don't believe this but there were rumors that he was a killer. Probably when he reared, he came down close to where the doctor had fallen. You know how rumors start. Since he's been here in my stables I haven't seen a mean bone in his body. I just think it's a damn shame that he's not being ridden." Duffy then spit tobacco juice through his bristled mustache.

Tilting his Stetson higher on his forehead he thought for a moment and then rubbed his boot into the ground. "Now I can't let this horse go to anyone but an experienced rider. Dwight Shuster told me that you'd done some rodeo- n'. Now I can't guarantee his papers, but his granddaddy is Roan Allen, the best foundation stock a Walker can have. I can't let him go too cheap. Game to try him, Raymond? "

"I don't see why not. Where's the saddle?"

We all stood back, watched and waited as Duffy saddled him and brought him out. Dad walked toward Chief and spoke to him directly. He whispered and rubbed his hand down his neck and through his mane. You could tell that he fancied him. Chief was a peacock. Every bone in his body knew that he was special. He liked himself, and so did Dad.

Dad gathered and overlapped the reins into his broad hand, and held them to the horn as he lifted his foot into the stirrup. Anxious, Chief stood and danced as though he was walking on hot coals. Dad positioned himself firmly in the saddle and laid both hands on the reins. The stallion stood, waiting.

Duffy backed us up, far enough away that if anything happened we wouldn't get hurt. Chief danced and waited, as his mane flowed gracefully on the crest of his neck. All my father had to do was purse his lips with a slight whistle, loosen the reins and this stallion was a sight to see. He tucked his head into his neck, raised and fluffed his tail, and went into a gait that we had never seen before. There was no up and down motion at all. He thrust his front feet out smartly knowing exactly where to place them. His back feet came forward, over striding the front. My father didn't move out of the saddle. Up and down the driveway Chief went, doing his fancy walk. He would twist his head, and throw his mane and tail into the wind.

It was a sight to behold. He was the most magnificent animal any of us had ever laid eyes on. When he got to the end of the drive, he insisted on coming back, but Dad wouldn't let him. There they were at the end of the lane confronting one another. Duffy was impressed. With one quick smack on the rump, and a little of Dad's heel, the stallion reared, and turned in the direction that Dad wanted to go. For a moment or two they marched out of our sight. Larry and I got nervous, as did the Shusters, but shortly afterwards he entered the driveway in a speedy running walk. They both knew exactly what they were doing. There is nothing more beautiful than when horse and man are one.

Dad dismounted and walked in front of the horse. Chief's head had a half white bald blaze, and his roan body glittered against the sunlight with mixtures of chestnut and white. His mane was almost flaxen, and his tail moved smartly toward the ground. All four feet had white stockings past the knees and hocks.

"If we can come to a price," my father said, "I'll take him. But of course not being worked at all, I'm going to have to put a lot of time into him."

We all turned and smiled at one another.

Duffy spit again, "Well, Raymond, I don't have to make much of a profit, but I've got to at least get my money back out of him."

Duffy handed the reins of the horse to Mr. Shuster. Then the two men walked toward the hay barn negotiating and discussing a mutually agreeable price. All we could tell is that they were confronting each other, like the stallion and my father had done in the driveway. When they returned Duffy took the horse from Pappy Shuster and we drove off in the car. Dad just smiled. Finally, about a mile down the road, Pappy Shuster asked,

"Did you buy him, Raymond?"

"I think so."

"You think so?"

"I reckon He'll deliver him by the week-end."

Larry liked the school in Marlton. He adjusted pretty well there. I didn't. I was allowed to wander and pick out flowers and day dream. I couldn't keep up with Larry and Judy and would get to school half an hour late. We'd walk to school about a mile and a half and they wouldn't wait for me. I would go through the fields and woods and pick pansies or violets or go along the main road and find old telephone insulators. Not being ready to grow up, I used to stutter a lot. I couldn't say f, s, l sounds.

I was given the first license to be me when I was in kindergarten. After sitting with the teacher and watching the other kids nap, she would allow me to water the plants on the window sills. When we were working with the building blocks, I would supervise the construction of the block castles and bridges by my classmates. I didn't want to participate within the class room. They saw me as a future engineer.

My teacher gave me a large pad of easel paper and paints, probably to keep me from interrupting the class. I couldn't stop painting. Squinting my eyes and lying on the ground in the yard, I would watch the clouds go by and imagine myself flying.

The school tolerated me most of the time. My parents did too. At the farm during family visits, they not only tolerated me but the women thought I was cute.

I loved adventure. I loved being in the woods, I liked to be in the earth. If I could walk through the rows of cornfields and get lost I was happy. I wasn't lost. I was with me.

IN 1941 the United States was tooling up for World War II. Jean was eighteen years old and working at the shipyard and going to hometown rodeos. Dad, at 27, was still a rodeo contender and very excited about showing off. He was also working at the New York Shipyards in Camden, New Jersey.

Two years later he rented the farm at the edge of Barrington. When we first moved I remember him having friends over, Marshall and Bob or maybe it was Jean Shuster and her parents. He'd play his guitar in the good parlor and share his life and his experiences at the rodeo with them. Sitting on the couch with a silk scarf and ten gallon hat, and his two 22 gauge side pistols with leather embossed holsters, he awed us by passing photographs of a silver mounted bridle and martingale that he'd won at the Woodstown rodeo for being the best calf roper. One of my favorite images is the picture I have showing him standing by an iron-grey horse in an open field with his chaps and ten gallon hat.

While he seemed at home, I always felt that he was from another era, once removed. I always knew that about him. He was misplaced in the twentieth century. You could never tell which world he was in. He could mesmerize us with tales of the Homestead and of the first Ballingers in New Jersey and end with stories about fox hunting and his various hounds.

My father was a rebel. He rebelled over a lot of things from his life at the Homestead. He never had much of a childhood. He worked like a man from the time he was less than ten years old. Part of this was economic. His childhood coincided with the Great Depression. Part of this was being the only male child on a farm. Part of this was that his father had severe asthma and osteoporosis or osteoarthritis.

Clara later told me that my father was like a dog. He would want to have sex in the morning, then sex at noon, and then again in the evening and that he never stopped and that it was abnormal.

With a man who is spontaneous and physical and in nature, the sensuality and sexuality of nature takes over. When you're out in the fields and you're plowing the earth or you're cutting hay, you're dealing with passion. You're sensual, and you're in the earth. You're in the harvest, the sun, and the furrow of the plowed field. It's a very sexual thing. You feel things deeply. My father was young and he had no other relationships. He was very alone and had never been loved and never been touched. Sex was also his way of being attached and of being connected. When you come in for lunch and you see your woman walking in a cotton dress to the kitchen cupboard, and reaching up high with her hips swaying, you want to be in that too. He was young and he was vital. He wanted to be in all of life.

Dad's life was lived in the woods with the hounds and in the plowed fields and the burning heat. When you come in for lunch do you transcend into something else or do you continue feeling the way you are? You're sweating, and feeling sensual and sexual. You're making love to life.

Dad was a very forceful man. Clara was in the house in a more mechanized world so she wasn't always feeling what he was feeling. He saw the sensuality in her. She didn't understand it. She didn't have his appetite because she wasn't in his world with him. If she were, she probably would have been making love in the hayfields or in the lofts.

Dad had his hopes and dreams. He was always looking to have the edge on everything. His dream began to become real when he moved from Pine Grove to Barrington.

Clara's first defiance was refusing to move and refusing to go along with his dream. After nine years of a reasonable marriage and three children there she was. As long as he was doing what she wanted, she was alright. As soon as he pursued his own dream she balked.

The war continued and Clara received her rationing stamps for the family, but there was talk of the war ending. Things were changing. Industry was booming and new factories were being created at a rapid speed, and women were going into the workplace and becoming more than housewives.

Shortly after my seventh birthday on May 8th, we were all over at the Homestead, and Grandmom had made me my favorite birthday cake. I was hanging upside down in the maple tree by the front side of the house and playing around with Queenie and Plunder. It was about four o'clock in the afternoon. All of a sudden I heard sirens, fire engines, police cars, and people banging pots and pans and screaming. You would hear people everywhere! I swung down from the tree and yelled for Larry and Judy. Larry came running. All the way from Barrington and even Haddon Heights, three and five miles away, you could hear the people yelling and cheering. The war had finally ended!! The war in Europe was over. This became VE Day, May 8, 1945.

In retrospect, Clara hated those two years she spent at Barrington and Dad did everything in his power to make it work. What he could not do was change his dreams to make them fit hers. That was the parting of the road for the two of them on the Barrington farm. She went one way and he went the other.

As a child you don't understand those things. Dad's temperament was frustrated, trapped, and sometimes violent. He scared us children. Larry, Judy and I clearly knew that he and our mother were not getting along. They argued and fought so much that we tried to stay away from them. We were parenting ourselves, making our own decisions and living our own lives. That was usually what got us into trouble. We didn't see the necessity of getting permission from either Dad or Clara to do something. Most of the time we were too scared to ask, and most of the time they were too self-absorbed to notice.

I'd walk to school and I always had to go to the bathroom. I never had to go when I left, but in the middle of walking to school I had to go. I'd either pee in my pants, or I had to stop and pee. Judy wouldn't wait for me.

One day I was pissing in the urinal and these bigger boys threw a whole dozen rotten eggs through the anchor fence on the window, and spattered them all over me. I zipped my pants up, and I got my penis caught in my zipper. I ran out with this rotten egg all over me and threw stones at them and rocks, and then I ran all the way home and told my mother what had happened. I didn't want to go back to the school, ever.

Another time I went to school and dirtied my pants. I had on long johns because it was winter time. I couldn't make it in time. I went into the bathroom and I took them off. I washed myself and I put my clothing back on without my underwear. I put the underwear in the toilet and tried to flush it. Then it ran, the whole toilet, all through the bathroom and clear down the hallway and it just kept running and the janitor couldn't stop it.

He came into our classroom and he asked, "Who flushed their johns down the toilet?"

I knew he was looking straight at me, but he really wasn't. I was so humiliated, and so guilty, I started crying and I got up out of the classroom and ran down the hall and out of the building and down the pike. I ran a mile and a half all the way home, crying, "I'm not going to go back to that school ever again!"

I was an emotionally disturbed child. I sensed things happening, and nobody else seemed to be disturbed about them. Life was often a very painful experience for me. I felt too much of everything. I wanted to go back to Granddad's and Grandmom's. My mother said I couldn't. The pain and loss were so deep. My grandparents had always been my security.

My mother had a bridge party and had some girl friends over. I remember her going behind that back porch where the privy was and smoking. She wouldn't smoke in front of Dad. She smoked Camels. I never told because I didn't want to get her in trouble, but I knew she did it.

Soon everything that Dad had worked to accomplish became worthless. There must have been brief moments of affection, because both Leslie and Sandy were conceived there. Maybe it was just an ill-advised attempt to make the marriage work.

When Leslie was born, we went to the hospital. They made us sit in the car and wait. I couldn't go into the hospital so I sat in the car with Judy, just waiting for Leslie to be born. I could feel the excitement. I knew the swelling of her belly, and I knew she was having the baby, I thought I could hear the cry of the baby when it was born,

When she brought him home, I wanted to hold him and feel his warmth. He was my little brother. We baptized him at the church in Barrington.

Judy would kick her heels against the back of the church pew. She had brown and white saddle oxfords. As we left to go home the cherries were coming out on the cherry trees, and we walked through the fields rimmed with barbwire. We elected to climb through instead of going home in the car. We had our good clothing on.

I felt punished by Dad as he enforced the work load on the farm in Barrington. Dad was desperate to prove that he could make it on his own. He burdened us with his life compromises, needs, and demands. His urgency to achieve caused a definitive lack of parenting. We, as children sided against him. Judy and Larry became the hired help, and I the 'Rebel without a Cause'. Our punishment was much too harsh for small children.

But as time progressed with our new calves, new crops, newly wallpapered home, rebuilt barns, school, and a new brother we started to feel better.

Then I was put in the flea barn.

I had made a bet with Marshall for a cigarette that I could jump from the top beam of the barn down forty feet into a load of hay. I tumbled like a wingless bird and managed to live through it, all for one cigarette that I didn't even want. This didn't seem equal risk and reward to me, so when opportunity presented itself, I stole all Marshall Simmons cigarettes. Larry and I smoked the whole pack, on Bridge Creek Road. We got as sick as dogs.

Dad had this little draft horse named Doc that reared up in the stable and hit his head and died. He fed him to the dogs. They dragged the carcass down and put it in an old eight by ten foot chicken coop. The carcass was lying in there for a long time. He had a lot of hounds then, and the hounds ate the whole thing, except for the bones.

The coop became infested with fleas from the horse carcass in the July heat. There were fleas covering each and every wall. Fleas! Marshall and his friend Bob caught me and threw me in there. They locked me in the flea infested chicken coop with a dead horse carcass. I almost died in there. Larry heard me yelling and panicked and ran for Dad. I was in there probably about fifteen, twenty minutes, and I was screaming and crying. My Dad and Larry dragged me out of there and poured kerosene all over me. When I came out I was covered with welts and flea bites over my whole body and in my ears and in my mouth. I screamed and cried. I was so sick. I was almost dead.

One afternoon, Pappy, Jean and Bud were over and a storm was heading in. My father had tried to locate the freelance combine harvester man. Not being able to find him, he had made the decision that in order to save the soybean field he would mow it, dry it in the field, rake it, and haul it into the barn, like hay. This way he could keep it from getting moldy or rotting. Then it could be used for feed or combine and he could come out a little ahead.

We all worked hard to get the crop off the field. The big hay wagon was top heavy and overloaded. Molly and Dolly, the iron grey percherons, couldn't get momentum. Dad was so exhausted he climbed down from the top of the load and left Larry there with his fox terrier, Suzie. Pappy took the lines of the Grays and whistled for them to go forward over the wooden bridge from one field to the next. Molly had always resisted the bridge but with the heavy load she was even balkier. Pappy thrust the reins over their rumps, yelling, insisting that they move over the bridge, jackknifing the wagon and turning it over with Larry and Suzie ending up under the fallen load.

In a panic, we all began to dig after him. Pappy held the horses while the rest of us dug. A minute later Suzie appeared from under the load. We could barely hear the muffled sound of Larry, calling for his life. Within a few long minutes, the four of us had dug into the load. Then Larry came crawling out, looking like a ghost, frightened and stunned.

Once Larry was uncovered, we got the other team and pulled the wagon upright and reloaded into two wagons, instead of one. It wasn't until late in the evening that we had hauled the harvest into the barn and finished milking the cows for the night. It was the end of the harvest. Barrington seemed empty. There was eeriness everywhere.

Clara was away for longer periods of time. Larry and Judy and I had started back to school. When we came home, our mother was not in our house waiting for us. Dad was already half done milking. Larry and I would help him finish the chores. Afterwards, he would quickly wash, dress up in high western gear, and disappear for the evening. We parentless children would try to entertain ourselves.

Very late at night, or early in the morning, we could see my father's car lights coming down the long narrow driveway. Some nights Clara would not even come home. Often, Clara would come back in somebody's car hours later, and Dad would come back equally late. There was a black cloud hanging over our new paradise. When my grandfather learned that we were left alone so often and virtually abandoned, he came up and gave my father hell. Today my parents would have had their kids taken away from them.

By late September, things completely fell apart. Nobody seemed to care for the seasons or the animals. Larry and I recognized the vagueness and confusion and wondered where we were going to end up.

After the incident with the overturned hay wagon, Pappy and Jean insisted Larry, Dad and I come to their house for dinner, since Clara was never at home. She had taken Judy and Leslie to visit her sister Edith, so they said. It was a nice feeling, sitting around the table at the Shusters' and having a hot home cooked meal, which we had not had at Barrington for some time.

Jean gave us towels, and a warm tub of water to bathe in. We put on fresh clothes, that she had in her drawer, all of them much too large, but they smelled and felt good and clean. It wasn't until late in the evening that we returned to our empty Barrington Farm.

I began to wonder, months later, after my mother and father's separation, and after Larry and I had moved back to the Homestead with Granddad, if the accident was an omen. Was it telling us that our world was being turned upside down? Without being aware of it, did we inject our feelings into the team with the overloaded wagon, forcing too much confusion, disorganization, and upside down expectations?

Larry got very angry. He would take Judy and me and put us in potato sacks, and drag us around the yard, trying to babysit us and make us behave. The more he tried the more ornery we got and he was starting to panic. We just became more and more impossible.

The big war might be over, but in our house in was just escalating.

My mother had gone with her sister Edith into Camden. She had bought a dress with sequins on it. It was an evening dance dress, and it had cost a lot of money. My father came in from raking hay, and he was very angry. He didn't confront her until later in the evening. They had started to argue in the daytime, when he was having lunch. His anger had festered until evening, when they were in their bedroom. My room was right across the hall. I was six years old, and I heard them in there fighting over this dress. He told her to take it back. Instead, she stuck it in the closet and put it in a box. I understood what he was saying about the price of the dress, and the money, and our clothing and our food, and here she was out dancing, and buying this dress with sequins.

Later, Judy and I went into their room. We took the dress out of the box in the closet and Judy being a girl "ooohed and ahhhed. " At the sight of all the glitter, she lost her common sense. I cut some shells off and we put them in a cardboard cottage cheese container. Judy started gluing them on things. She was a little eight year old girl. Clara saw them downstairs in the living room. Judy had put them on a piece of paper glued into a drawing.

Clara went upstairs and opened the box and threw it on the bed and started crying. She was very upset. My mother used to use a fly swatter to spank me, but, she used her hairbrush this time. Then she put Judy over her lap, and spanked her so hard with the back of a mirror. Judy had welts. My mother's anger and frustration became extended to Judy. Judy was really hurt badly by that.

Their fights were tremendous. We had put a heat duct through the floors and there was one going up into my bedroom and one into the hall. I would lie down on the heat grid listen through the ducting. I could hear them fighting, and I could hear what they were saying, and I would listen for hours instead of sleeping. I'd want to know what they were saying and what was going to happen to us. It just got worse and worse and they'd leave Larry and I and Judy alone most of the time in the evenings.

After Granddad came, Dad realized that Larry wasn't old enough to take care of us. My father started entertaining at the house. He'd bring friends over and he'd bring out his guitar and sometimes he'd have his Stetson hat on, and he would play some western music. Often he'd ride Chief down the drive and awe people with his dramatics.

Another evening I stood at the kitchen door on the back porch, and heard my parents having the most violent fight I'd ever experienced. I heard them actually hitting each other. I heard the screaming and I heard the passion, and the pain coming from the room. I felt the concern and the threats and the desperation in their voices. It was the most frightening thing for a child that you could ever imagine.

It was after this fight that Dad told Clara, "If you walk out of here you can never come back. You make the decision but if you walk out that door, don't ever plan on coming back." Dad's disappointment was not coming from anger. It was coming from lost expectations. My father couldn't get Clara to do what he wanted. Not only did they not stop and think about what they were doing, but they kept on having babies when their relationship was wrong in the first place.

When Clara left it was her last stand. She thought that Dad would want his children and because his family was so important to him she could hold him hostage and she would have him back where she wanted him. We children also thought our mother would come back, the same way she had when she first refused to move to Barrington and then showed up two weeks later.

Astonishingly, Clara didn't realize that Dad was strong enough to give up everything and then rebuild all over again, as long as he had his sons. With Jean he now had someone who would be a fully engaged partner who shared his dreams, waiting in the wings.

After that fight Dad went out in the barns and to the fields and Clara was left in the house. She called her sister Edith and they arranged something. The next day it rained and that's when she left. I think she went with Edith for a couple of days and then she came back and took the furniture. When Dad came home that night the furniture was all gone. The afternoon that she left for good she took nine-year-old Judy and one-year-old Leslie and was pregnant with Sandy.

I DO REMEMBER HER LEAVING. It was at the end of the season, when the leaves had completely fallen. There was starkness in the air. Each cloud neatly slid itself in front of the sunlight, as though it were selecting a filter to fit the hour. They continually blinked the room in and out of darkness.

Too frightened to confront the issues, I hid in the living room behind the door.

The room became dimmer as each hour passed. I heard Aunt Edith's car come to a stop on the long and narrow driveway.

How quickly my mother collected her things, I thought. I watched them through the window, as they loaded the car. I heard the hysteria. I saw it all through the embroidered lace curtains. They hung in the farmhouse window like a scrim on the set of a tragedy.

"Mommie-e-e," I cried, "Mommie-ee,"

As she disappeared down the driveway, I cried out wanting to know why my mother was leaving us. Why me, her favorite? What could I possibly have done to make her leave?

My outcry echoed through the rooms, resounding like a huge and empty canyon. I stood for a moment on that very spot where my mother would sit in her special chair that faced the window, where she would sit for hours crocheting and watching us play in the yard. Stunned, I went through her embroidery on the curtains, through every connecting pattern, looking for an answer.

Through every single thread of needlework I searched, hoping to find a clue.

For hours I sat sobbing in great lengthy jerks, until I had felt the stitches cutting me, as though they were being sutured into my very own flesh. I was caught up, wrapped in the netting, fighting to be free.

I sobbed harder and harder. Still not one intimation, not one little hint of why she had left. I cried through most of the night, until my tears, the lace, and the rain on the window were one.

When I awoke the next morning I found that I had somehow been taken to my room and put into bed. Maybe it was all just a bad dream. I became mute throughout the next three days. There were braided red furrows from the lace mapped out on my skin to remind me that it was very real.

My sense of loss was deepened when Dad decided to auction off the farm and almost everything on it. In the days before the auction, I would enter the rooms with the greatest expectancy and faith that she would be there, reaching out for me, with her rounded smile and her auburn hair, holding me close to her bosom.

I could even smell the perfume and feel the softness of her through the cotton dress. Every intimate memory was embellished with the expectation that I would someday find her.

That was the end of our new Paradise. It wasn't long after that that the auctioneer came.

He put paper numbers on all the cows' rumps we were milking in the morning. He chewed an old cigar and he had a big canvas hat which he wore down on his head. He kept a lot of cigars and pencils in his pockets, and he wore rubber boots with his pants tucked in. He had a wooden cane and he would touch the cows and observe them as they were being milked. Then he'd number the cows and he'd write notes down on his clipboard.

We finished milking, and Larry said to me, "We're going to sell them all. We're selling everything."

Larry was angry. Larry got angrier and angrier. I felt lost and left out.

That afternoon hundreds of cars came in and everything was brought out onto the driveways and into the yard, including our things from the house and all the cows in the barn and all the machinery that we'd worked for three years to build and to have. I saw it all get auctioned off in front of me, everything except the team of Percherons and Chief and a palomino mare.

The truck that Pappy had fixed was the last thing that the man came and got. We waited, and little bits of snow started coming down. It was cold, the ground was freezing, and we stayed there that night with kerosene stoves. We were really cold.

The next day around three o'clock, it seemed to get dark early. The mist was coming in and you could tell it was going to snow. Then it started, big flakes, and they just kept coming down. You could feel the stillness of the snow. It was so white and it felt deadly.

My mother had left and taken Judy and Leslie with her. Leslie had been sick with asthma that whole year and was in the hospital several times. We thought he was going to be sick like Granddad.

It was cold and damp and Larry and I were all alone. We were leaving the farm forever. We had spent two whole years, forever to my seven-year-old mind, building that farm.

Dad yelled, "Come on, boys, we're going to go now." I said to myself, "Where are we going to go now, Daddy? Where are we going to go? I want Mommy back."

Dad and Larry took the harnesses and put them on two of the horses, so we wouldn't have to carry them. Dad led Chief, who was very anxious and frightened. Larry led the two Percherons. I think my father must have tied one of them behind the other. I just walked alongside, at the tail end. The snow got worse and added to the wind. My hair was getting frozen and my eyebrows were wet. My nostrils and my toes were also frozen and I could hardly walk.

I held my hands under the thigh of the horse just to keep them from freezing. I wasn't tall enough to reach the horse's belly. We walked. It seemed we were walking for miles and miles. It felt like we were never going to get off that farm. It was probably no further than three or four miles. It seemed like it took a whole day and all night.

We finally got to the last field. The oncoming night had a misty, damp, cold, smoggy grayness, about it. It was eerie and the snow just kept coming and coming through the stillness. There was a feeling of deadness and damp-ness along with the cold. I had no house anymore and no mother. There was nothing. We finally got to the end of the fields and found the telephone poles. They reached out like sentinels. Our fence line was down below where Dad had barb wired all the fences. Dad took out a pair of pliers with the cord dangling from it. On one end and he started cutting the barbed wire that he'd stretched so tight. It screamed like a violin string in the wind and the snow. You could hear the wailing as it broke the silence and squeaked and crawled thrashing out in the cold. It was giving us a warning. Dad cut the second wire, then the third, and the fourth. The fourth sounded like a startled quail or grouse escaping from some bird-eating beast. The fifth and last wire sprung back curling like a huge spring. That whole area had been closed off since Dad had rebuilt his rented farm.

We walked through the town streets with those horses. I felt abandoned. We marched from the edge of the farm through the town on the village streets. It was still snowing heavily. There was snow all over the trees and on the sides of the streets. People looked out of their windows. Some came out and some even opened their windows and hung out and watched us leading these horses through the village. When I looked up I wanted to hide. I didn't want to be seen. My mother had left us. My father had been fighting with her. He had sold everything and we had nothing.

I had come from a Paradise where I was 'Master Raymie'. I wasn't anything anymore. I had nothing. No mother. No father. No home. No nothing. I was nothing. I was ashamed and embarrassed and humiliated.

Jean had come over and asked if we wanted her to cook for us the night before we moved. It was just Larry and I, and Larry was out fooling with the chickens since there were no cows in the barn to be milked. We left the next morning.

We put the horses in Pappy' Shuster's stables and then Jean took me in and she rubbed my hands together and she took my wet clothes off and tried to thaw me out. I cried and she held me in her arms. She asked, "Would you like a bath?"

She gave me a warm bath and she washed me with a wash cloth and soap and water. It felt so good to have somebody love me and take care of me and she did the same for Larry. She had two twin beds and she put Larry in one. My father was very familiar with the place and he walked around like he lived there. I guess he'd been staying there a lot. Jean put me in a cot in the corner off the bedroom. I saw that she had records and a record player and she had a nice life. She read me Aesop's fables.

I kept demanding, "Read me another. Read me another one." I didn't want it to be over.

No one had read to me in ages.

I finally asked her, "Are you going to be my mother?"

She tucked me in and I went to sleep.

I liked Jean very much for caring for us and treating us the way she did, but I also felt guilty about liking her. Later, I started to get nasty and angry at her and made it difficult for her. We just started off on the wrong track for a long time. I didn't give her a chance, not because I didn't want to, I just didn't know how to. As a little child I wanted to be faithful to my mother yet she had broken her faith with me. She was gone. My father thought I was only seeing what I wanted to see. That's not true. I was a little child who was trying to be loyal to my mother, not to Jean, this strange new person. I couldn't pretend that I liked Jean when all I really wanted was my mother. I couldn't do both. For me it had to be one or the other.

Later on, Larry and Judy were able to smile with affection toward Jean without really meaning it. Their biggest fear was being totally abandoned. I refused to do that. Consequently I didn't have the love from either one. I just didn't know how else to look at it as a child. I thought for a long time after my mother left that somehow it was my fault. I think kids pick that up when they're little. We never fully comprehended back then why Clara had gone and Jean had replaced her.

All Dad and Jean had to do was gather his children before them and explain what had really happened rather than lie about it and continually be deceptive through their own guilt and misguided morality. It became a tragedy for him and all of his children. At 72 years old and after 46 years of marriage Jean, his second wife, finally confessed to me with great emotional sobs, that they had lied to us all out of shame. Not only did it devalue the wholesomeness of their living relationship and marriage, but it also destroyed part of their children's faith in their parents and their own sense of their personal identity.

AFTER DAD LEFT TO GO OUT TO RENO, we were sent to Grand-dad's. Judy and Leslie were still with Clara. I had nothing of my parents. I was always telling lies about where Dad was. The boys from Pine Grove would make fun of me and beat me up. They would say things like, "We know your mother left you. Did your father have to leave you too, 'monkey face'?" Grandmom never took Larry's part. She just stood there and watched the Italian boys beat him up. She thought Larry was ornery. He was repeating the first grade while Dad was out West.

The nights were the worst. I slept with Grandmom the whole time Dad was gone. I kept having these nightmares and waking up in the middle of the night, crying and screaming, telling Grandmom that I wanted my mother. I wanted my father. I wanted to go home. She said you are home Raymie and she would just hold me until I fell back asleep.

I had received two postcards. That was all I had to show that I still had one parent. The first one was a lone coyote crying in the night, which personified my pain. The second was a gold diggers pack mule, waiting for its take.

Dad had gone out West with Jean to get a divorce in Nevada. Pappy had arranged it and it only took six weeks. I felt that he was gone forever.

WHILE JEAN AND MY FATHER WERE OUT WEST, my grandfather let Clara come and visit us. She came at twilight, when the sun was just going down. She had taken the bus.

She walked down Elmwood Road, about three quarters of a mile and turned down our orange gravel driveway. I had been anticipating her arrival all day. They had told me she was coming. During Clara's visit she stayed too late, and it got very dark. The moon was about half full, and I could hear the crickets. It was damp, and moist, and getting very cold in the evening. As she walked back down the driveway, I called to her again. I was very worried about her going out there alone.

After she died, I went to her house and I found the bus schedule with her old crocheting needles. She kept the schedule of the bus all those years.

Clara was a beautiful woman inside and very vulnerable. She was lost at the time and didn't know what she'd done wrong. Maybe she hadn't done anything wrong. She just wanted a different kind of life and she wanted to be loved, and she wanted to love. She wanted to love her children. People blamed her for leaving us, leaving her children. It tore her apart.

She told me,"Raymie, I loved you enough to let you stay with your father, because I knew your father could give you boys what you really needed, what you'd already had a taste of. To take you away from that and put you on cement sidewalk would have killed you. It would have killed both of us."

Judy got so homesick being with her and being away from us boys that Clara had to bring her back. Judy would hold her breath and turn blue and Alex, Edith's husband, and Edith, Clara's sister, would smack her to make her stop it. She thought that if she refused to breathe she would be taken back to the farm and to her brothers.

My grandmother had given Larry and me two drawers for us to use in this wonderful big hutch. I opened my drawer and I went through all of my stuff and I brought out my scrapbook with pictures of thousands of horses that I had collected. When Clara finally got there, I didn't say I'd missed her. I hugged her and kissed her, but I selfishly took her to the couch sat her down and shoved this scrapbook in front of her face, and insisted that she go through the whole scrapbook with me.

I pushed Larry away, and Larry just sat there until she finally had Larry come and sit on the couch next to her. I was on my knees on the floor in front of her. I opened the scrapbook and I remember, literally, taking my hands and taking her face, and pulling her face toward me and the scrapbook. I think what I was doing, was trying to show her through the horses in the scrapbook the wildness inside of me... recognizing the wildness of her, something that we had in common. I tried to communicate to her that we were the wild horses, she and I.

My father used to say to me, "You're just like your mother, you know. You're trash. You're no damn good. She's trash!"

It was very painful, but it was also very exciting for me. Dad couldn't see her for what she was, just the simple excitement of her. Neither Clara nor I really belonged. Somehow, with that horse scrapbook that I had made, I thought we would be the same.

During the first days of Dad's return, I had tried sitting in the kitchen of the Homestead in his lap and going into his arms as I had always done. I witnessed a change.

He said "Come on son, you don't need to do that. Get down now. Your father's talking."

He was in his new life with his new wife and was trying to cut off from his world with Clara. That world included his children with Clara who were still with him. That shutting off was the end of my seven years of intimacy with Dad. Judy had been equally shut off and traumatized. Almost seven months after Clara left with Judy and Leslie, Judy came back to us. We had always been inseparable. Leslie was a sick asthmatic baby and she had been his caretaker. She must have been terrified to have that responsibility without her brothers.

JUDY HAD ENERGY, like our mother, and didn't know what to do with it. She was always active. She had long red ringlets of curls. They would dress her up perfectly in the morning, but by night she would have her socks ripped,

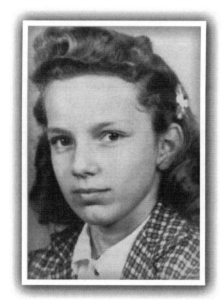

her knees skinned and bleeding, and her clothing and her face would be dirty. Her sash and her dress would be ripped and she would be happy. She was full of life and strength of feeling. She was a natural part of the Homestead. Her time there was probably the happiest time in Judy's life.

I don't really know what went on when Clara took Judy away from us to live with her in Merchantville. Clara created a bridge of pain that Judy couldn't get across to regain that sweetness. She didn't even want to look across the bridge. Judy was nine years old when Clara gave her back.

When she returned she behaved like an abused child, which in fact she had been. Emotionally abandoned at the least, she had a defined impression in her mind.

In the spring of 1946, when Judy and Leslie were given back to my father, my grandfather picked up Leslie and Judy from Clara and gave her a check for $25 to pay for Judy's dentist bill. Judy had seen her grandfather hand over the check to Clara and Judy was sure that it was a payment her father made to get her back. Judy lived with this horrible interpretation for years. All she was worth was $25. It wasn't until Judy was fifteen and we were living in Culpeper, Virginia that she learned that the check was actually repayment for a dental bill. Judy never got over that feeling of only being worth $25.

When we moved back to the Homestead, Judy was eleven years old. It was hard for all of us, moving back, especially with my grandparents and Aunt Ginny still living at the Homestead. The family had a confrontation because, at that time, they despised the ground that Judy walked on. Instead of seeing her as a troubled child who needed extra care and love, they blamed her for "acting up."

At thirteen, when Judy reached the beginning of her womanhood, she was emotionally scarred and very immature as well as lost and angry. She had a chip on her shoulder, although physically she had grown into a beautiful young woman. As a child with her auburn ringlets she could out do Shirley Temple. As time passed her deep-set eyes became a scowl and the big question was why? Why had her mother taken her from her father? Did her father not want her? Why did her father offer to take her back for $25? Did her mother not want her?

Judy lost herself early in life. Her only close companions were her brothers Larry and Raymie. We were a trio of childhood conspirators surrounded by fields of clover and hopscotch, wrestling on the picket fence lawn. No matter how much Judy played at being a tomboy or ripped her clothing, her ringlets stayed in place. By her eighth grade portrait, there were already lines under her eyes skating over the black shadows.

Academically she did well in school. Her personal, unanswered and unmet emotional needs wore on her like a shroud. Her secrets were only shared with me, her little brother. I innocently felt I should answer her with a positive remark like, "Don't worry Sissy, I'll protect you." As her body started changing and growing she seemed even more lost. "Who would want me?" she used to ask.

Later on, Frank Peters, a young paratrooper, came around. He fell in love with Judy. She had no idea what that meant and got angry with him when he mentioned it. She screamed at him, "How could you love me? You don't even know me!"

Judy had not learned to love herself. How could she be expected to understand someone else's love for her?

Frank continued dating her and taking her to the movies. He wrote long letters from wherever he was stationed telling her how he could make her happy. Judy avoided his letters. Eventually Frank stopped writing to Judy.

Then there was Earl Bailey, who worked on our farm. He had come from a poor sharecropper's family. Earl had worked hard and bought a shiny used blue Plymouth. He made it look new and treated it as though it were. He worked for my father during the harvest season. At the time, we were bringing in thousands of bales of hay and filling two silos, and there was only Larry and me to help. Leslie and Skip were too young. Earl was a big relief.

When the harvest was over, Dad was so impressed with Earl that he decided to keep him on through the winter milking doing odd jobs around the farm. By that time, 1953, Larry had quit school in the eighth grade in Culpeper. This was his first year working full-time at the farm. Earl was two years older and had the street smarts which Larry lacked. Earl was masculine, well built, and fairly sure of himself.

Larry always had Dad directing him and he had given his heart and his whole being to his father and the farm. He knew one day he would own his own farm and raise his own family. Earl wanted the same thing, and he wanted Judy to do it with him.

Earl went through Larry and got his first date with Judy. As far as Earl was concerned, he was upgrading and Judy was a fine young woman. By their second secret date, they had fallen madly in love. Larry and I believed that Dad had an inkling of what was happening. Judy was appearing at the barn too frequently. Dad took Earl aside, and told him that the relationship with his daughter would not happen. He told Earl to go and find someone else. Judy wasn't right for him. Earl didn't show up for work the next day. By the weekend he was back at milking, begging Larry and me to help him see Judy.

"Take her to the Movie House with you. I'll pick her up in front of the theatre. I'll pay for both of your tickets." This was too good for us to pass up.

The next day, Dad found out. He fired Earl Bailey on the spot and told Judy she was grounded for the month. She locked herself in her room for almost two days and wouldn't eat and wouldn't come out. Dad and Jean were beside themselves. They knew she needed help, but did not have the faintest idea of how to help her.

Judy went into the US Air Force directly out of high school, right after I did. She met her future husband Nick when she was stationed in Oklahoma, and their first daughter Paula was born there. At that time you could not remain in any of the armed services if you were pregnant. Nick and Judy came back to Dover AFB in Delaware and Judy came home to Kenton when she was expecting her sons Pat and Pete. Jean's youngest son, Ashley, and Pete are the same age. Judy's youngest child, Penny, was born while they were up in Presque Isle, Maine.

Nick was a good father and husband, but totally and completely chauvinistic. Judy made the mistake of literally waiting on him hand and foot. Dad approved of that arrangement and liked Nick very much.

MY FATHER REBELLED over a lot of things at the Homestead. There was always a tremendous amount of anger in him. I can't believe that it all came from my mother. I remember him in the hay barn when I was four or five years old loading a wagon. He was cursing, and he was angry. I cared about his pain and his anger and how resentful he was.

I asked him if he was hurting. He said he was alright.

He kept on forking the straw. It was during the period when my mother was still living with us in Barrington, and he had a lot more love for me then. He was a different man on the farm, before my mother left. He had changed, but there was more than anger in Barrington.

My Dad had his guitar and he had his six guns and he had his chaps. He was a real cowboy. He could lasso and he could do the 'wedding band', where you put the rope all the way around yourself and throw to the floor and come back up again toward your head standing up on a horse. The man was quite a performer. He was a dandy and he was swift and smart and good-looking. He had great horses. He would have been a natural for rodeo shows or Hollywood.

This is where I get my whole theatrical flair from. It didn't come from anybody else.

Dad was an incredible storyteller. People would come around to listen to him. He would start out with one or two people, and before long there would be ten listening to him, riveted. The world for him was so large, but when he moved to Barrington all that fell apart.

Initially, I think he really hated farming. He connected it with his life struggle. He worked so hard. His big dream that he shared with Jean was that they were going to go out West, buy a ranch, raise horses, and maybe have some beef cows. They weren't going to have a dairy.

He never got over those childhood dreams and fantasies. He shared them with Pappy and Jean, and Pappy suggested that he go see a lawyer. The lawyer said that the quickest way to get a divorce was to go out west. They couldn't wait to leave.

The only problem with the dream was that at thirty years of age he had four children and a pregnant wife.

Jean, when she first met Dad, embraced his world with him. She rode the tractor, was out horseback riding and fox hunting with him. When she came to the farm I saw them in the hay loft together. Then they were in the horse barns and the fields. I saw what they were doing and how they were handling each other. Jean immersed herself in his world. Clara did not.

Pappy Shuster used to come over to the farm in Barrington and get corn for Jean's horse, Sheba. He helped my father with things. He fixed the truck and put in the electricity. He liked my father and loved being on the farm. Sometimes he would bring us gifts. Pappy was only sixteen years older than Dad.

Jean went over to Barrington to babysit for Clara and Dad. Even Mrs. Shuster got to know Clara. At this point it seems there was this kind family trying to help Clara and Raymond survive in their marriage and trying to befriend them. During this period of time the relationship with Jean and Raymond grew more physical and perhaps Clara saw it.

In the meantime my mother was meeting her sister and going to dances in Camden the same way she did while we were living in Pine Grove. Dad was still working at the shipyard. Camden was actually closer to Barrington than it was to Marlton.

I remember her going out in the evening without him, and I remember him primping himself in the mirror in the living room and going out as well. He was not with my mother. Who was he going to the rodeo with? Not Clara.

Once in Barrington we went to a horse show. They had country and western music from a band and there were rope tricks. I saw a Will Rogers wannabe standing up and telling jokes. Bleachers were on both sides and horses were performing, doing calf roping and all kinds of stuff. Dad took us but we were not with Clara. I think we were with Jean and her friend.

In the evenings, ten year old Larry would be babysitting us, and dragging us around the house in a gunnysack. One of my mother's friends came over and asked, "Who's taking care of you children?" She called Granddad who saw there was no one taking care of us. He sent over Ginny.

Larry and I were up in the hayloft and watched Jean sliding into my father's arms and kissing him. I went into the house and told my mother that they were there together.

"I don't know what they were doing. She was just sliding down him," I said.

There was a lot of violent fighting after that. I always thought that I was to blame for it, because I told. I was only six and had no idea of the consequences. Through time and insight I learned that I was not responsible for what happened, but I did carry that burden for years. My parents were not compatible and never would be, no matter what Dad and Jean were doing in the loft that afternoon. I loved my father and only wanted happiness for him.

Clara was pregnant again and angrier and maybe she consciously or subconsciously thought, "Let Jean have these five kids and the cows and the horses and let's see how she feels. I'm out of here!" Clara went to her sister Edith who said, "That scumbag!! Come live with me. We can go dancing and play cards."

Next thing Edith's car was parked in the driveway and Clara was moving out furniture without thinking of the consequences for her children.

Jean's father, Pappy Shuster, had gone to school with Dad's mother. The close friendship that developed between my father and Pappy Shuster was no coincidence. The Homestead wasn't that close to Haddon Heights where they lived. Pappy worked in the shipyards in the summer months and taught school in the winter. It would have been unlikely that Dad and Jean would not have crossed paths at the shipyard. Jean worked in the supply department and the pay office. It also seems unlikely that Jean, at twenty-one years of age, would have just shown up in Barrington. Dad mentions an unnamed man at the yard who told him that a farm in Barrington was available for rent. It might have been Pappy who recommended the farm.

Pappy always seemed to have been the one who was at the center of it all. In the beginning Pappy discouraged Jean and Raymond's relationship because he was trying to help make Raymond's marriage work. When he saw that it was not going to work, he accepted and perhaps encouraged the relationship between Jean and Dad. Dad's life was one he dreamed of.

I believe that while Dad was working at the shipyard at nights, and while Jean was at the shipyard, they knew each other, and Pappy was aware of it. Jean had met Dad and they talked rodeos and horses and farm life. Maybe Pappy told Dad not to get involved with his daughter or maybe Pappy was just as enamored of Dad as Jean was.

Jean gave Dad unconditional love. She filled a very deep hole in him. It was the lying that created the most lasting damage. Jean later adapted puritanical religious beliefs in order to find redemption as well as punishment for the relationship. Jean didn't want her children to think she took a husband and children away from another woman. Both rigorously maintained the lie never thinking that maybe it was not so bad after all.

Shortly after they returned from out West in May 1946, Dad had an appendicitis attack. Clara came to see my father when he was in the hospital and when she realized that he was married to Jean, she blew up.

Once again we lived with Jean's parents in Haddon Heights. Then my beloved Sissy came back. Dad was helping out Grandpop at the Homestead, and we never saw him.

WHILE DAD WAS IN THE HOSPITAL recovering from his appendix operation, he was reading the paper and spotted an ad for a dairy farm manager in Lyndell, Pennsylvania. With the exception of Leslie, we all followed to live in Lyndell while Dad managed the Bruno dairy. He worked there for three months.

Bruno was a dentist out of Philadelphia. The bad news was his Polish wife was left to manage Dad. Nobody managed Dad. Mrs. Bruno insisted that Dad get rid of all the Holstein cows that he had purchased and buy Jersey cows because their faces were cute! Cute didn't work for my father. So, he quit. He said that if she wanted Jersey cows, she could buy them and milk them herself.

Jean and Dad had moved from her home in Haddon Heights, to a run-down farm house on the Bruno property in a condition very similar to the house at the Barrington farm that he had bought with Clara. It was a shell of a house with nothing in it. It was cold, it was musty, and it was dirty. Jean moved in and worked to make a home out of it. She was happy to buy furniture, happy to go out and look for things for it on a budget, and she refinished old furniture and redid the house and painted it.

Dad and Jean left Pennsylvania after Grandpop came and asked Dad to come back to the Homestead. He had had the first of several strokes in August and couldn't handle the farm anymore. Dad agreed but we needed a place to live. Grandpop promised us the half of the house where Aunt Ruth was living. The next thing I knew we had moved back to the Shuster house in Haddon Heights while waiting for Aunt Ruth and Uncle Bob to vacate the smaller side of the Homestead where they had been living due to the shortage of housing caused by the war.

Larry and I went back and forth to school, and we went back and forth to the Homestead in Marlton. Judy and Leslie stayed in Haddon Heights. When

I went to school that fall, I wouldn't talk to anybody for three weeks. I just wouldn't talk. Then when I talked, I just started crying all the time. Larry buried his pain differently. Judy agreed with everybody in order to avoid the pain and the confrontation, which is how most of the girls at the time were taught.

I sassed back constantly. In retrospect that was probably the best thing I could have done, because I got some of my anger out while Larry and Judy buried theirs.

Living in Haddon Heights was very painful and lonely for me. I felt totally abandoned by everyone. The drumming in my head was the echo from my soul, fluttering in its darkness. The emptiness cried out to be filled, but I could not open the door. I would not let anyone in. That September when I first started the second grade in Haddon Heights the teacher called the roll and asked if I was there. I screamed at her, "No! You can't see me. I'm not here." After that I was silent. She was very worried about me, and called the Shuster's to ask what could be done.

The next day on the playground the kids yelled at me. "What's the matter, dummy, can't you talk?" I picked up a fallen branch from a tree and whaled it around my head, screaming at the top of my lungs, "I hate you, I hate you. I hate all of you." I chased them around the school ground. I chased them so fast that part of the group was coming around behind me, as though they were chasing me. I fell against one of the swing's poles and my nose began to bleed as they piled on top of me. Screaming and pushing my way out of the pile of children's bodies, I threw the stick at them and ran off of the school ground down into the woods where I stayed until dark.

On the way home that night I turned off of High Street and down into Broad across the railroad tracks toward the north end of the village. Randomly, as I passed the houses, I would pick the one that I thought would be most likely to be the home of a happy, normal family and I would climb over the hedges and look in their windows. I saw people reading their papers and listening to the radio. I saw children sprawled on the carpet doing their homework or sitting at the table eating dinner. They were families living out their lives together, lovingly and caringly while I observed through the base of their window. Sometimes I would smash my head against their window sills and cry out in pain.

Finally, when I reached the end of Broad Street I turned back down toward the Shuster's and walked in through the front door with the blood from my forehead running down my white shirt. My collar had been ripped off and my buttons had been pulled from their sockets. I couldn't fight any more. I was giving up.

The next day the Shusters forced me to go to school. Finally, after four days and my teacher's attempt to get me to speak, Mrs. Henning suggested that I make birds and paint them. For the remaining part of the week I made paper mache birds, great numbers of them in bright colors gleaned from Pappy Shuster's Audubon bird book. I created them so realistically that the children became fascinated by them. Awed by the skill and the color, Mrs. Henning asked if I would explain them to the class. That was how I began to talk again, by explaining the great variety of birds that I had closely watched on the Barrington farm when my mother was there and when we were a whole family. The year passed very slowly. My grades were poor and I was angry and defensive.

I was still lost but I started to repair and get stronger after I got involved in school. I met a boy named Walter who had a friend, Cecil Gilmore. Cecil's father was a missionary who operated the Wally Mission in Philadelphia. On Friday nights I would go with them to the mission to listen to the sermons. The preacher would play an accordion and he'd tell tales from the Bible. To me he was wonderful. He was a story teller and wild-eyed and exciting. He liked women, he played music, and he would tell stories and dramatize them and passionately act them out. I'd sit in the front row and watch him, and he'd say, "Come on down here boy, I'm going to save you!"

I'd be saved! I'd get down on my knees and he'd preach and he'd cry out. "Son, you're going to be saved. You're not a sinner any longer!" Afterwards we would go downstairs and have coffee. I'd never had coffee before.

Pappy Shuster and his son, Bud, used to make huge model airplanes. Some of the wingspans were six feet long. Because I was so withdrawn Pappy got me interested in building model airplanes. This was how I found my love of flying, and why I went into the Naval Air Force.

When we lived with the Shusters in Haddon Heights, Dad would wake up ten year old Larry at five o'clock each morning and haul him down to the Homestead in Marlton where Larry took care of all the calves. Afterwards, Dad took him to school. Jean was now expecting and heavily pregnant. Of course Larry would fall asleep in classes. He didn't learn a damn thing and they put him back and said he wasn't very smart. He couldn't learn. He couldn't memorize spelling words. No wonder! He couldn't stay awake. He couldn't concentrate. He couldn't focus. He had practically put in a day's work before school.

Dad would bring him back to the Shuster's house at six o'clock in the evening, after they finished milking and Larry would eat dinner. Then Dad put him to bed at ten o'clock at night and got him up right back up again at five o'clock the next morning.

Larry had wanted to go to school in Marlton. That's where he had gone to school before and he liked it and he wanted to stay there. I went to school in Haddon Heights with Judy and wouldn't talk, but Larry was in an even harder place. From the very beginning he was beaten down to a pulp. He had constant earaches. He would go out to the farm in the early morning with bad earaches and cotton stuffed in his ears. His eyes would be tearing from allergies as he was feeding the calves and helping with the milking. Amazingly enough, no one wondered why he wasn't doing well in school!

Larry had no real love other than from Judy and me. He couldn't even stay with Grandma and Granddad where he could have had some love.

Dad grabbed him by the head of the hair one night right there in the house in Haddon Heights when he came back late at night from farming.

"Why can't you remember how to spell that word?" He shook him.

Larry just cried and said, "I don't know why, Daddy."

I stood right there by the fireplace in Haddon Heights hearing. "I don't know why! I'm trying Daddy."

We had no family. We were living with strangers. There was nobody that we knew.

Dad left the Shuster's house early in the morning to work at the Homestead and came home so late that I barely remember seeing him. One weekend when Dad was home the man next door told him he had seen us kids selling outdated newspapers.

A boy in my school had been delivering newspapers and making money and we figured why couldn't we do it as well? We didn't understand that they were selling current papers. I had found a whole bunch of *New York Times* and I took them all down to Pappy's cellar. We folded them back properly and threw em' on the porches in the neighborhood and asked people to pay us for the paper. They gave us money. I used the money to buy gifts for Judy and a big shoe box full of combs, hair pins, ribbons, and jewelry for Margaret and Eleanor, two girls who I liked. I was too embarrassed to give the box to them directly, so I put the gifts inside of a hole in a tree at school and wrote them a note telling them where the gifts were. The girls were twins.

Dad found out and appeared at Haddon Heights. It was the first time I had seen him in ages. He told me to give the money back.

"Well I can't give the money back. I've spent it. I gave it to my girlfriends."

He took me down in the cellar with a belt and whipped me for being dishonest and selling the newspapers. Then he went away. The next time I remember seeing him he was exercising Chief, his roan stallion, in the baseball field. Judy and I used to fly kites there with Pappy.

This was the most tragic year of my life. I was in a home with Pappy and Mrs. Shuster and Bud. I was never sure that Jean or Dad were ever there. Nobody cared where I was. I could walk home from school alone, and then continue to walk for miles around the neighborhood in the dark. Judy and I began stealing from the little five and dime store in town.

We were caught by the police, and they asked, "Where do you live?"

We answered, "We don't live anywhere."

They let us go. "You tell your parents to keep a rope on you and take care of you. If you come back again, we're going to see to it!"

After they threatened us we ran out of there and ran home. We ran through the park, and down through the hill where the school was, down through the woods, and down past the Davis' home. It was dark. We thought we were going to be arrested and God knows what else.

Judy and I were always getting into trouble. I think Mrs. Shuster knew but she didn't want to tell anyone. It might have just been too much for Jean to handle.

I stuck a nail through my foot at the swimming hole over in Marlton. I jumped off the edge right on to a twenty penny nail. Larry held me down on the floor and Dad poured the iodine bottle up and down through that hole in my foot. Then I did it again in Marlton on the manure ramp with a pitchfork. I was trying to raise the plank and the fork slipped and went through my foot. Now I had two holes, one on each foot. Then I got another nail through my hand.

If I had been old enough, I would have had a serious breakdown. A lot of those emotions and feelings stayed with me and continued to build until I got in the Navy.

December 25, 1946 was the last Christmas we spent at the Shusters. Later in the year we moved from Haddon Heights to the Homestead's big house and lived in the left side. Aunt Ruth had finally moved out. After living with the Shusters for eight months we were back at the Homestead. All seemed right again in my world.

The right side of the house was the bigger side and the original side, the operational side, and the side of power. The left side had been the summer kitchen and they had taken a quarter of the living room area and a bedroom upstairs to make it into a separate house. Attached to the house was a wooden section where the tenant farmers used to sleep and there was a third floor where Larry and I slept. It was a very small space for a family with five young children. It was only after my grandparents moved into a bungalow in Marlton that we moved into the other side of the house.

During the transition of taking over the Homestead, my family appeared to descend upon my grandparents like a plague of locust. Granddad, having been born and raised there, and Grandmom, having lived there for thirty-four years, had planted not only their herbs and gardens, but were integrated into the wholeness of the Homestead with both body and soul. My grandparents had no desire to really accept the ascendancy. In their minds they had decided to let my father and his new wife take over, but the wholeness, intimacy, and spirituality between them and the Homestead was still protected.

At the time it appeared that Granddad was better resigned to and more peaceful about the transition than Grandmom and her daughters. During these raging disputes my grandfather would stand in the background on the porch behind the wisteria and watch his family feud in the back yard. Grandmother, Dad's own mother, would pound at my father's chest, and then point a finger at Jean, his new wife saying, "You have no rights here yet, you haven't earned them."

For me, it was traumatic enough that my mother had left, but to watch all of this was even more devastating.

Very little time passed before Granddad had his second stroke. I wanted to blame all of them for the strain he suffered with this constant turbulence. During this difficult period Granddad would take me with him for long drives in his car, supposedly to go fishing, but many times we would just sit in the car or at the edge of the woods and talk. He would try to explain what this rivalry was all about. I could see in his eyes, as he talked, that he felt the way I did. Oftentimes on the way home we would just sit quietly as he drove, because we knew what we were both feeling. He would look over to me and wink his eye and ask if I would like to stop for a candy bar or an ice cream cone. Then, he would put his hand on my shoulder as he drove.

"It's alright, Raymie, it's going to be ok if thee take care of thyself. You're Master Raymie, you know that. I'm a Raymond, and your father's a Raymond. We must stick together. Do you know what the name Raymond means? It means wise protector. Someday that's going to mean you. You must learn to forgive your father, who is doing the best he can."

My grandfather was so strong and able to teach me how to hear my own inner voice.

When my grandparents moved to Marlton, we moved from Ruth's side of the house to Granddad's. I carried our things from one room to the other. We just opened the door and carried the stuff through. Dad took the old kitchen and made a pantry out of it and moved the new kitchen over into the old dining room.

I had liked the old way, how it had the refrigerator in the corner as you came in through the door. There was an Indian match holder that hung on the left side of the door frame, and a coconut Aunt Jemima that Lois and Ginny had made that hung on the right side of the door as you went through the kitchen. We had an electric range with the two steamer vats on the side that kept the food hot. The warming oven came out under the hood. It stood where the old wood stove had been, and the double sink with the drying basins on each side under the two windows overlooked the back fields. Everybody used to play in the kitchen and sit around the counters and talk.

There was a little table off the porch in the back where they used to feed the hired help, and where Grandmom used to set her pies to cool when they came out of the oven. I was always sticking my fingers into those fresh hot pies, and I'd get my fingers smacked, too!

Judy's position on the farm was to take care of Jean's and Dad's children and iron, and clean, and cook. Jean's great gift was adapting. When Dad married Jean she wasn't able to do much. Judy became a tool that enabled Jean to break into being a farmer's wife. Judy knew what Dad wanted.

Jean was able to start out her life with my father without the same pressure that Clara had been under. Clara had started out fresh with nothing, except pregnancy and the demands of being what my Grandmom wanted her to be. Jean was equally ill equipped and untutored but she was able to have her children and raise them all and still read books and look at her soaps because Judy was there to do the work. Judy resented this enormously, and would go out in the barn when we threw in the hay at night, and tell Larry and I how mean Jean was and how Marjorie was a spoiled brat. Jean's children got all the love and Judy felt she got nothing but hard work. She was constantly doing the dishes, and cleaning up and cooking and ironing all the time, without feeling any parental love.

Larry had made a big red model barn on a platform with matchstick fencing, driveways, trees, cows, tractors, and machinery. Larry loved to play with that farm. He was getting older and he decided to give it to Leslie as a gift that following Christmas. Leslie was far too young for it. Within a week he had destroyed the whole farm. He ripped up the fences and the trees. Larry was furious and so was I. Subsequently I did a terrible thing to Leslie.

Judy was pushing Leslie on a sled out behind the barn and he asked me to push him. Dad was coming around the barn with the tractor and the spreader. I purposely pushed him in front of the tractor. Dad wasn't going very fast so he was able to stop. He got off that tractor and tanned my hide.

I was still so frustrated and angry with everybody. Larry was going to be a dairy farmer. He had given Leslie his model farm. Leslie was going to be a farmer too. I was going to be ... nothing. They weren't sure what I was going to be. They ostracized me. After Leslie destroyed the model farm and I shoved him under the tractor I thought, "See what you can be now."

I was very frightened, distraught and lost. Jean got me some pastel paints. I was actually quite talented and used to draw and paint. I didn't feel talented. I felt freakish. I was in such pain after being condemned by my father who told me to "Stop being a sissy, be a man."

After my father whipped me, and reminded me what I had done, I realized that my artistic talents were going to cause me even greater suffering.

When Jean bought me the paints it was an incredibly emotional thing for me. I went home to my room. At first, I wouldn't use her paints. I never showed my paintings to my father. I'd only show them to Jean, privately and secretly.

I loved the farm. I liked cows, but I saw a broader picture. I saw a universe outside of that farm and I saw people and things happening that were more exciting to me than just being on the farm. I wanted the farm, but I wanted everything else as well. Dad couldn't understand that.

Deep down I knew that Dad loved me in his way. I knew that I loved him, but it was never confirmed in terms of his saying to me, I love you son. I love what you are and what you do and how you are. That acceptance didn't come during my childhood. I had had none of that validation through all the years of adulthood, years in which I didn't speak to him or see him. A year and-a-half before he died I got that confirmation for the first time.

PART IV

Ballinger Sisters

LOIS BALLINGER (17), RUTH BALLINGER (25), BOB DICKINSON (25)
POP, RAYMOND BALLINGER (51), 1942

Ruth Ballinger

I WAS BORN THE SECOND CHILD and the first daughter at the Homestead just before Christmas, 1917. My Mom named me Ruth. Dr. Brick came to the house, and Aunt Anna helped Mom deliver. There are just about three years between my brother Raymond and me. Lois was born eight years later and then Ginny, six years after Lois.

The farm at the end of our lane, across Elmwood Road, was an Evens (Evans) farm, and that was where Clayt Evens lived. He was a cousin to Grandmother Sally Ballinger, and a bachelor and a recluse. He had gone to college and was well educated. Clayt would read all the time and had a big library. He talked about everything and anything. I used to go over there. I think earlier that an old cavalry soldier lived with Clayt.

Cousin Clayt was over at the Homestead all the time. When my Uncle Herm and his wife Mary first married they moved in with Cousin Clayton, as Grandmother always called him. He would wear these overalls that were ten sizes too big, all tattered and torn. He'd take a piece of twine rope and put it around the waist and tie it together, and he let his hair grow long. Grandmother would cut his hair for him every once in a while.

One time Clayt was climbing through a wire fence and he caught his head and he came over. Clayt called Sally "Sarah." "Sarah, will thee look at my scalp"?

He had scraped it over the barbed wire, and he had a gash that was pretty bad. She tended to it and bandaged it and it took quite a while to heal up. Afterward Clayt got my father to go up to town and he bought a pint of ice cream for each one of us to celebrate.

I thought I could never eat a pint of ice cream, but I did! Of course he was nice to all of us, and we were all nice to him.

We were great ice cream eaters. We had the cows so the milk and the cream were easily available.

Pop made great rice pudding. He used a big pan and baked it in the oven. My mother used to make a tomato dish with lemon sauce. I didn't like it because it was too sweet. Pop liked it in a side dish with lemon butter and all kinds of relishes.

Pop was not a loud man. He had a good sense of humor. He just didn't explode with it. He'd sit back and chuckle with the rest, especially in his older years. My sisters, Ginny and Lois, would always be laughing and joking about something. He'd sit back and not say anything, but you'd see him shaking with laughter.

We had this work horse, a heavy horse, and Raymond loved to ride him.

Pop told him, "You're not to do this."

Raymond was with some of his friends and Pop was away one Sunday. I was home, and I heard a lot of commotion out the window and there was old Soldier rearing up. He fell over. I thought "Oh, boy, somebody's gonna get it." Somehow it didn't hurt the horse or Raymond.

As young girls, Father did not allow us in the barn around the cattle and the men, so we didn't have to do any of that type of work. We tended the house and grounds inside the yard. We took care of the flowers and we mowed the grass.

My father was always in charge of the vegetable garden. We weeded. Pop got up early and had an early breakfast. He worked hard and at noontime he wanted a meal. We would go out into the garden and pull beets and pick peas and bring them in and wash and cook them. I haven't had anything so good since then.

At the end of the summer we'd get a big wooden box and fill it full of dirt. The carrots and the beets that were left were stored in the cellar.

My mother canned a lot. She had a big cupboard in another of the root cellars with shelves which were always full of fruits and vegetables. We canned tomatoes and peaches and pears. My father would go to the market and get her purple plums. She loved those. We'd take a bushel of them and can them, and have fresh pineapple too. Of course, we would eat as much as we could while we were fixing it.

There were wonderful fruit trees on the Homestead. We had an apple orchard out in the front by the lane.

It was always a big time on the first day of hunting season. All the friends and relatives would come over and the men would go hunting and we had to help Mom fix dinner. We always had a big family dinner with a white linen table cloth. There was an extra long one for special occasions when she opened the table. We had to set the table, make a salad and a fruit cup. Mom always baked pies.

I never met my Grandfather, David T. He died two weeks after I was born. Uncle Josiah, my grandfather's youngest brother, would come to hunt with his two sons and Uncle Harry and Uncle Evens. Uncle Herm and Uncle David never came. They were not hunters.

We didn't get electricity till 1928 when I was eleven. We had a big old black kitchen stove and I had to get up early in the morning and light the fire before we could cook breakfast.

When I was thirteen my baby sister Ginny was born. My mother was not well. She had a kidney problem. It wouldn't even be daylight when I'd have to get up and cook. I was going to school but I would still get up in the morning, make the fire, and cook breakfast for my father, my brother, and Jake. The men got up somewhere around four in the morning and did the milking. Jake had been with us since he was eleven years old. Often we had another man or two, depending on the season. They all had a full breakfast, potatoes, ham and eggs.

We had a wood box in the winter time in the corner. When we were kids, we had no plumbing. There was a big tin bathtub, and we put that on top of the wood box and we took a bath by the stove in the kitchen, or we'd freeze to death. We had no heat in any of the bedrooms, and I tell you, they were cold. We had really cold winters. My mother told me when we were babies we slept with mittens and caps on, and of course blankets. It was a big deal when electricity came through. In the summer time we didn't use that big stove because it threw out a lot of heat.

I did the oil lamps. Pop's sister, Aunt Anna, would come over. We'd take all the oil lamps out of the rooms and put them together on the kitchen table. We had thirteen to fourteen lamps, plus a couple of Betty lamps. First we would fill all the bases of the lamps with oil. We'd use a small funnel and a little red gallon can of oil. Afterwards we would clip the wicks with scissors, or reload with new wicks if they needed them. Last we would take a basin of water mixed with white vinegar that had gotten too old for table use, to cut the oil soot off the chimneys. You had to be careful washing the chimneys because they would break quite easily. Then we would remount the chimneys and place the lamps back into the rooms. This took a good two hours or more every day.

Of course, there were the chamber pots! There was one under every bed, with a lid. We had slop jars. They were large porcelain buckets, with handles. You would go around the rooms and dump what was in them into the slop jar! Then you would take the empty chamber pot and lid, wash it down with lye soap, dry it, and put it back in its place for the next evening. We would take the slop pot to each room. That took another hour. Finally we would dump all of the wash basins and rinse and wipe them down, then refill them with a bucket of fresh water for the following morning.

Sometimes it would get so cold in the bedrooms that by morning there would be a slight shell of ice over the water. The beds had to be made and the sheets washed and changed once a week. Quilts and pillows were shaped, pounded and laid out for fresh linen. The rooms were vacuumed out. We used a little push vacuum broom that you ran over the carpets, and a damp mop to wipe around the outside perimeters. That would take another two and a half hours. The total time for daily house work was around five and a half hours.

Aunt Anna would do the housework most of the time, but if it wasn't completed, I would have to help after school as well as help with dinner, and do my homework. When my sister Lois got old enough she would help.

When electricity came we put in a refrigerator and an electric range, plus plumbing!! We had a real bathroom with a hot water heater in the basement. We already had cars before we got electricity.

Pop got his first Model T with yellow wire spokes, a touring car. You had to crank it and keep putting water in the radiator. That old Model T was all open, so in the winter time if it was cold or raining you had curtains that you snapped on that were made of isinglass. The edging frame of the curtains was made of leather, to keep it flexible. Pop sold the Model T and got the Model A. The Model A had windows and a windshield that went out a little. It opened up at the bottom and you could wind the windows up and down. Boy, we thought we were living high!

Earlier, they had electricity in the town but they didn't hook it up in the country until much later. First they had to put up poles and wire all through the countryside. We had severe winters with tons of snow. In the country we got the big drifts. You could look out the dining room window and the snow was not too far below the window sill.

During one storm they had to dig a path from the house to the barn. For me, as a little child, it looked like a tunnel since the snow was so high. We had to go out to the Marlton Pike to get the school bus. If the snow was bad my Father would take us with Gamwood and a little wagon. The wheels would go through the snow. One especially bad snowfall he had to get the hay wagon with the big Percheron horses because the snow was so deep.

When I was in high school they sent us home early because a blizzard was coming. I was tall and the snow was up to my knees just from morning till mid-afternoon. It was so hard to walk. You had to pick your feet up. My mother was standing at the front door, watching and worried. She couldn't see me, because it was snowing so hard.

Mom would bake bread a couple of times a week. My Grandmother would bake more often. After a while it got delivered. Freihofer would come to your house, and then later the Bond truck came.

There was a butcher shop in Medford, Johnson's butcher shop. Johnson had a truck and went around to the farms once or twice a week. Grandmother would go out to the wagon and pick out the meat she wanted.

Trucks from Philadelphia would travel out to the country with their wares. That was always a big thing for little kids, because they had all kinds of pots and pans and utensils and trimmings. People sewed a lot and there were notions and items that we didn't see every day.

Marlton School was just eight grades. When I started they didn't have a kindergarten. By the time Lois went they added it on. We were transported by bus to Moorestown High School. Later they changed the contract, so I had two years at Moorestown, and then they shipped us to Haddonfield for the remainder of high school.

We had the hog killing in the winter when there was snow on the ground. All the neighbors pitched in and helped. When another farmer wanted to do his, my father would help him. The Evans family had this great big metal tub. They built a fire and boiled the water. It had a smoke stack in the back. My father would shoot the pigs, and then they would dump them in there and peel the hair off and gut them and let them hang in the shed overnight. It was cold, so they would keep well. The next day they would cut them up.

My mother and my Aunt Anna and Grandmother Sally worked as long as they were able. We girls would help grind up the hog meat for the scrapple and the sausage. My aunt and my mother would sit there doing the sausage skins. They used the intestines. They'd soak them in salt water, and let them sit. They had a board and a sharp knife, and they'd scrape and scrape the lengths. Then they'd soak it some more and they'd scrape some more, and then they'd turn it inside out until it was pure white when it got done. Then they would stuff them and tie them in lengths.

That was fantastic sausage. It was good scrapple, too. It would keep a long time in the winter. My mother would also can some of the sausage. After she had the electric oven, she used to can inside.

My father would smoke the hams in our smoke house, and wrap them in gauze and hang them in the attic. It was cold up there. They were pretty well gone by summertime.

Pop had five or six beehives. He kept them out along the Lombardy poplars. He would add the honey from his bees to the brine to sweeten the pickling of briskets and corned beef.

My mother made a lot of our clothes. It was a lot of work. That was your whole life. The trade off today is that you go to a job, you make money, and you buy food. If you grew your own food, you'd work at that instead of a job, which I think is much more harmonious. We canned tomatoes and beans and all kinds of vegetables ourselves.

Mom had a small herb garden in the yard. Pop grew parsley, basil, and chives. We had a grape vineyard and we made grape jelly. We would gather wild elderberries and we'd take apples and cook them for the juice, and my mother would make jelly out of these.

Mother sewed cheesecloth into a cone shape. She'd fill that with the apples or grapes from whatever she was making. Then she would tie the top and we'd twist it so that the juice came right out for elderberry juice and apple juice, then elderberry and apple jelly that was delicious.

She used to make the best corn relish. You can buy it in the store, but it doesn't taste the same.

At the end of the season we'd pick the green tomatoes before they cut them up. The tomatoes got chopped up into little pieces, with raisins and suet and Mother made the best mincemeat pie. There were a lot of raisins and apples. It was so good.

When Ginny was born my mother wasn't well. In her younger years mom was very ambitious. She would have gotten my father's midday meal cooked plus feeding the men that worked for him before I came home from school,. After Ginny's birth, when I came home from school at three o'clock, the twelve o'clock dinner table was sitting just as they'd left it. Boy that used to burn me up. My job was to clean it up. I couldn't stand seeing those old dishes all dried up. It was terrible to get them clean after they'd sat there. That used to annoy me something terrible.

She'd be sewing or maybe reading, if a new magazine came in the mail. She'd sit and read all day. It wouldn't bother her. It's just a difference in personality. Me, I couldn't do that. If I had something to do, I couldn't read until I got it done.

My husband Bob was quite a character. He always played with all the kids. After he came out of the Navy, we were still living at the Homestead.

Pop was hard on my brother Raymond, but he probably deserved it. Pop took him out to the woodshed when we were young. I was six and Raymond was about ten or eleven. I thought what's he going to do to him? I was scared to death. I think he only gave him a whack or two.

Pop was very gentle with us girls, very respectful. He never said anything in front of us that was a little bit shady. After we all got married and our husbands were around he would joke with them. We all liked a little joke too, but Pop would sit and look kind of funny if he thought we'd heard. I guess he figured after we got married it wouldn't hurt.

Mom, with the rumored Welsh temper, would spout off to Pop rather than the reverse.

When Raymond and I were young, I was sixteen and he was twenty, we all got going around with a group of young people in the Medford area. Uncle Evens' kids, Dave, Albert and Irene, lived close by at Kirby's Mill. We'd get together most Saturday nights at somebody's house and have a watermelon party. Dave at the time had been dating Clara. When Clara met Raymond, she liked him better.

I always thought Clara and I got along alright, and it was great that my big brother had a wife. Then I started working and we moved away. We returned to the Homestead after Bob got out of the Navy.

Raymond took over the farm in 1948. Pop's health was deteriorating. His asthma was very bad. In June he went into the hospital for quite a while. Bob and I were helping out.

We lived on the Homestead when Raymond was in Lyndell with Jean and the kids. Pop asked him to come back and take over the farm. Raymond needed us out so he could move in. He got a little uppity when we couldn't find a house. Houses were just plain scarce after the war and we didn't have a whole lot of money. I didn't really hold any grudge. Lois and Ginny thought it was just not right. Raymond only wanted to get in to help Pop.

Raymond was going back and forth from Haddon Heights to run the farm. He was building an extension onto the barn and he had put up a silo. Bob and I stayed on the other side of the house until June. Pop was going to go to Arizona because he was having difficulty breathing. I believe a good part of his anxiety came from trying to keep up with the farm. With his asthma that summer, the farm was too much and his health had deteriorated.

Lois Ballinger

I WAS EIGHT YEARS YOUNGER THAN RUTH and eleven years younger than Raymond. I came along in 1931 and they named me Lois.

In the early morning during berry season, we'd hook up a team to the large wagon. Then, we'd drive into the deep woods near Taunton Lake to pick  wild blueberries. Pop would drive, with Jake, Ruth, me and Aunt Anna. Sometimes Raymond would go. I must have been about six or seven, and I liked to go everywhere with Pop and he liked for me to go. Sometimes he would let me drive the single horse buckboard.

Every morning Sally B. swept the front walk that went out from her kitchen to the front gate and every afternoon Sally B. got herself, 'fixed up'. She'd wash her face, brush up her hair, and change her clothes. Then she would read the Bible.

One morning around the first week of May after she swept she went upstairs to make her bed and had a stroke. She couldn't speak. My father would ask her "Can thee hear me, Mother? If you can, squeeze my elbow." She could barely touch his hand. Her throat was partially paralyzed, and we would try to give her water with a spoon, but very little of it would get to her. She lingered for two weeks and then she died. She starved to death. Sally B. was taken to the old cemetery where David T. was buried, Eldridge Quaker Cemetery. My mother and father were both buried at the Colestown Cropwell Meeting House Cemetery, part of the Quaker meeting house in Mount Laurel.

The last meeting the family had was to divide Grandmother Sally B.'s possessions. There was no will, and a terrible family feud erupted that provoked continual hard feelings with Pop's brothers, mostly because of their wives. It changed everything. It had always been so much fun with those week-end gatherings and dinners, and now there was tension.

Harry's daughter Sarah ended up with a lot of things. After Sarah went into a nursing home, they were sold out of the family. Ruth wanted to have a woman come in and put a price on everything and then have a sale so that everyone in the family could buy something if they chose. Sarah needed money to live in the nursing home. Uncle Harry and Aunt Ida had this old colored man that worked for them for years. He told Sarah that he had a friend who could sell all these wonderful antiques for her, and without asking the family Sarah let him take them all.

One day my sisters and I decided that my mother needed a change, so Ginny and I got her to cut her hair, and Ruth gave her a perm. Then we decided that she needed a little bit of make-up. We kept Mom away from Pop and the men in the barns. Mom was always against drinking but this one time we told her what she needed to do was to have a little glass of wine before the meal. When we sat down to the table that night we called her to come on in.

My father looked up at her, and he looked again. "Well, Alice, what have you done to yourself?"

High school was fun, I had friends. We used to spend the week-ends either at their house, or at my house. I wasn't permitted to date until I was sixteen. I started driving after I was married when I was twenty-one.

I was playing softball with my nephew Larry, and reached up to catch the ball, missed it, and it hit me right on the bridge of the nose. The following day was my graduation from high school, so I refused to go and get my nose taped. I have had sinus trouble from that all my life. I was a good student and after high school I walked right into a job at the bank in Camden. I should have studied more but when you're young you don't think of those things.

Pop loved to go with me to the movies. We had to go clear over to Moorestown but Gary Cooper was playing there. My mother would not go with him, because she was ashamed of the way he looked, because he was so bent over. Ginny wouldn't go with him either. I went gladly. He appreciated it.

Mom was very proud, stubborn and arrogant. These are the qualities my brother, Raymond, inherited.

In the summer I went with some of my girlfriends down to Cape May. The Naval Air Stations were at Wildwood and Atlantic City. I met a young man. Of course I was young and stupid and terribly impressed by him. Back then, young men were nice and they were gentlemen. You didn't have to worry about being beaten, or murdered, and this young man was also getting ready to go overseas.

Dick Cuthbertson was from Kansas City and I brought him home for the week-end. Dick was very impressed with our Homestead and my family, but my father didn't like him. Pop said he talked too much and he thought he knew everything. He went overseas shortly thereafter.

I met Don in 1944 on Saint Patrick's Day. I was eighteen and he was twenty. I saw Don and I picked him up. It was a strange thing. I guess we just looked at each other...and....Don came back the next weekend. He said I was his dream girl. We would go up to Fort Dix where they held dances for the soldiers. Everyone donated part of their time to the servicemen. I remember in particular one little sailor from Duncan, Oklahoma. He was the nicest kid.

They would all be passing through, getting ready to go to war, and it was terrible. I would bring soldiers home for a meal. My mother would get irritated because she got tired of it. But I found it very interesting, because I was curious about what the rest of this country and world was like, and being able to meet people from different parts of it was a great thing for me.

The war was going on hot and heavy. The boys were coming home without arms and legs to the Naval Hospital in Philadelphia. We would be asked to go over there and just talk to them.

I had met Don when the war in Europe was ending. Don was headed to the Pacific for a year. I had just known him a few weeks before he left. He asked me to wait for him. I continued working at the bank for three years. I took a bus for a half an hour to get there.

When the war was over, we decided to get married. We got married in Moorestown. Granddad was there, and Pop gave me away.

Virginia 'Ginny' Ballinger

I WAS THE BABY NAMED VIRGINIA but I was always called Ginny. I was closer in age to my nephew Larry than I was to my own brother and sisters. My brother Raymond was seventeen years older than me and my sister Ruth was fifteen years older. My other sister Lois was only six years older. I was really the baby.

We had this huge old white bull, a Holstein, and his horns were cut off. He used to break out of those big white boards they used to put on barnyards. We were in the hammock one day. I was about six, and my nephew, Raymie, had just been born. Our bull got out and Lois saw him come running toward us. You never knew where he was going and if he got to you, he'd kill you, because he was real mean. Lois ran and she just left me in the hammock, swinging. She saw the bull, ran off inside the picket fence in the yard, and left me in the hammock!

I told her, "When you get married, I hope you have a whole bunch of ornery boys as ornery as you are. Then you'll know what I went through." Well, it worked! She got four boys, Don Jr.,

Gregory, John, and Matthew, and they were ornery too, just like her. Don, Lois's husband, was a test pilot. Don passed out one time when he was flying and almost killed himself. It was something to do with his sinuses.

I was shocked when I went down to visit my brother Raymond at his own place in Delaware. He had deer running all around his fields and he didn't shoot any. He said he was not crazy about hunting and he'd never really been.

He's been crazy over fox hunting ever since I can remember, but that's different. They chase the fox but they don't shoot them. He used to go on Sundays. Clara would go to church and take the kids with her and he would go fox hunting with his friend Buck, up there in Taunton.

My brother's friend, Buck, used to have a pet crow that would sit up in the mulberry tree and eat the mulberries. Buck would stick his finger out and call to him, and he'd come down and sit on it. Buck used to keep rattlesnakes in a barrel and he would reach down in there and grab the damn things, bringing them up and show them to us. I didn't bother looking at them, but the crow, that used to fascinate me.

I was four years old when Clara came to the Homestead and married Raymond. I thought she was great. Clara was like a mother to me, more than my own mother was. She taught me how to knit and I spent a lot of time at the bungalow, because I grew up with their kids.

They always used to go grocery shopping at the Giant Tiger and Clara would take me. It used to be like a supermarket. The Acme took them over. Afterwards we would always go back to Mount Holly to her Mom and Pop Williams and have cake and Jell-O.

I was three years old when Clara first came to visit and then all of a sudden they were married and Larry was born. I remember holding him as a little tiny baby. Then Raymie was born. He was the orneriest one of the bunch.

When I dream, it's always about the Homestead - things that happen to me now, I'm always at the Homestead. Even after my Dad died I dreamt about him for years.

He used to embarrass me. First he used to say," This is my baby." and pat me on the head. When I got to ten or twelve years old, that became kind of embarrassing. Later, he'd always say my "Right-hand man." I went everywhere with him. We got up at six o'clock in the morning to take the milk. I would freeze to death in that old truck with no heater.

They had a milk box that set down into the floor of the milk house. It was like a big chest and I used to have to keep that clean. I did other chores, like helping to feed the cows. I was an outside girl. As I got older I had to cut the grass and clean the house. Lois and I took turns.

When one daughter got married and moved out, the next one took over.

While cleaning the house, you had to move the furniture around to sweep underneath. I liked to move the furniture and put it in a different place. I still do. If you ever come home from work when you're not supposed to or sneak out and come back in the dark, you're going to fall over the furniture. You never know from one day to the next around here.

They still had the teams when I was young. One time I took a walk to the springs to get some tadpoles. We had a little short horse and I guess he had a heart attack. There he was on the other side of the barbed wire fence lying on his back in the ditch with his legs standing up. Rigor mortis had set in. He was stone dead. It was terrible.

We used to put the tadpoles in a big jug in the house and go down to the pond every day after school and get fresh stuff for them to eat. We'd keep them until they turned into frogs. There was a little frog and he hopped out and got into the sink and we couldn't find him. We used to have an old cupboard in the kitchen to keep your dishes in. It had a dough board that we'd pull out and make a pie crust on it. This frog had hopped under that old oak hutch and died there and dried up. Mom liked to have had a fit.

February 28 was my birthday, and every year about that time we would have a big storm. When we had storms then, they were storms. The snow would be up to the window sills. The wind would blow and the snow would drift and the electricity would go out. That happened once while Mom was making my birthday cake. Mom had the woodstove moved out into the little workshop where Dad kept his tools. He had a shoemaker's kit and he would mend and resole everybody's shoes. There was a wonderful tool chest out there with his draw knives. He took a cedar shingle and carved a flat arrow for me, with a catch on the end of it. Then he cut a supple willow stick and hooked the arrow head to it, then taught me how to thrust it toward a target.

Grandmom Sally B. was wonderful. She was almost blind. She wore a little knot on top of her head and was very neat. She wore long black dresses and sat in the chair and rocked all the time and crocheted monkey lace. She used to sew it on her underwear, her slips and just about everywhere.

Ruth never learned to swim and neither did I. We used to go out in the boat with Pop fishing. I always sat there and each time Pop said, "You're a darn fool ever to go in a boat if you can't swim."

I never heard Pop cuss. He used to get mad and say "Christ Almighty," but I never heard him cuss. He didn't drink. He didn't smoke. He used to smoke those medicated cigarettes for asthma, and I never heard him be abusive to me. Only one time did he get mad at me and holler. That was when I was a teenager, and that was after he was sick.

That was just the way he was. Mom used to fight with him and she'd be hollering and cussing, and fighting. He'd never say anything. She'd cuss at him, and hit him too on the head with the dish rag, because he'd sit there and not say anything. After a bit he'd get up and go out.

Pop was milking when a Delaval salesman came by. Raymond and Pop were busy trying to get these twin calves to suck. Their mother's bag was feverish and Pop wanted them to suck and bring the fever down before the mother got mastitis.

Pop had told the salesman he was busy, and to come back later. The salesman kept persisting, and without saying a word Pop stepped out of the box stall with his asthma and bent back, and lifted the salesman by the shoulders and he hung him on a nail that was sticking out of a beam. He told him to stay there until he finished and then he'd deal with him. Larry was under a cow busting his side laughing. It scared me, so I took a bucket of milk and ran into the milk house. I know the Ballingers are all hot tempered but I never saw Dad get that mad.

When my brother Raymond was nineteen he was riding Gamwood. Raymond loved this horse. There was some ice and the horse slipped and fell on him. That's how he hurt his hip and why he limped sometimes.

After he was married to Clara he bought a paint horse, Domino. Raymond kept the paint at the Homestead and he'd ride him back and forth to the bungalow where he lived. He knew how to handle any horse, but Ruth's husband, Bob, didn't. Bob got on Domino at the bungalow to ride him back to the Homestead. It's a wonder the horse didn't kill him, because Bob had never been on a horse in his life. The horse was stable sour and ran all the way back with Bob, right down the Marlton Pike. The worst part was that Bob was still in the Navy and wearing his white uniform. Bob just let the horse go and held on to whatever mane he could grab till he fell off. His white uniform was never the same again.

Raymond really knew how to handle horses. He used to do tricks on the paint. He would gallop the horse and slide down one side going under his belly and coming back up the other side, like the Cowboys and Indians used to do on TV. He was a great horseman.

I drove the horses while Pop was sick in the hospital. Something was wrong with his stomach. He had some kind of sac in his stomach, and they had to dissolve it. Pop had never been in a hospital before. I had to drive the horses with the wagon through the tomato field. Bob loaded the tomatoes on the wagon. I liked working outside.

I was fourteen when Raymond and Clara broke up. I didn't really know what was going on. I was just told that Clara had left. The only reason I knew something had happened was that Mom was out in the garden pulling carrots, crying her heart out. I went out and asked what the matter was? She didn't want to talk about it. She couldn't talk. Mom just couldn't explain her feelings to anybody. She'd just stand around and cry. She said I was just too young to understand.

At this point Pop's back was causing him a lot of pain. We didn't realize that he had osteoporosis. When he was younger, he was a handsome looking man, tall and strong, with copper colored hair, but his back was always curved ever since I remember. It got that way before I was born. People used to make fun of him, and look at him strangely, but it didn't bother me. He was my Pop.

When he died they came to Mom and wanted to know if they could break his back because he didn't fit in the casket. She had a fit. Well, can you imagine that? Having to break his back so that he would fit down in the casket? She told them "No." They had to take all the lining out and rearrange it inside. That was terrible.

They always called my brother Raymond Junior, or Buddy, so they wouldn't mix him up with Pop.

We had collie dogs when we were young. Lois's collie had gotten old and sick. The vet came that used to tend to our cows. I saw it. Nobody else did. The dog went over and lay down and died, and I saw it. The vet had given him a couple of pills to put it to sleep. After the pills it went over in the grass, lay down and died.

Lois didn't know what happened to her collie, but I saw the vet sticking those pills in. I wasn't supposed to see it, but I did.

Larry used to ride his little scooter all the way from the bungalow over to the Homestead. This little boy would ride that big old scooter about a mile, through the fields past the Quaker school, down by Cooper's fields and across Elmwood Road almost every day.

My nephew Raymie had to milk the cows since he was about three or four years old. Raymie didn't do it so well when he was little. He didn't like the idea. It's not that he was a sissy. He just didn't want any part of it. He'd sit around and be mournful. Larry, he'd get right in there and milk them real fast like a man. He didn't care. Raymie didn't want any part of that.

Pop used to tell all the kids, "Just twist the tail around and she'll give you milk." Then he would say "Pull the back tits down, and she'll give you chocolate. Pull the front ones down and you get vanilla." Some kids believed it.

I spent a lot of time with Raymond's kids. I grew up with them like they were my brothers and sisters. I just was around them all the time.

There was an old courting buggy that Mom and Pop used to use sitting behind the corn crib that was connected to the carriage house. They kept it in the garage all those years. It was like brand new. All of a sudden they decided it had to go, because they had to use the garage for something else. Larry and Raymie used to play in it and bounce it up and down.

We had this mean old white bull that would be looking over the fence in the barnyard and bellowing and bellowing. He'd get so mad. We just kept an eye on him in case he got out because there was no place to run to. The kids played around that carriage for hours, while they were milking, and that bull bellowed for hours.

Old Jake grew up on the Homestead like family. Grandma Sally raised him from a boy. He was around until he got so old that his brother took him to Medford to live with him, and he shut him upstairs. You'd ride by and look up and he would be just sitting there just looking out the window. It was a shame.

Jake used to eat in the kitchen, at the pie table, and when he'd eat he'd bite the fork which gave him an old sawed off tooth. When I set the table I always gave him the same fork because his was all chewed up from his bite. After Raymond left the farm we used to let Jake sit at the table with us, and everyone treated him well. Grandma washed his clothes like one of the family. I don't know where he came from, or who he was. Why she took him in, I don't know.

They used to saw wood with this big blade. In the fall, after the harvest season, they would cut firewood for the winter. Jake and Raymond would haul wood with the team, and sometimes the neighbors would help. Cutting wood was a big occasion, just like it was for pig killing, or filling the ice house, or splitting rails for the fence line. The man that brought the saw was loading a log in and ran his arm into the saw. I was very young and this was right before I started school. Everybody was yelling and hollering and running around as if something had happened to them.

Pop had an old sharpening stone. He had taken a bicycle and fixed it so it would power the stone making it turn as you pedaled. Pop would sit on that seat and pedal until he sharpened everything on the place. He'd sharpen all of Grandmom's scissors, peeling knives, his drawing knives, axes, hatchets, sickles and scythes, any blade that he could find. Everything was always sharp.

You know childhood memories are the most vivid of all memories. They are the richest, because they have been with us the longest, so they're the strongest.

Don Mikell, Lois' Husband

I WAS DELIVERED BY A ONE ARMED DOCTOR, Farnell. He came to the farm. I don't recall ever seeing the man. In those days they didn't make up birth certificates. I had to apply for a delayed birth certificate after I graduated from high school and before I went into the Air Force and married Lois.

We moved east of Morristown, Florida to north of Morriston, from one farm to another. We were dirt farmers. We grew everything you could to make a living. We grew our own foodstuffs except for flour, ate a lot of grits, had plenty of beef, plenty of vegetables and because we grew vegetables and shipped them we got some peaches and pears. Of course this was during the Depression.

I was the oldest of three brothers. There was another one, but he expired soon after birth.

Dad acquired some acreage west of the town of Morriston, and built a house when I was about a year and a half. I grew up chasin' hogs and cows and killing rabbit snakes, anything you could think of. I was two and a half years old then.

We used to go out in the summer time, before the days of the screw worm and we'd mark and castrate all the pigs, and chase them down on foot. We castrated them with a sharp knife, and then turned them loose. When screw worms came along, you didn't dare break the skin on an animal. They had a fly that laid its eggs along an open skin break, and within a matter of hours the live maggots would be consuming that animal. Within a few hours after this maggot fell out into the sand, he would hatch into a fly, and take off, and do it all over again.

They would destroy a cow, because when their eyes would start running the damned bugs would get in there and eat the eye. You would use benzene and it would kill the screw worm by freezing them, but it would also just about kill your cows. The only thing you could do was shoot them and burn them to get rid of the bugs.

After the war was over, they finally eradicated that fly by sterilizing male flies and releasing them from airplanes all over the state until the things died out. I think it came out of Mexico.

My mother, Sadie, had to work right along with my Dad. We'd start at daylight. We were picking cucumbers, okra, or whatnot, and she'd leave a little early if we weren't finished by ten o'clock in the morning. She'd go and fix lunch, and we'd usually finish up by noon. You had to get the darned stuff shipped out. These were some tough years (1923-1938), but we had plenty to eat though we didn't have a heck of a lot of money.

If you didn't pay your taxes, your place was gone. My Dad, Lester, had lost one little quarter section because he couldn't pay the taxes on it, but nobody came along and bought it out from under him. Eventually the neighbor down the road paid the taxes on it and got it.

I played every sport I could get my hands on, basketball, baseball, and football. I was real skinny, and could run. We were kind of a rag tag little old outfit. We didn't even have uniforms for twelve guys. We played six man crews because we didn't have enough guys to field an eleven. And then the war came along.

I was just out of high school and working for a construction company. I helped build Buckingham Gunnery School at Fort Lars, the air base at Boca Raton, and the one at Boca Chica, and the one at Williston.

I joined the Aviation Cadet Corps in 1942. I applied for pilot training, and I was selected as an aviation cadet candidate. I went to Miami Beach for thirty days, and then got shipped out to Galesburg, Illinois, for college training in a detachment program that was beginning to fill up. After three months in Galesburg, we started the classification during which I was selected for pilot training, and then I went to pre-flight training and from there to Corsicana, Texas, for primary. I advanced to Enid, Oklahoma, for basic training, and then moved all over the country.

I went to Foster Field, Victoria, Texas, for advanced training and worked on the T-6 and the P-40. I was commissioned at Foster Field the fourth of August, 1944.

They shipped me back to Richmond, and then to Goldsboro, North Carolina, where I took my P-47 checkout of basic. It's still an operational base. I ended up at Dover, Delaware. That's where I met Lois Ballinger.

Lois and I met at the USO at the Naval Air Depot in Philadelphia in 1945. I probably just walked over to her and we danced. I was pretty brassy in those days.

I shipped out of Dover to Richmond, to another pilot pool, and then to Seattle, Washington. I spent six weeks in Hawaii and flew out of there on a DC - 4, to Yashima, just off Okinawa, and joined the Four Hundred Thirteenth Fighter Group, Twenty-first Squadron. In a year, I got in two missions, and then the damn war ended.

I got on a DC-4, and flew down to Manila for the initial surrender ceremony. I watched them showing pictures of the white painted bombers with the green crosses on them. I just stood there on the air strip where they landed with about ten thousand other guys. We circled that airstrip watching the Japanese come in and surrender.

I stayed in Manilla for nearly a year from the time I got there to the time I left, because I had no points. I was a fighter pilot, period. Then, of course, we lost all of our enlisted people that took care of the airplanes. I never saw any planes close enough to shoot at. We'd go out on fighter sweeps and tool around and then we would go back to base. The war was virtually ended by then.

They had dropped at least one of the atom bombs by that time.

On Okinawa there were these skeet ranges. We had the planes and the equipment, the shotguns and the ammunition so we shot a lot of doves. That was a big deal over there. During the war, you'd never see a bird. When the war was over, they came back by the millions. We did a lot of crazy things like pushing equipment, airplanes, and everything you could think of off the end of an airstrip in Okinawa. We just whiled away our time and flew every minute we could 'till we got home.

I came home in June of 1946. Lois and I were married in November in Morristown, New Jersey at a Presbyterian church. Sarah Ballinger, Harry's daughter, made the wedding dress. I bought the material in Shanghai. We had a three day honeymoon. We didn't have enough money for anything else.

When we came back we rode a train to Philadelphia, got across the Delaware to Camden, picked up a bus, and came up the pike. When we got to Marlton we waded through snow, waist deep, from Elmwood Road to the Homestead. The roads were open but man! The mailman hadn't even delivered the mail that morning. Lois was crying, tears running down her cheeks, she hurt so badly, "I'm done froze to death!"

When Lois and I were first dating, I went to dinner at the Homestead right away. Her mother Alice didn't like me, I could tell. I was only up there for an overnight and the next day her brother, Raymond, was there. We were never what you would call close. We weren't around each other that much. I'm about nine years younger than him and we chopped corn and chopped silage together.

His kids were just wild scary kids, always into something, chasing around. Larry, Judy and Raymie. Leslie was a baby and he would be playing with Ruth's daughter.

I tried to help out at the farm. I was visiting, and kind of earned my keep! That first summer we used a team and a flat bed wagon, cutting all the corn by hand with a machete. The next year we used the tractor and the harvester. Pop dropped his inhaler box into the conveyor, and it stopped working. I grabbed it and jerked it out of there. Like to scared him to death. He thought I was going to get caught by the auger. Pop and I were throwing the corn off the wagon, and Raymond was up inside the silo, leveling whatever we could pump up there.

I think I helped save that man for a couple of years. When Lois and I came back from Wichita, Kansas, her pop was getting pretty down, and didn't want to do anything. He was down psychologically. I went over to see Dr. Monroe, and I asked, "What would be the damage, what would be the harm, if I took him hunting?"

The season was coming up, and old Doc Monroe said it would be the best thing in the world that could happen to him. Alice was madder than hell at me, because I went back and I stood and talked to him. She heard me, and I said something about "Let's go up to the deer woods and go hunting this fall."

He perked right up! Well, she didn't like the idea, and I don't know who else didn't like the idea, but I understand there was a couple more. We went deer hunting anyway, with the agreement that if he got tired he would say so and I'd bring him home. He had a ball!

After the hunting season was over, they always took the meat to a butcher and then the men would divide it up between them and then they would have a big banquet at the deer club.

We went over for that, and spent a couple of mornings at the deer camp. You couldn't see your hand in front of your face, but we got there, and we never did have to bring him home.

He and I would go fishing. Of course there were all kinds of fishing.

Ginny was still home when we got back from Kansas. I was only about 23. There was this painted horse that Bob rode. That horse almost killed me as well. I never got on another horse since.

If I had my life to live all over again I don't think I'd do a hell of a lot of anything different.

Ginny, Virginia Ballinger

BOBBY MOORE WAS WORKING at the farm that year and I thought he was cute. He had hooked the sleigh to Silver and he took us all up and down the driveway, and clear around to the Marlton Pike. We went out but we couldn't ride on the road because the horse wasn't shoed for it. We went alongside of the highway and the snow was really deep. The horse stepped in the snow and went down in the ditch and threw me out of the sleigh. I stuck my hand out and I hit the horse's rump. I thought I'd broken my arm. All I could hope for was that the horse wouldn't kick. It took me a long while to get up. I was stunned. That was the last time I went on a sleigh ride. Raymond just laughed. Bobby wasn't knowledgeable about harnessing a horse and he didn't have the harness on properly.

Raymond tried to break a chestnut draft horse, Amos, for one of the Westcott boys. He took him out in the back lot and covered his eyes with a burlap bag, so Amos couldn't see when he jumped on his back. The horse sure felt it and he reared up and went over backwards and almost killed Raymond.

Instead, he took that old white horse 'Silver', the one we used for the sleigh, and trained him for riding. Raymond was already married and living at the bungalow in Pine Grove with Clara.

My brother used to go home for dinner to the bungalow from the farm. Clara always cooked for him and after dinner he'd come back to the Homestead. Sometimes I used to go with him. He would drive the old Model A that he bought off old man Budden. It had green spoked wheels and a rumble seat. He'd drive real fast and he'd turn into our orange gravel lane on two wheels. The car was like a little box, sitting up in the air, and I was always afraid it would overturn. He used to scare me to death. Years later when I told him that story he said he never turned like that. I must have been with somebody else. Sure.

Raymond's friend, Marshall Simmons, used to give Raymie and Larry cigarettes to smoke which made them sick. Marshall spent a lot of time at the farm in Barrington when Clara was pregnant with Leslie. Marshall used to scrub the kitchen floors for her, she was so sick. She got very puffy and swollen. She got that way with Sandy, her last child, too. Clara wasn't supposed to have any more children because her kidneys were failing, and she was in bad shape.

I used to come to Barrington a lot. Pop would drive there in his old truck to help. Pop would get to the top of the big hill and put the truck out of gear and let it coast down the hill to save gas.

One day Raymond came running toward the house, "Get Mom!" he yelled. "Quick, get your clothes. We've got to get Clara to the hospital, she's gonna die." They took Clara away in the middle of the night. It was before she had Leslie. I think she might have been miscarrying, but didn't. It was a big emergency, but no one would tell me what was wrong.

Was she alright? What happened to her? They wouldn't say a thing. I was fifteen years old and considered too young to know. I stayed with the kids.

Lois and I never shared a room. I had all these Alan Ladd pictures and scrapbooks of all the movie stars. I helped Raymie make scrapbooks of horses.

We used to take the bus from Marlton to Camden almost every Saturday, just to see Roy Rogers on the silver screen. Roy Rogers came to one of his restaurants around here a couple of years ago. He was shaking hands with the men and kissing all the women, so I turned my cheek up and he kissed me. I thought that was something.

I loved the land, I like nature, and I love horses. I'm crazy about horses just like Dad was. I've raised them all my life, and I love cows. I love to be in the woods. I love being around nature a lot. I just didn't like dairy farming.

Larry wasn't the same as me. I was fourteen and Larry was ten. Larry would sit down and milk a cow as if he'd been doing it his whole life. He could keep right up with the men. He milked those old Holsteins with the big bags, and he just kept right up with them. I used to sit on a little stool behind Larry as they moved from cow to cow. Occasionally I had to jump up to get out of the way. I'd draw or read a book.

I didn't want to be behind a cow twenty-four hours a day, seven days a week. They were shoved down my throat. I was made to work, and Larry and I used to milk those one hundred twenty head every night and every morning before we went to school. We did it with machines, surge milkers with straps and six fourteen quart buckets that had to be continually carried to the milk house, lifted above my head and poured over the aerator. Larry and I milked those one hundred twenty cows every night and every morning before we went to school, and we didn't get much appreciation for it.

When Raymond came back to the Homestead to live he and Larry had to do the milking. Larry would milk with the men and Don would be sitting there watching and saying, "I come from a farm."

Don would sit down and he'd milk one cow and he'd put his thumb into his palm against the tit to milk. After a bit he's hollering, "My thumb is hurting."

Big deal, you know! I come from a farm. I can milk the cows! Really?

They tried to tell him you can't milk like that, but he couldn't get any milk out of the cow the other way. He had to stick his thumb in to squeeze and that was the only way he could get milk. I thought that was funny, it cracked me up! I couldn't get over that. Here Larry was just a little kid and he used to sit there milking the cows with the men and Don was a man out of the army and he'd milk one at a time.

You got used to it. But I still didn't want to milk cows seven days a week, night and morning.

PART V

Raymond and Jean

JEAN SHUSTER ON SHEBA, 1942

Dad, Raymond Ballinger

I NEVER MET JEAN 'till her father, Pappy Shuster, brought her over. That's when I met her there at the farm. That was after Edith and Clara left, or right before she left. Pappy came over one night to get corn for Jean's horse. He had been coming over there for some time and I didn't even know he had a daughter. I'd bought this big truck from those boys in Haddon Heights, a Chevrolet with the high sides on it. Pappy helped me start it. We went to the corncrib and he helped me load corn. We took the truck over to his garage and that's the first time I ever laid eyes on her. Pappy had been coming over at different times. He just liked to be around the farm. I never saw her even when I worked at the shipyard, hell no. I stayed in Barrington until the boys finished school that year, and then we had the auction and we left. It was after VE-day.

I did not leave Clara for any other woman. There is no truth in that whatsoever. I can look anyone right in the eye and it's just not so. That's something that's somebody's fantasy. I realize now that maybe I should have sat the children down around the table and had it out. But they were only kids. It was hard to explain without running their mother down, and I didn't want to be responsible for that. That's the reason I held back.

Clara had threatened me and said she would leave if I didn't go back to the shipyard and I told her if she left not to come back. I told her that that day, in the parlor as she was loading things up.

I had come home that October day with some feed and there was a Mayflower moving van backed up to the front steps. She'd loaded all the furniture, everything but the stove, and left me the kitchen table and chairs, some dishes, and a bed and a bureau. I came in there. She was there, of course. Edith was waiting in her car for her with Judy and Leslie. Larry had gone to get feed with me and was still in the barn. I think she waited for me to get home so she could hand Raymie over to me. We were screaming at each other. It started raining and she drove off with Edith in her car.

Clara was pregnant with Sandy when she left with Judy and baby Leslie. She had Sandy the following February.

When Clara left, I gave her money each month until she brought Judy and Leslie back. I'd sent Pop money when I was out West getting a divorce and he'd give her so much a month. When the divorce came through I was to pay child support for Judy and Leslie, which I did. But then Judy begged to come home to live with her Daddy and her brothers and then Clara didn't want Leslie. He was in the way. She would have had to take care of him without having Judy to do it.

Pop went to see her when I was in the hospital with appendicitis. Clara told Pop to tell me that if I would send her a check for $100 I could have the baby. That was Leslie. I have the receipt signed by her. In return for $100 from Raymond E. Ballinger, I hereby give him custody of Leslie.

I spent the next fifteen to twenty years trying to make up for my mistake with my children. I may not have been the best father, but I did the best I could under the circumstances. This was why I took Judy and Leslie back. Jean and I kind of figured out the children would all be better off together living back at the farm. I know it's affected all the kids and me too, but that was the best we could do.

After I sold the farm in Barrington and married Jean it was hard for all of us, having to move back to the Homestead, especially with Mom, Pop, and Ginny still living there. Ruth had been living on the other side of the house and had to get out when I took over the farm. This caused a lot of friction, especially with Judy because she was in the house and the boys were in the barn with me. When we moved back, the resentment between the two families was hot and heavy, and Judy was an easy target. She was only five years younger than Ginny and she was easy to blame for any real and imaginary thing that went on in the house. Judy's anxiety was evident. A lot of that was caused by her insecurity of having been sent away and sent back with the divorce and the family breakup. Then, of course, she was only eleven years old.

JEAN HAD BEEN GOING WITH GEORGE BAKER, a guy with thick glasses who used to have a horse. She'd come over to my Barrington farm with Pappy for corn. Pappy was fascinated with the farm. He'd always been interested in farming, but he never had a chance to farm. He had been coming over quite a little while before I ever met Jean.

After Clara left, Jean would come over and help take care of the kids and then she would take us all over to their house for supper with her mother, Mrs. Shuster.

I think when I first met her, Jean was working at the Haddon Press, a book publisher in Camden. There was a lot of hero worship there on her part. I was a farmer and I knew how to do so many different things with my hands. I rode horseback and I still used to rodeo a little bit. Jean was crazy about that stuff as well as the horses and the cows. I think Jean put me on a pedestal so damn high that if I fell off, I would have broken my neck. I was different than any man she ever went out with. Jean was nine years younger than me, and I had four children. If Pappy objected, I never heard him, and she never told me. I'm sure that there was some hidden objection by her mother Sarah Elizabeth. Pappy was the kind of man who wouldn't say anything. That's the way he got along with his wife and his sister, Beulah. If there was any problem he just turned around and walked away from them.

Clara had left me with only part of my family and taken the other half. A week later she tried to come back. She actually wanted to come back! She was crying and carrying on and I told her," No." I had told her the way it would be when she went out that lane. I felt like my dreams had been sabotaged. Clara just wasn't satisfied there in Barrington, and that's all there was to it. She went out of that door with our furniture. That killed any feeling that I had for her.

I'd get up in the morning and go out and milk and then come back in and get the boys up and dressed and cook their breakfast and send them to school. I did that for a month. Clara left in October and I sold out in November. Eventually I had to auction off everything to survive. At that point my cows were gone, the barn was gone, and my home was gone. Everything was gone.

That last couple of weeks Mrs. Shuster got us to come over to their place for supper a lot. During that period, Jean came over and washed clothes a few times just to help out. We became intimate through that.

My parents never said much about the divorce. Mom didn't approve of it and took it hard. Pop would always stick up for me.

They thought Jean was too young and kind of scatterbrained. Jean rode horses, went around with dungarees on, and was a little bit ahead of her time. My mother knew Pappy Shuster from when they were kids in Sunday school. Alice was a Baptist. Mrs. Shuster's mother was Stoke Sutton's daughter. They lived not too far from where my mother was raised.

Pappy had come down to see Mom one night and brought Mrs. Shuster and Jean to visit the Homestead. We were still in Barrington but Clara had left and we went there for supper with the boys. Pop was in the barn with me and said "That girl has a crush on you, boy. I was watching. She's got eyes for nothing else but you. She seems nice enough."

I wasn't looking for something like that, 'cause I was too bitter and filled up with what had gone before.

But on January 10, 1946, Bud, Jean's brother, and I drove out West so I could get a divorce. Pappy was teaching mechanics in Philadelphia, and he had rebuilt the engine in that '34 green Ford. Bud had always wanted to go out West, but after we got out there he got homesick and turned around and got a bus ticket and came home.

Jean came out after I was divorced. I sent for her and we were married in Virginia City. As far I was concerned I'd had enough problems with Clara, but Jean wanted to get married and she loved the life I led.

Carson City, Nevada
Jan. 22, 1946

Dear Clara,

I hope this letter finds you feeling better than you were the last time I saw you. I hope you have found a doctor and gotten everything straightened out for the coming event. If you have, please let me know the particulars. I have had quite a trip but have not yet found a good place to stay for awhile. The housing conditions out here are just as bad as they are back home.

I can sure play cowboy for fair out here with plenty of wild horses and thousands of cattle and sheep. As soon as I get settled I will write again and give you my address. I have been thinking of you a lot and wondering how you are feeling and getting along.

Am looking forward to receiving the letter you promised when you get my address. Remember me to Sis and tell her to write me a little letter too. Also remember me to Edith and Alex and the rest. Hope you received the cards I sent. I will be home soon and bring the boys down to see you right away as I promised. I want to tell you now that no matter what happens, or what papers you receive from out here I will do my share as I promised as long as it is humanly possible regardless of what the law says. I am going after a job tomorrow but I don't expect it will be much as this is a slack season on the ranches out here. There will be plenty of good jobs when the spring roundups start. But I will be home before then. I hope you will not be unreasonable about all this, as I now feel that it is the best for both of us and the children too.

The country sure is beautiful out here and the weather is remarkable. The other morning in Arizona it was six above zero and I was quite comfortable outside in just a sweater.

Don't forget no matter what happens I will always think of you as I have in the past and I will be looking for that letter you promised you would write when you get my address.

This is the hardest job I have ever had to do. I have been hours trying to write this letter. I can't think of anything more to say so please try to be reasonable about everything and do what you think is best and may God bless you.

I still don't know why things had to turn out like they did, but I guess it couldn't be helped.

So with good wishes and lots of luck I will say
Goodbye,
Raymond

P.S. Don't forget I will be thinking of you and praying for you every minute, and please don't forget to write as soon as you get my address.

Carson City, Nevada
Feb. 3, 1946

Dear Clara,

Have finally found a place to bunk for awhile. Places are as scarce as they are back home. I am staying at a ranch outside of Carson City. Carson City is in Washoe County and is the smallest state capitol in the U.S. about 2,000 people. The dome of the capitol building here in Carson City is made of silver. As you know Nevada is a great silver and gold mining state. I was in an old gold mine the other day in Virginia City a short ways from here. Carson City is located in the heart of Eagle Valley and surrounded by the snow capped Sierra Nevada Mountains, a very beautiful valley.

The weather is very unusual here, always warm in the daytime but down around zero at night but you would never know it was that cold. Have not worn anything but a sweater since I have been here.

I hope you have received my first letter and that it finds you feeling better than the last time I saw you. Did you and Judy receive the cards I sent before?

Please remember me to Judy and all the rest of the folks and tell Judy to write Daddy a little letter. Hope Leslie has gotten over his cold and is feeling better.

Have you found a doctor and made arrangements yet? I sure hope so.

If you have time please let me know the particulars about the baby's arrival so I will know what to do when the time comes.

I hope you are feeling better and wish you the best of luck from the bottom of my heart. I keep thinking of you often and wondering how you are and what you are doing. Don't forget you promised to write to me as soon as you get my address. So I will be looking for a letter from you and Judy in about ten days. It takes about five days each way for mail to come from New Jersey. Can't wait to get home and see you and the children and to know how you are getting along.

Don't forget your promise for I will be home soon and will keep mine.

So don't forget to write and tell me everything as you promised I will be waiting for your letter.

Best wishes & good luck,
Raymond

Carson City, Nevada
Feb. 11, 1946

Dear Clara,

I hope you have received your letters and cards. I was not sure whether you get your mail from Camden or Merchantville, so I hope I guessed right on your address.

I am still looking forward to that letter you promised so please don't let me down. I hope you are feeling well and that the children are all well. I heard from the boys the other day and they are fine. I will be home soon and bring them down to see you. You don't know how much I miss you all. I guess no one will ever know now.

If I hadn't started this mess I don't think I could have gone through with it. But maybe I can make up for all the suffering I have caused you when I get home. By now you most surely have gotten everything settled, so please write and let me know the particulars. I think of you often and wish you the best of luck in what lies ahead. Have you gotten any papers from out here? If you have I hope you will sign the papers and send them back as soon as possible. If you don't sign them it will take a little longer for this to go through.

I have a job offered in another state and as my money is running awful short I want to get to it as soon as possible so I can send some home to you. There is no work here right now but now that I have started I have to stay and see it through.

If you do sign do not worry about our baby not having a name because a divorce would not come until March and even then it would not make any difference about the name unless you wanted it changed from Ballinger.

Don't forget no matter what you hear or what you receive. I will live up to my promise and do my duty to you and the children with everything that is in me. Although it is breaking both our hearts please try to be reasonable and we will get this ugly mess over with as little fuss and suffering as possible.

Please remember me to Judy and all the folks and tell Judy, Daddy misses his little curly head and tell her to write daddy a little letter. I expect Leslie is getting to be some boy, sure do miss you all.

Please write and tell me everything I will be waiting.
Best wishes,
Raymond
R.E.B. Box 119. Carson City Nevada

Carson City, Nevada
Thursday Evening Feb. 21, 1946

Dear Clara,

   Received your letter yesterday, was very glad to hear from you but I was also very disappointed and hurt that you had not let me know before February 5 that the baby was born. I was very proud and happy to hear about our daughter and I like the name you gave her very much, I guess it is about time you had a chance to pick one yourself.

   I am also very happy that you are feeling fairly good and I hope and pray that you continue to improve and are soon yourself again. I also hope the baby comes around alright. I think you did right by taking her home. At least you won't have that no good old man of yours always bothering you this time. Ha! Ha! I am not trying to be sarcastic or rub anything in.

   I received a very startling letter from my mother on February 18th. She told me about the baby and about your dad's visit and what he said. I had not told them about the baby as I thought it didn't concern anyone up there or around Marlton. I knew there was a lot of nasty talk going around Marlton about our separation and I didn't want to make it any worse. Mother was very upset and she thought because I had not told her that I was hiding something about us and the baby. So I wrote her a return letter immediately and told her everything in plain language and I think she understands now. I spoke very plain not blaming you or sparing myself. Naturally she feels bitter toward you for leaving me and the children, just as your folks feel bitter toward me for what has happened but I guess that is to be expected and neither you nor I can help that. It is only human nature.

   I know your Dad don't think much of me from the way he talked to mother. Mother said your father was there on a Monday evening and was very nice to them, said he only wanted to talk to them and to get them to give him my address, said he took no sides with either one of us but it is hard to believe that.

   I don't know why you had not written me so I could have sent you money for the bills. You know I told you to let me know as soon as you made arrangements and I would send you the money.

You should have told your Dad all this. I don't know what he thinks of me not knowing this. He told mother if you knew my address you wouldn't give it to him and that you wouldn't like it if you knew he went there.

He told them you were in the Cooper Hospital and were penniless except for five dollars your mother had given you. I don't know what they thought of me right then. Said he had paid the bills so they could take you home. He also said he supposed he would have you dumped in his lap and he felt he could not or should not have to bear these expenses. And he was perfectly right. This was certainly some mixed up mess and I sure do feel terrible about it all. He said you told them that I told you I wanted you to get out and what else could you do. Clara, if you did tell them this you know deep down in your heart that it is not true. You knew that I really wanted you to stay just as much as you wanted to stay but we were both too damn stubborn to admit it or give in.

Your father told them that he knew what and who was responsible and time would tell, said he would talk and have his say when the right time comes.

What did he mean by that? I certainly hope you did not tell him there was another woman, and you know who I mean. I thought I made you understand how I felt about that, that day we said goodbye before you left,

You said you understood but I guess you were just telling me that. The whole Shuster family was very good to me and the boys after you left and nobody blames you for what happened. They are really very fine people when you get to know them like I do. I wish you had given the Shusters more of a chance. But what is past is past and we can't do anything about it. I want to say again that I am glad you stuck to your own name for the baby, it is beautiful. What were you going to name a boy if it had been one? Where in the world did you ever get trench mouth, been kissing another man, Ha! Ha!

Don't be too hard on your Dad when you see him, he was only doing what he thought was right. I guess I would have done the same thing had I been in his place. I was certainly worried when I did not hear from you and I knew something must have happened.

This is some place out here, gambling is legalized in Nevada and all the towns are full of saloons and gambling halls, open all night. The streets are just a mass of lights at night. I haven't tried my luck yet, you know me, just no gambler I guess. In fact I haven't got anything to gamble with. About the divorce papers, I was certainly surprised when I heard the way they talk about a divorce out here. To them it is all in the day's work. I still can't get used to that it really shouldn't be that way but this is the West and it is still pretty wild. Plenty of cattle rustling still going on.

One fellow killed a man right here in Carson City the other night with a six gun and only got from one to five yrs. in state prison. It was a gun battle and he said he shot in self defense. We never hear of these things back home. The hills around here are full of wild horses, something else I could hardly believe. Some of my rancher friends are going hunting for them in about a month. They catch them and break them in for saddle horses.

Now about the papers, if you sign them I will only have to stay here one more week, but if you don't it will take another 30 days. I cannot make you sign them and I guess I have no right to ask you to sign so I will try to explain the situation and you can use your better judgment about signing. As I told you before I left, I had very little money left after paying all the bills and now after sending you yours and all, I have a lot less. In fact I have got to make a little more before I can come home. Work is awful scarce out here this time of year and I can barely make enough to meet my expenses. That is the reason Bud come home. I think I told you he was coming with me before I left.

I can get a job in another state but I can't take it until I finish here. If I have to stay here another 30 days it will take about every cent I have and I cannot earn enough to send you anything for expenses and you know that I want to do my share as best I can. I will sell the car if you want me to but then I wouldn't be able to go anywhere or even get home. But I do so want to help and do my part.

So if it is possible physically and if you feel that you could, please sign them. It would make things so much better for both of us. That is all I can say so you do what you think is best and I will abide by that.

As I have written you before this is such a beautiful country out here but there seems to be something missing I guess you know what I am trying to say. I miss you and the children so much especially since Bud went home and I am out here all by myself. I have too much time to think. The people out here are wonderful but it is still not home and I get so lonesome. After all, we've been together for eleven years.

I did not know that I was such a sissy until I got your letter. I thought the rain [tears] would never stop, Ha! I want you to know that you will always hold a place of honor in my heart. I have tried to think that you didn't, but I know it is entirely impossible. I can never forget the happy times we had and the tough times we went through together. I know now that I have been no prize package.

I want to put the blame for what has happened on my own shoulders where it belongs. I hope and pray that you can find enough room in your heart and forgive me just a little for all the trouble and heart ache I have brought you. I know now that I was not big enough to give you what you deserve. I wish there were more like you. I pray that your future will be bright, and that you will find the happiness you deserve with someone that will appreciate you.

I mean this more than I ever meant anything in my life. This trip and this country has made a man out of me, I hardly know myself sometimes. I weigh 183 lbs and am as hard as iron. But I think so much differently about so many things. I was very much hurt and disappointed when you said what you did about Jean. I thought you trusted and had a little more faith in me than that. I don't know what kind of a man you think I am. Although I guess I can't blame you for feeling that way, I guess I have given you reason to. I hear from Jean and the Shuster's quite often and I know that she is not home right now, and I expect it looks bad to some people but what they don't know won't hurt them. I expect Marshall Simmons started this as Mrs. Shuster says he is always asking questions. As you well know people are always ready to believe the worst. I wish I could be there to ram it back down their throats. I don't know why people have to be like this.

I would surely like to see Leslie. I bet he is sure some boy by now and I sure miss Sissy more than I thought I could.

This country is so big it has made my heart a lot bigger and I see things so much differently I hardly know myself. As I said before if you can possibly sign the papers and get them back here quickly you would save us both a lot of trouble. I can stand it but I do so want to help you and the kids.

But you do what you think best and let me know as soon as possible. Time is getting short if you are going to sign, please do!

Before I forget, please remember me to Edith and Alex and tell them some day and in some way I will make up to them for what they have done for you and me and the children. I must close now with love to you all.
Write soon.
Raymond

P.S. I hope you got my money order the other day. I did not know a thing when I sent it.

Miss Judith Ann Ballinger
Thursday Evening
2236 Merchantville Ave
Feb. 4, 1946
Merchantville, New Jersey

Dear Judy:

I received your letter along with Mommy's and I sure was glad to hear from my little girl. I want to tell you that I sure do miss you and I can't wait till I get home to see you, Leslie and that new baby sister. I am glad you like her and I know she must be awful sweet and I like her name.

I am glad you are getting along good in school. You are a smart little gal, Old Curly Head. Way out here a lot of the schools only have one room just like in the old days. I must close now so give Mommy, Leslie and Sandy all a big kiss for me and I am sending you a big one in this letter.

XXX

I have some presents for you when I come home.

Love,

Daddy

WHILE I WAS IN RENO Larry and Raymie stayed with Pop and Mom at the Homestead. Judy and Leslie were still with Clara, down to Edith's place in Merchantville. Everybody was helping me out. At that time they blamed Clara for walking out and leaving the children. I didn't pay much attention to it, but I was bitter. I had the sale in November and by January, I had left to go out West.

You had to establish residence for six weeks in Nevada to get a divorce. It took Bud and me ten days to get out there with the Chevy. We found a place in Carson City to stay. We thought we could get some work while we were there, but we just couldn't find anything. Of course, Bud didn't know how to do anything. Bud had never been away from his mother, so he got a bus ticket and went home on the Greyhound, and I stayed in Nevada.

I tried to get some work but I didn't have any experience with irrigation. I was thirty-one years old.

Jean and I got married March 4, 1946 in Virginia City. I bought her wedding ring in the Bucket of Blood Saloon. That's quite a place, the old Piper Opera House in Virginia City, right there at the silver mine. The magistrate was a woman who married us, and she got the sheriff to come in as a witness.

The first night we spent alone together was right there in Elko, Nevada, and then we drove through Idaho, Utah, and Colorado and came on home.

When we drove out in January through the southern route we stopped at the Grand Canyon. We came back by the northern route. We were home by the middle of May.

I was barely back when I had an appendicitis attack and went into the hospital. I think Clara still harbored the thought in her head that she would get me back. When we got the divorce, the lawyer said in order to make it binding, you'd have to hire a lawyer. If Clara didn't have one to represent her, it wouldn't be binding in some states. I had to hire another lawyer. The lawyer sent papers to her and she signed them and sent them back. Although she knew we were divorced, she still had hopes, I think, of us getting back together.

They operated on me for appendicitis. Clara came to see me after a couple of days. Jean was sitting there at the bedside talking to me. I guess it hit Clara all of a sudden, that she had lost me. Clara blew up. There was some bitter stuff that rolled out of her mouth right then, I tell you. I told her to have enough decency to be a lady, and not act like a fool in front of everybody in the hospital. Clara quieted down and turned around and left, and that's the last I saw of her.

Before we broke up, Clara came to visit the Shusters while we were still in Barrington. We went there as a family in the early afternoon to visit. Mrs. Shuster had taught Clara about canning. It was the Fourth of July and Mrs. Shuster gave the kids a bunch of noise toys, wooden spoons and pots and pans to bang on to celebrate the Fourth of July.

I tried. I wouldn't try to skin nobody, or beat anybody or do anything like that. What hurts is my own children don't want to believe me when I tell them the truth. How will they ever know if they won't listen and believe? Jean will tell you and so will I that we made some mistakes. We shouldn't have rushed. We should have waited longer after the divorce.

I had kids and nobody to take care of them. They needed a mother. I had sold my cattle and every source of income that I took pride in. It was my first start on my own and all I had left was four children to be taken care of.

Of course, I was lonely too. With a young girl that puts you up on a pedestal and bends over backwards to wait on you hand and foot and does everything for you, I couldn't help but love her. It felt right.

175

My Mom and my sister said it would never last. Jean was too young and she would get tired of this life and taking care of somebody else's kids. But it has lasted forty years, and we are still together. You can't help but give Jean credit for what she took over.

She was a girl that had never had any responsibilities and didn't know how to boil water. She took over four kids. You know she must have thought a hell of a lot of me. The kids weren't easy on her either. I was worse yet! I was hard on Jean because I was bitter, and I took it out on the kids, the farm, and on everything around me for three or four years, before I started softening and trusting. I loved my kids and I loved her. But that bitterness would build up till it exploded.

Jean and I came back from out West after we'd gotten married. We didn't stay at the Homestead, but in Haddon Heights with her parents. I was going back and forth to the Homestead. The boys were finishing school in Marlton.

I knew that Raymie and Larry were having some difficulty, but I was so damn bitter and confused trying to straighten out my own life, that I wasn't able to deal with their problems. That's why I wanted them staying with Mom and Pop at the Homestead.

Virginia Ballinger (Ginny)

————

WHEN RAYMOND AND JEAN RETURNED FROM RENO, my brother had an appendicitis attack and went into the hospital. Clara came to visit him. I think she was there to get him back. She seemed shocked to hear he was married to Jean, and there was a big fight. He claimed he had told her but she didn't listen. He said again that when she had walked out he had told her that was final.

Clara asked him about Sandy, the baby she had had while he was gone, and he asked how he would know Sandy was his. Clara said he had everything and she had nothing. Raymond responded that she had Judy, Leslie, and Sandy.

That was when she told Raymond that she wanted to give Sandy away to her brother-in-law's brother, Will Wilkins, to raise. Raymond had worked with Will at the shipyard and liked him. She also said that Judy was missing the boys terribly and that she couldn't afford to keep them. Raymond said he would continue to give her money, but she wanted to give Judy and Leslie back. Jean wanted to keep Sandy as well. Raymond felt that she would be better with Will and his wife.

Two days after Clara's confrontation with Dad and Jean in the hospital Pop went and got Judy and Leslie.

During that time Raymond had been going through the newspapers and spotted an ad for a dairy farm manager in Lyndell Pennsylvania. He told Jean that after he helped Pop plow the lower west field he wanted to go out there and work so they could get a fresh start in their own home.

Raymond and Jean were still living with the Shusters at Haddon Heights. Ruth and Don were living in the other side of the Homestead. Raymond was helping Pop out at the Homestead. I had just turned sixteen and I was playing house on the porch. I looked up and here comes my brother walking in. He was black from the waist up but he had white hands. It was him but I barely recognized him.

Raymond had gotten dizzy while he was pushing a wheelbarrow load of manure off the board at the Homestead and fell off the ramp, face down in the manure. He walked to the outside spigot to get washed up and I got scared. Something was wrong with him. He was a hollering and hollering. Everybody came out to see what the matter was with him was. He got gotten dizzy because he was working too soon after the operation. His blood pressure was low and now he was all covered in manure.

Shortly thereafter Raymond and a pregnant Jean left for Pennsylvania with three of the children, Larry, Judy, and Raymie. Leslie stayed behind with Jean's mother.

Dad, Raymond Ballinger

I FOUND OUT ABOUT DOC BRUNO who was out in Pennsylvania. He wanted a farm manager. Having worked and lived all his life in Philadelphia, Pappy Shuster knew all of that countryside. When Jean and I went out to talk to Doc Bruno, Pappy went with us. Doc asked us to come back after he had talked to a few other people.

Jean and I went back a second time and we met him at his office. He had a big dentist's office on Walnut Street in Philadelphia. He didn't live out on the farm. He would come out on weekends. They had fixed up the main house.

At first we lived at Lyndell, Pennsylvania in a big stone house on another farm that Doc owned. Then his wife stepped in. She was the boss. She wore the britches. Doc was mild and easy and he made a lot of promises but when it came time to fill 'em, she wouldn't do it.

When I got to talking to the other people that had worked there, I found out some of the things that she had done. I was scared to death. She was just out to beat everybody. She had been a legal secretary for some big law firm in Philadelphia, and she was just like a lawyer. She was sharp and had a mind like a rat trap. She knew all the ways to make contracts and the minute you made a misstep she'd clamp right down on you.

I had been there about two and a half months. I had done the plowing, planted the corn, and got up some hay and of course milked cows.

She come out one Sunday afternoon and brought this contract for me to sign and I sat right down there and read it myself. She said she wanted to see how I was going to do, before she brought the contract.

She just had everything in it for herself. If I had made one error, I couldn't collect a thing. I wouldn't be able to move my cows or the household goods that were mine. She'd have me tied up for months in litigation. I said I wouldn't sign it, and she told me I had to and I said I don't think I will.

Then it just went from bad to worse. Dr. Bruno never showed his face. She did it all. She went back and got some more papers drawn up. She was a close friend with a secretary to the head of Supplee Wills and Jones, which is Sealtest in Philadelphia. Mrs. Bruno went to her and had them withhold all my milk checks. I couldn't even get any milk checks!

Part of the cows were mine. I'd borrowed some money to buy cows from Herb Tallmann up there in Middletown where the nuclear power plant is now. The Brunos were going to furnish half the cows and I was going to furnish half.

I had used my own money for gas to work the land and plant the corn seed. I was supposed to get reimbursed. I went there in the early spring and I was there till the middle of August. There was an old man who was milking for them, a retired farmer, but he didn't want to do it anymore. He was just helping them out. That old man told me about George Kraph who had one of the top Holstein herds there in Lancaster County, Pennsylvania, and that's saying something.

Kraph had fifteen school buses he was working on and he didn't have any time left to put into his farm. He had an apartment in one part of the house that he had been renting out. Kraph had about five hundred laying hens, Rhode Island Reds. He sold hatching eggs. He had thirty purebred Holstein cows and he grew all the feed for them, plus seven or eight acres of tobacco. Some Amish people come in and they took care of the tobacco.

I started to work for Kraph and drove back and forth to Lyndell. Bruno's wife sent me a notice that I had to be out by the end of August. Lancaster was only eight or ten miles from Lyndell.

I was to get every third heifer that I raised out of his herd to keep for my own. At that rate, I would soon have a herd of cows built up. If I went back to work with Pop, I'd have some good cows.

In the meantime Pop came to see me, and we talked it over and decided the best thing for me to do was to try to rent a house where I could still work for Kraph and move out from Bruno's.

Instead we ended up moving back to Haddon Heights and working for Pop. Pop had had a stroke and came up to Lyndell to get me. He was in bad shape. He begged me. He realized that he couldn't work the farm by himself. After his being so adamant about not needing me when I came back from out West, he needed me now.

Jean said we could move in with Pappy at Haddon Heights. I told her I didn't want to do that, especially with the kids. I wished I never had. That was the first hard feelings there ever was. Mrs. Shuster got edgy with all of us. There were just too many people and too many young kids that weren't even her relations. Once she slapped Larry in the face. Oh man! He got mad. I don't know if he cussed her or not, but it was nasty language. I didn't want it, but I didn't know what else to do. I traveled back and forth to the Homestead to work.

Ruth didn't want to move out of the other side of the Homestead. Pop didn't want to say anything to Ruth, because she was his daughter.

We stayed in Haddon Heights for the entire school year. It was a nine long months. I couldn't get into my own house where I worked because my sister was living there.

We lived at the Homestead on the small side for two years before I bought it. We lived there a total of three and a half years. That's all I ever wanted to do. My taking over the tradition of the old family farm meant a lot more to me than it did to anyone else in the family.

I never had any trouble with my sister, Ruth. Mom didn't approve of Jean and Ginny sided with Mom. Pop liked Jean, and Jean adored him. Mom said she was trying to get around him, because Jean helped Pop hunt eggs because his health was bad.

Jean loved doing anything that was new to her.

Mom had a vicious mind when she wanted to, I tell you.

181

When Jean and I were first married, Jean was careless. She'd leave her bobby pins lying around or a little ring on the tub. She never had had to do anything before. Of course I've seen my sisters do the same thing. Jean used to wash her hair every day of her life and take a shower or a bath every night. We weren't used to that. We'd bathe once a week. If a little hair was left on the wash basin Mom would come running to me, "Jean has the drain plugged up!"

About that time Judy was acting up. Mom starting yelling at me and Mom grabbed my arm. I gave it a yank and she fell down. Ginny tried to say that I knocked Mom down. It was not the truth at all. I am not that kind of a man! I helped her get up, but she was just so damn mad. I finally threw a bucket of water at her to cool her off. Ginny hit me with a clothes bag.

Years later, when we were living down there in Virginia, Mom became very fond of Jean. She told me, "I never thought I ever could feel like I feel now. She's certainly a wonderful girl."

I HAD LOST THE FIRST ELEVEN YEARS of my adult life from the time I married Clara until I got divorced. Those years cut deeper than anybody will ever know. I put a hell of a lot of money, work and dreams into that farm at Barrington. I kept everything inside of me and it just kept building up till I couldn't take it anymore. It was so difficult with Clara running off all the time. If it weren't for my kids, it would have been a complete loss.

Those were physically the best and the strongest years of my life which could have added up to something. If only I had married someone who co-operated with me. Re-gaining those eleven years became an obsession. I had to prove myself all over again, and make people realize that maybe I wasn't such a bad guy after all. I felt that all I truly needed was a partner who would co-operate with me.

In those days most men were pretty naive about women, and I was no exception. My first girl friend had died of tuberculosis and I didn't know where to turn. When I met Clara, she was street smart and knew how to handle a man. I was the complete opposite. I had never been off of the farm and was easy to manipulate. Clara was not a bad woman. We just were not meant to be together.

Clara continually dreamed of a kind of life that I never wanted to be part of. I had to get up at five o'clock in the morning, for Christ sakes, with cows to milk, fences to put up, seeds to plant and hay to harvest. I didn't have time for anything else. Clara never seemed to give up on trying to change me. But, things were quickly changing. With four kids, I had to have a certain amount of income. Everything was more expensive, food, clothing, and taxes.

When I came back from out West, married to Jean, I didn't have any money. That's why I took a job in Pennsylvania, managing that Bruno farm.

When Pop asked me to take over the Homestead, I still had no money, just barely enough to buy the ten cows that I put in with Pop's.

I was only out West for six weeks. While I was gone the boys stayed with Mom and Pop in Marlton. Judy and Leslie were over with Clara. By the time that Judy came back to us, Jean and I were married and we were all together.

After we married, we bought two palomino riding mares, Sundown and Sunny. One was a little smarter than the other. Pappy had converted a three car garage into box stalls. We had kept Chief there. When we were in Reno Pappy took care of him and a black Tennessee Walker for a neighbor.

Jean had lived in Merchantville most all of her life. They had lost their home in the Depression and went to live with her Aunt Beulah. Pappy had had a garage he couldn't manage. His partner ran off with all the money and he didn't even know it. Aunt Beulah's husband, Mr. Fry, got him into teaching school. He loaned Pappy some money and he went to school at nights. That's when he got on his feet.

I had met a man in Denver. The man milked thousands of cows and each man had a hundred cows to look after. He wanted me to manage a hundred cows for him. He furnished a home and salary and a share of the profits beside the wages, but I was homesick for my kids. Things were upside down. Afterwards I thought many times it might have been the best thing just to have been away from the whole business.

Raymie and Judy went to school in Haddon Heights and Larry went to school in Marlton. Larry'd come up with me when I came to milk. He'd feed the calves and get his breakfast there with Mom, and then go to school. I'd bring him back at night. We did that for several months till Ruth finally moved out. Larry always wanted to be up there on the farm.

After I bought the Homestead, Pop supplied the rest of the money to put up the new silo and plant the alfalfa. We tore out the old horse stalls and used the space for stanchions to make the dairy larger. I laid concrete and built an extension on the other end of the barn close to where the new silo stood. I did most of that myself. Pop helped a little, but his health was pretty bad and getting worse.

I bought everything just as it was, the horses, cows, and machinery, all of it. I believe at the time Pop had about eighteen to twenty milk cows that tested three percent butterfat! If he shipped a couple of cans of milk a day he thought he was doing alright. I had to have income. I didn't like tomatoes and sweet corn, and cantaloupes and watermelon and cabbage. No way! I'd had enough of that in my lifetime.

Pop had bought the farm from Grandmom and her brothers and sisters. As long as Sally B. was living she got half of what he made on the farm and she owned the furnished home and whatever was grown in the garden. In 1928 he had paid her $12,000 for it. There were 102 acres left and of those only 50 acres was tillable. The rest was meadowland. I paid $12,000 for the Homestead nineteen years later, in 1948.

Before I could buy the place I needed a certain amount of income. We went to the Medford Bank and they gave me a mortgage for $8,000. That was a lot of money then. Pop then took a second mortgage for $3,000 so he would have money to live on.

For the first year I paid both mortgages. It wasn't easy but I wanted to get it paid off.

We didn't have any furniture. Jean had a friend in Merchantville who worked in real estate with Prudential Life Insurance. Jean got in touch with him. Three days later two assessors came out and took a look at the Homestead. Within a week we had a new $11,000 mortgage which paid off both mortgages. Pop had his money and I had a fresh start.

Unfortunately, that was not the main difficulty. We were living with Jean's family and I was going back and forth from Haddon Heights.

When Pop asked me to come back he promised to talk to Ruth about moving. Ruth and Bob didn't want to move out. They said they couldn't find a place.

The last thing I wanted was to live with the Shusters again, but there was nothing else I could do. In the beginning it was Jean and I and the two boys, but then Clara sent back Leslie and Judy and their house had gotten pretty crowded. I couldn't say "No" to Pop, the man was in severe pain and dying.

Things went pretty good that year except for the traveling. It was hard on Larry, his staying in school in Marlton and getting up at five o'clock in the morning. Raymie and Judy went to school in Haddon Heights.

My hands were tied and there was nothing I could do. Pop couldn't buy a house and move out till I came up with some money from the new mortgage. Finally I told Pop that I couldn't go on traveling back and forth twelve miles every morning and night. My sister Ruth and her husband Bob were not offering to do one earthly thing. I had to talk to her. 'Course that made her firing mad, not to mention Bob.

Ruth and Bob finally bought a house in Cherry Hill. When Ruth moved out we moved in.

Ginny had cancer on her lip, probably from smoking. She was going with a guy, Frank Davenport, who was much older than she was. He was nothing but a truck driver, and he got to seeing her. Ginny was too young then, about sixteen. Pop didn't like it at all. Ginny was seeing him on the side and I guess Frank got her in a bad way. Frank stopped coming around. That's when she met and married Bobby Moore. Bobby knew it wasn't his child but he married her, and they had three more children.

When Bobby got out of the service he couldn't find any work. Ginny asked if we needed somebody to help out, and I hired Bobby and rented another farm and we milked in both places.

After World War II no one could make a living farming 100 acres. I had Pop's cows and horses, but he didn't have much equipment. I built an extension, a silo, a laying house for Jean's leghorns, and a lot more. We were running back and forth with all the equipment milking at two farms. I had also rented some more land from Mr. Bowker alongside of the Homestead. I was running all over killing myself to make up for lost time. After moving to town, Pop still used to come out every Sunday morning of his life. He'd walk around in that flat top straw hat and talk to me about the cows and the farm.

Pappy couldn't do anything with Bud, Jean's brother, and he asked me if I needed some help. He wanted to send Bud to me. Bud came up here and I paid him $60 a month and fed him. He helped out for a while.

I'm used to jumping in and getting something done. You had to lead Bud around by the hand. He couldn't drive a team of horses through the gate without getting hung up on one side or the other. You couldn't tell him anything. He got up on a loose truck load of hay with no rope. As we came into the lane he fell off. He cracked a vertebra. He was in a cast for a while. It was easier not to have anybody, than to have somebody like that.

Every time Bud ran that wheelbarrow full of manure up on to the chute, he would forget to gather momentum and he'd end half way up and have to come back down, or dump it over the side instead of into the spreader. He was so angry that he couldn't get it up that he backed down to the barn to get a new running start. He'd push it clear up the chute right over into the spreader, wheelbarrow and all. Larry and Raymie would be there watching him. There would be Bud standing in the middle of the spreader in four feet of cow manure yelling 'Help!' and two boys laughing their heads off.

We had an old black cow with curly horns who loved to kick. Bud was wiping her down, and testing for mastitis. He stepped in without saying anything to her, and she let him have it. She kicked him right down into the gutter. He came crawling out of that manure crying,

"Where's my hat? I've lost my hat! "

I told him to get back in there to test her before we put the milker on her. He yelled for about five minutes that he was going to tell his mother. That's why I took both of my boys to live with me. I just think they needed a man around.

Bud then took a job at the Everson Leatherworks or Woolworks in Camden driving a delivery truck. He was going over to Philadelphia and his mother, Mrs. Shuster, like to have had a fit.

That was the whole trouble with the boy. She never gave him a chance. She tied him to her apron strings his whole life.

I didn't have any guilt about selling the Marlton Homestead. I just saw I wasn't gonna be able to make it there. I couldn't keep my bills paid and raise my family. The taxes were almost $1,000 on 102 acres. The old Ballinger farm close by was almost $8,000 in taxes. They had rezoned it for residential or commercial property to get away from agriculture.

THE LAST DEER I KILLED was in 1950 before we moved to Delaware. I had to get up at two o'clock in the morning, milk the cows, and clean out the stables and spread the manure. I needed a lantern to see where I was going and to keep the manure from freezing in the spreader. It was right in the middle of December when deer season come in. I'd have to feed the chickens and the hogs, and tend to the horses. We still had the teams of horses. Then I had to get my breakfast, change my clothes, and be over there to the clubhouse ready to go at daylight. That takes it out of you.

When Jean and I were first married I had complete charge of the hunt. I had to organize everything. There were two captains under me. I was thirty-four years old.

Dan Horan, our hired help, drank hair tonic that he got at Kruger's Store. He promised me that he wouldn't get drunk and that he would look after things while I was deer hunting. Then he went and got drunk over there to Kruger's. Jean found out and she called up Mrs. Foster who came down to the club and told me that my wife wanted to see me. The man had got so drunk that she was afraid he would burn the place down. I had to go home. Damn!

We had several guys in the club that were slackers. They wanted to take a stand everywhere and not drive. That's where you got most of your shots, on the stands. The drivers would drive the deer to them. They didn't want to get into the briars and bushes. Some of those drives could be over three or four hundred acres.

In order to calculate which way the deer would run, you had to figure out the drive from where the road was and according to the way the wind blew. It changed from day to day. If a deer is used to going a certain direction, that's where he's going. They'll run into the wind all the time. A fox will run with the wind, so the scent won't blow back to the hounds.

A lot of men in the club who knew them woods as well as I did could get turned around, and they wouldn't know which way to turn to get back to the truck. I was always different. We killed more deer the first year I took that club over than we had ever killed in the history of the club. One of the men hadn't hunted before and he killed my fox I had running. I had asked him not to. The fox came out and he let on he couldn't help it. He offered to go down to Maryland and buy some young foxes and to pay for them and put them out. He just couldn't keep from pulling that trigger.

We had two captains and a red and a white side. They were young men. We had three or four older men and we never had 'em drive. We were incorporated. Most of the time, I would wind up the furthest away from the truck, because I would put men off at flank to keep the deer from slipping around. The deer would come ahead of the driver and wheel around and come back and slip out the side. As long as we got some deer, I didn't mind.

This last year that I hunted was a warm Saturday morning for December. I was dragging. I'd been going with only a couple hours of sleep. We had kept the cows in the stanchions. I still had to get the milk ready and be gone by daylight. We'd gun until dark. Then I'd have to come back and do the whole thing all over again. I'd fall asleep at the supper table.

I was just tired and worn out. I happened to look over in the woods and there was a pond that had flowed over an old swamp gum. It was about twenty feet off the ground. I got up into the tree and I could see deer out of the tree better than I could on the ground. I unloaded my gun and tied my rope around the trigger guard and sat down there with it across my knees. I was just disgusted. I could hear the drivers about a mile away. The sun was rolling down on me and I just went right dead for sleep.

I woke up and looked down in the woods. Close to me was a deer. I could see his head. I sat there and we eyeballed one another for what seemed five minutes. He wasn't moving, and I wasn't moving. I thought if I move my gun barrel around real slow he wouldn't see it. He turned and away he went! It was a wide rack buck. He started right away from me, and I shot right in the tail and down he went. I guess I killed him, but I never shot one like that in the rump before. I unloaded my gun and I started down the tree. When I got about eight feet off the ground I jumped.

I heard him. I heard him, trying to get away. He had gotten back up when he heard my noise. I loaded my gun and I ran after him. Of course I couldn't see anything but I could hear him going. I shot again, but I shot clear over him and too quickly. He was getting through the woods faster than I could run.

After a bit, we got into a little open place there. By that time, the drivers were getting pretty close, and he was going right back in to them. I knew if he went much further, I couldn't shoot him, or I might shoot somebody. So I just up and shot him right up in back of the neck. Of course, he just dropped. I had to carry him all the way out of there clear around across the cranberry bogs about a mile and a half.

That's the last deer I killed, and that's the last year I hunted.

I went fox hunting around Milford Neck in Delaware and asked if anyone knew of a big farm for sale. I was complaining about the taxes and running all over milking cows at two barns. I heard about a nine hundred fifty acre farm for sale with four houses, four barns, and 700 tillable acres for $35,000. There were also 250 acres of timber.

The woman who owned it had been married to a doctor who had died and her only son was a dentist up in Connecticut. They had raised twenty-five or thirty work horses that were more or less wild. Everything was in good shape and they had vineyards in the front of the house.

The man running the place was stealing their share, and the woman found out. I spoke to her and made an offer. I was late getting back to the Homestead and Jean had already gone to bed. I crawled in and woke her up. "I want you to start packing tomorrow" I said. She thought I was crazy. I told her about the farm and that the taxes were only $100 on 950 acres. We were paying $900 on 100 acres. We were both excited.

It took me two days to get up the courage to drive to Marlton to talk to pop. As usual, Pop was alright with it. He blowed up a little bit. Mom was still bitter about my marriage. It was his family farm. He understood how impossible it was to support my family and to make a living anymore at the Homestead.

I went down to Camden, talked to the real estate man about selling the Homestead. In a week he brought the Jaggards out and they bought the Homestead for $35,000. I immediately went right down to Milford Neck and bought that farm. I'd given Pop $12,000 for the Homestead and had sold it for $35,000.

I sold part of Milford for $12,000 to Ralph Franklin and I also got $7,500 for timber. I still had the three houses and three barns. I put up a couple of silos, and more stanchions and built a milk house.

What I hadn't counted on was that the flies and the mosquitoes got so bad for Jean, the kids and the cows. It was pitiful. The cows wouldn't even go out to pasture and the children were full of bites getting all festered up.

I finally had the farm bureau come in there every week and spray and a day or two later they were all gone.

Jean didn't make friends easily. She was kind of shy, like I was. I had originally hoped that some friends of ours would move there with us. Jean's best friend was Sadie Franklin. They had bought some of our property but decided against moving there, and instead hired a man to farm it. George Bluff was his name. Bluff was just as ornery as cat shit and ran a pitchfork through one of the heifers that Franklin had bought off me and killed her. I had given Ralph Franklin a good deal on the land. Franklin turned around and sold the land for a big profit. That didn't set too well with me. Ralph would sell his brother or his father out for a buck. I knew that, but I didn't think he'd do it to Jean and me. Sadie and Jean are still friends.

Part VI

Jean Shuster

JEAN SHUSTER WITH LESLIE BALLINGER, 1946

Jean Shuster

MY FIRST JOB WAS WORKING AT HADDON PRESS. It was on Westfield Avenue in Haddon Heights and I was a copy holder. I literally held the copy and read it to a proof reader. If there were mistakes she had to change it and make the corrections. You had to read the commas, the question marks, and the quotation marks.

I was always a good reader. One of Zane Grey's books came out and was being edited. I don't know whether it was a first print, or being re-printed. It was called *Majesty's Ranchos*, and it was a sequel to *Light of Western Stars*, one of his best books and one of my all-time favorites. Zane Grey would spell here "hyeh" and you would have to spell it out so she got it right.

My friend Janet had taken a secretarial course and was a typist at Penn Mutual Life Insurance in Philadelphia. She got me a job as a clerk in the filing department and my pay was $16 a week. I worked at Mutual Life until I decided to go to the New York Shipyard in Camden.

I had things that I wanted to forget. I had the mistaken idea that I could do that by putting myself out on the docks or on the ships and I could work, work, and work. Times were changing for me to be able to do that. I had no duties at home.

My mother did my ironing and washed my clothes. She packed my lunch when I went to work. I did not want to be in the house. I wanted to be out in the world, making a living.

Daddy had a brother, Harry, who later died from Hodgkin's disease. He was working in the office at the shipyard, taking identification pictures of all the workers. Harry had sense enough to see that I most definitely did not belong out working on the ships and he started me in the supply room where the material chasers came for whatever the men on the boats needed. Eventually I went from there to the payroll office.

My mother was very upset. She did not talk to me for two weeks after I started working there. I was making $40 a week. That was a lot of money then. If I worked Saturday, I got time and a half with double time for Sunday.

While Pappy was teaching an automobile mechanics class at the trade school, we bought the house in Haddon Heights. Though we lived in town I was, in my heart, a country girl.

Before I got my horse, Sheba, I had had a pony and a cart. Daddy had sold his boat to get me that pony. I wanted a horse so bad. I started saving $20 a week when I was working, and that's when I bought Sheba.

When I got Sheba I didn't have sense enough to be scared of her! I didn't have any sense, period, at that time. I learned the hard way. She was part thoroughbred, and she was not happy. If you were with a group, she had to be out in front. One day I was riding her down a short lane. As she turned to go on the highway, her feet slid out from underneath of her, and down I came. I landed on my back, and it hurt! What I should have done was get right back up on her, but nobody made me do that, and as time went on I became afraid of her. Eventually I did get back on her and ride.

I became involved with this one "cowboy." There was a place up at Maple Shade called the Totem Ranch which was a bar and a night club. I was under-age, but I was going there with Janet. The man that I was dating was very undesirable. Mother and Daddy found out. Daddy didn't have a car at that time, but he got somebody to take him up there. He told the "cowboy" in no uncertain terms that I was underage and he needed to stop seeing me.

My love for horses probably had a great deal to do with my initial relationship with Raymond. I met him for the first time at his farm in Barrington when I went there with my father looking for hay.

Raymond was a big good-looking man. He was really overpowering. Pappy and I continued to go back there and buy hay. I was always Daddy's girl and I went where Daddy went. Raymond had these huge horses which was very exciting to me. Those Percherons were such beautiful animals and of course Larry loved showing them off to me. I don't know whether he could reach them at that time from the ground to put the bridle on, but he sure did try. He was only ten years old. Of course this was all very romantic to me. At that time I was working for the New York Shipyard. I had never seen Raymond at the shipyard. Daddy had known him, and he became very friendly with him.

Pappy was never happier than when he was fooling with an engine. That's why he got along with Raymond so well. He was always outdoors, and that's where Daddy wanted to be. Once I got Sheba I considered it to be the end of all. Then Raymond bought Chief. He was gorgeous. I couldn't believe Raymond on that horse. Of course, I feel in love, with Raymond and the horse. Daddy loved that horse as well.

I never wanted to be in the house and never did do housework once I went to work. I just did me. When I got the horse, I was outside even more. That's what Raymond and I had in common. I loved to be in the fields, and I would help with the hay. In Jersey I drove the horses to the hay-rake and I drove them to the hay wagon when they were loading it. When we got married, we were going to raise horses.

We didn't raise horses, we raised children.

One day Raymond and his friend Marshall came by and asked me if I wanted to go with them to get ice. I asked Mother if I could go, and so I went. The next time that Raymond went after ice, it was just him and me. That was just the beginning and it went on from there. Eventually we started holding hands. The attraction was strong, believe me, on both sides. Without a doubt.

Clara was still living with Raymond at the farm in Barrington. I just fell in love with him. He was very romantic. In the beginning I felt that I was more in love with him than he with me. I never expected anything to come of it.

We would go riding as often as we could, on Sheba and Chief. Raymond wasn't the type of man to fool around. If he had been satisfied at home, he wouldn't have looked twice at me. He really wouldn't. This is the only excuse that I have. It was some months after that when he told me that he was going to get a divorce and we were going to get married. I didn't really believe him at the time, but, I didn't really know him, either. As far as he was concerned there were no ifs ands or buts. That's what was going to take place.

I thought I knew him inside out, upside down, and every which way. Clara told me in no uncertain terms that I did not know Raymond Ballinger. Of course I looked at her, and I said, "You've got to be kidding. I certainly do know him. I know him better than anybody in this entire world." But of course I didn't.

The Ballingers standing in the community was defined and strong. They'd been there forever and were very well respected. But the war had brought so many changes, and that white picket fence couldn't isolate the Ballingers anymore. Men came and dated Ginny and Lois. Ruth got married. Alice was prejudiced and did not like change.

After I fell in love with Raymond, things really did change. I felt that somehow everything would work out. The only idea I had then was that I loved children and I loved to babysit. I believed that all you had to do with children was to love them and keep them clean and neat and put a roof over their head and food in their mouth. If you loved them, they automatically loved you back.

Raymond had children, and I loved them. Judy was such a pretty girl. Her hair was so beautiful, curly and red. I just looked forward to being with her. I didn't think beyond a day. Alice tried to tell me. She said that I did not know what I was letting myself in for. I didn't! I had no idea! But I was sure things would work out with Raymond.

Raymond didn't quite know how to go about getting a divorce. Daddy knew a judge who had offices in Camden and we went to see him and he told us what our options were. That was when Raymond decided to go to Reno. I quit my job and I went out West with him. That was not the thing to do at the time. No one really knew. Instead they made up stories that were far worse. Bud wanted to come, and we decided to take him. Raymond also thought it would look better. Bud returned sometime earlier than we did. It took us a week to get there and a week to come back, and we were there for six weeks. It was the cheapest and easiest way to get a divorce.

It was a great trip! I was very excited about it. I was in love and there was never any question of doing anything differently, as far as I was concerned. If Raymond could have found work we would have stayed longer. Our dream was to have a ranch out West and raise horses. I was homesick. I couldn't wait to get back home, but now I think maybe it would have been better if we had stayed.

After the auction of Raymond's farm in Barrington, Larry and Raymie came to stay with my parents for a few weeks. Then they went to the Homestead and Judy and Leslie remained with Clara.

After we had returned from out West, we had a very positive outlook on life. We lived with Mother and Daddy, a very big mistake. Raymond worked at the Homestead and he came back to my parent's home in Haddon Heights every night that he could. Ramie and Larry also stayed at my parents. Then Judy and Leslie came there to live with us.

I don't know if Clara knew that Raymond and I were developing a relationship at the time or if there was anybody else in her life or not. There certainly were rumors. I don't think she did know because it came as such a shock to her when she found out we were married. Raymond and I returned from out West around the middle of March. One month later Raymond ended up in the hospital with appendicitis. Clara came to visit him in the hospital, and that's when she learned that we were married. I believe that Clara had expected to win him back and when she realized that wasn't going to happen, she insisted that Raymond had to come and get Judy and Leslie or she would put them in a home. She was bitter and was using them as a vehicle to get back at him.

Judy believed what she heard. A nine year old girl doesn't know! Raymond and I decided we couldn't allow that to happen, regardless of whether she meant it or not. He gave Clara money. When Judy and Leslie arrived, Judy was sick to her stomach.

Raymond had gone to get Leslie. Granddad might have gone with him. My parents were in shock. What they said doesn't bear repeating. What would any parent think of their twenty-three year old daughter who was married to a man with four children, the oldest one being ten? But still, they took us all in.

Leslie didn't know Raymond when he came back to us. That upset Raymond so much that he cried.

When Raymond and I and the children were living in Haddon Heights with my parents, Clara came to the house right around the end of December, just before we went out West. I was sitting there looking very domestic with some mending in my lap. Clara was by herself and the conversation was very formal.

Alice said that I was crazy for taking on all the children. When I said that I would take the baby, Sandy, she threw up her hands in holy terror. Raymond said absolutely positively "No" and Pop and Mom were not slow in telling me what they thought. Mother and Daddy never said anything to me formally, but I certainly can understand what their thoughts must have been. I would have most certainly taken in Sandy, Clara's last child.

I would go to the Homestead with Raymond every chance that I had. Larry did too. My mother was left with Judy, Raymie and Leslie. They walked home for lunch from school. Judy did get into my mother's jewelry at one point in time, but she didn't take anything. Mother had told her that she was welcome to look at anything in the house and handle it, as long as she asked first. Judy went in the box and rearranged it.

Shortly afterwards, we moved to a dairy farm in Lyndell, Pennsylvania. Pennsylvania was so different. I didn't have anything there. Raymond was gone working all day and it was just me and the three children. We had left Leslie with my mother in Haddonfield. Then Pop Ballinger came down and asked Raymond to come back to manage the farm at the Homestead.

When we came back to Marlton from Lyndell, we lived with my parents for nine months. I found out that I was pregnant when we were up in Lyndell. I didn't have the faintest idea. I was so excited!! That's what I wanted. We had married in March of 1946 and Marjorie was born in late November. Alice didn't miss that timing one little bit. I didn't have sense enough not to say anything but then I didn't even add it up. I didn't think of life as responsibilities. The days were too full, and I didn't have time to think or the inclination to do so.

At that time my parents didn't have a lot of money, and neither did Raymond's parents. Raymond gave me $15 a week to pay for food for us all, two adults and four children. In addition to caring for the children, I was doing all the housekeeping, laundry and everything. I didn't know why he only gave me $15, whether that was all he had or all he gave.

I remember Mother telling me once that she was in a store and she had found a wallet. There was no one around, and she didn't know where to take it. There was $60 in the wallet. She ended up using it all to buy food. It was very difficult financially for my parents. They never said anything about our dependence on them, but there was an undercurrent.

Marjorie was born while we were living in Haddon Heights. I didn't know what was going to happen. I went to Cooper Hospital expecting to see the doctor when I got there. The nurses put me into the labor room, and then after a while the water broke and the pains began. I never saw the doctor until I was in the delivery room. I had been having back pains most of the afternoon and I went to the hospital around seven and she was born two minutes past midnight.

Sandy, Clara's daughter had been born in that same hospital ten months before.

Bud, my brother, had one job in Camden where he learned how to drive. He was more of his Mother's boy, and I was Daddy's girl. Bud never knew how to relate to people, even less than I did at that time. He had one other job and he up and quit and he never worked again. Our parents never forced him to do anything.

Later they bought a farm in Marlton with the idea that that would give him a living. It was the worst thing they could ever have done. They just kept him sheltered and protected. Bud wasn't very bright, but neither was he dumb. There was never any incentive for him to grow up. In fact, they encouraged him to stay a little boy. Bud was very slow as a child. He didn't talk until he was around four or five. I was the only one that could understand him. He was very backwards. He never could do anything with his hands. Daddy had no patience with Bud. So how Daddy had the patience he needed when he became a teacher, I will never know.

Raymond forced the boys into doing things they had to do and doing them right, and consequently they were done right. He took the time and he made them do it. Daddy was just the opposite. Daddy was the one that did the farm work and fixed all the equipment himself. Bud ran the errands and took Mom where she had to go.

I can understand why my husband had a low opinion of my brother, Bud. When we were first married, Raymond worked so hard that he would fall asleep at night in a chair and you couldn't wake him up. You can imagine what it's like when you're first married. I wanted him to come to bed and I knew he couldn't get his proper rest in the chair. I kept on and on and on and he ended up getting ugly, he really did. This was my fault probably, because I should just have gone to bed and left him, I really should have.

Raymond was in the bathroom shaving and cleaning up after farm work and putting on fresh clothing. I think it was Memorial Day. I always hated to be late. We were invited for dinner up to the Homestead. Raymond moved at his own pace and in his own time, and when he felt like getting ready, he got ready. He was in the bathroom, shaving, and I kept telling him, "We've got to go, we've got to go, we're going to be late.'

Finally, he shoved me back against the wall, moved out of the bathroom, and slammed the door.

That Memorial Day was the same one that we found out his cousin Everett had been killed in a motorcycle accident. Grandmother answered the phone, a big black heavy telephone with the cloth covered wire. She turned pale all over and ran to get Pop in the field. By that evening the whole family was at the Homestead.

When we were finally living at the Homestead, I saw that Alice did things in a special sophisticated way and I wanted to be just like her. She was the one responsible for all the food and I realized very quickly how well she did things.

Raymond's sisters, Ginny and Lois, would arrange tomato slices on a plate with some green peppers or parsley and I'd never seen that done. It was the little things that were so refined. Her canned peaches were like no other peaches you'd ever want to eat. They were just perfect, absolutely perfect, and they looked like fresh ones. The whole farm area was ... it was romance. Raymond was romance. I wanted to be just exactly what Mother Alice was. I was in love with

Raymond. I had him on a pedestal. I knew that he loved me. I did everything to please him, even with all our children and our moves. I did everything that I could. I don't know what Raymond saw in me at the beginning.

There were so many good times. I can remember when we slept out on the lawn and the rides that we used to take on Sunday afternoons.

Then, after we were married, Raymond started fox hunting again. Back then he was so busy on the farm that the only time he went hunting was at night. When we were first married, he took me a couple of times. I don't have the perception and the knowledge of animals that he did. I think it has to be born in you. It's something he had with those cows and with those dogs. When he went fox hunting he didn't always see the dogs, but he knew the sound of each one. I am convinced that with those cows if he saw a cow that he had ten, fifteen, twenty years ago in the middle of a herd, he would have been able to pick it out.

I like animals, I always have, but I just don't have that intuitiveness. When I went fox hunting unless I could see the fox, it didn't mean anything to me.

After we married, I was faced with reality. It came as a shock. Raymond had told me that he was a farmer. That's all he wanted to do. That was fine with me. He also told me that he was a fox hunter. That also was fine with me. I'd never known anybody like that before, but when you come to the reality of it and you have to live with it, it's a hard life.

Here I was on this farm, and I had no way of going anywhere. I had four children, and was carrying another one. Saturdays and Sundays I was left. I had a brand new husband and I wanted to be with him, but he was off in the woods with his dogs and a fox. There was nothing for me to do. We didn't have a television then. There was absolutely nothing to do.

Pop was very helpful and kind to me. Alice was not. Part of that was my fault.

Granddads' chickens were for all of us and there weren't enough. Alice had some eggs set aside to hard boil and I wanted some, and I got them. It was either Pop or Raymond that interceded.

I wanted my own way. There's a difference between being self-centered and being selfish. I was self-centered in that I did what I wanted to do, and it never entered my mind that what I did would have any effect on anyone else. It wouldn't have made any difference to me if I had known, because I would have done it anyway.

Being married and having children changed that. I didn't see that anything was wrong with me or wrong with what I had done to come to live there. I thought that my ways of doing things were just my ways.

Back in those days you didn't have shampoos and conditioners. I washed my hair with Lifebuoy soap. Afterward I used the old tar soap that you would get in a tin can. For conditioner I used vinegar and water to cut the soap out of my hair. Alice had had the new bathroom for only ten years. It was still primitive living at the Homestead in 1947. If the bathroom had been there for forty years, it would still have been new to Alice and she did not want that vinegar used in her bathtub. She was as sure as anything that it was going to cut in to the porcelain finish. Once again, I got my way. I washed my hair and I used the vinegar, and that was it. I went to Raymond and I never even thought how else I could have done it. I think there could have been another way, but no, only my way would do. So, Mom and I had another confrontation.

Again, Raymond interceded and he simply told me how things were, and what was expected of me.

During haying season you cut and the rake in the morning. You haul the hay in the afternoon. I'd make a visiting cake and take something to drink out to the men in the afternoon. Afterwards I had to start to have dinner ready. Raymond told me the time that he would be in and when he wanted dinner. I didn't have any other choice. That had become part of my life. I'm not saying there weren't times when I wished that I'd never seen a stove, or an egg. I can remember getting two compliments from Mother Alice. I got one on my pie crust, and one on my chocolate cake. It was just a recipe from a Crisco can for Devil's Food Cake! It was very moist, and it was a very good cake!

When Raymond had gone down to Merchantville and brought Judy and Leslie back, Judy didn't say anything at all and she was sick. Raymond was very concerned, and very tuned in to Judy and Leslie. Judy knew what was taking place, but she never would say anything. You never knew what she was thinking. Larry was very quiet as well and very angry inside. I didn't see it at the time.

Judy might have been angry, but most of all I remember her confusion. She didn't know what was happening at any given moment, more or less in her future. She had been threatened, and had heard her mother say that if her father didn't come and get them, she would be put in a home. Raymie was more talkative than Larry.

Leslie was very sick with asthma. I had never seen anyone with asthma, let alone a year and a half old baby. When he first came to us he had an attack. I walked the floor with him all night. I was certain he was going to die. Leslie didn't have any color, and even his ears were like wax.

We took him to a local doctor. The doctor took one look at him and wanted to know where in the world he'd been. I had to give him this dreadful medicine and Mother helped me a lot.

I wasn't frightened. I was too stubborn. If I felt uncertain and if I had any problems, all I had to do was go to Raymond and he would know all the answers. He was nine years older than I was and I figured that he knew all there was to know. These were his children and I assumed that he knew them and I only had to ask and he would straighten it all out.

Of course I had problems with Judy, and I asked him and he couldn't straighten it out. When Judy came to live with us she was very quiet and withdrawn. Judy reacted well to personal touches and she loved personal compliments. She also loved getting clothes and jewelry. She would respond to outward things like the happenings of the day and things that she did in school, but never her internal feelings.

I was very concerned. I knew that Judy needed more than she was getting from her father or me. I asked Doctor Monroe about it, and, and he wanted to know if we went to church. He thought that might help. The boys seemed stable, but I was concerned about Larry. He had constant infections in his ear.

I tried to help Larry with his spelling and schoolwork. I was told that he had a difficult time in school. There was a spelling bee and Larry couldn't do it. I didn't know anything and I went about it all in the wrong way. I remember taking words out of the dictionary and trying to help him learn to spell them. Larry reached a point where he just stayed up at the Homestead, period.

He was sick a lot and I think that Alice wanted him there. His one eye was so weak and it was always watery when he was sick. I think he loved being there, but it kept him out of school, deprived of the education he needed.

Larry had a confrontation with my mother at one time. She asked him to do something and he absolutely refused and talked back to her. She slapped him.

Raymond always favored Larry. He was the first-born, and he seemed to be following in both his father's footsteps, and Pop's. That was evident to everybody. Mother Shuster didn't particularly like Larry because he wasn't open. Raymond was also like that.

Raymie was just the opposite. He was very outgoing. We knew immediately when he was upset, angry, happy, or whatever. Raymie was always my father's favorite. When Raymie was going to go to New York to be an actor Raymond said, "That's totally useless, totally, totally useless." He didn't want to hear about it. He wasn't interested in the least. In his mind it was not the thing that a man ought to be doing, certainly not one of his sons.

Leslie was just a baby when I got him, and I lost patience with him. Larry and Judy were always very protective of Leslie, why wouldn't they be? Judy had taken full care of him as an infant. I don't know that they trusted me.

I never felt like I could get anywhere with Judy or Larry. I would do things that I thought were supposed to please them, or make them happy, and they just didn't respond.

Raymond was impatient with all the children. I didn't know him in his relationships with his children. Once Judy was carrying in some dishes and she dropped a plate and broke it. That child absolutely froze. She fully expected a whipping. She didn't get it. I know that I intervened. I think he said something to the point that she shouldn't have been carrying so many and that she should have been more careful.

Larry and Raymie were with Raymond even before Clara left, so it wasn't as big a transition. Judy had been removed completely from us, and then she was sent back which was very devastating to her. Raymond told me things that the family had reacted to in Judy that I just simply could not believe. She used to crawl around underneath the table and look up the ladies' skirts. Every kid does that, but not in the Ballinger family. They took it the wrong way. It was totally unacceptable that anybody knew it, especially to her Grandmother Alice.

I made one terrible mistake and Alice came to me very upset. She told me that Judy was out in the barn and a calf was being born, and she didn't think that she had any business being out there. So what do I do? I went runnin' out and yanked Judy back into the house. She was with her father and her brothers, and what could have been more natural, especially with her father there? Of course that was a sign of the time, and again of the Evans family.

Mother Alice was always correct. She sat perfectly with her feet always together. That was the way Alice was brought up, and how she was underneath.

Marjorie was my mother's first grandchild, and she felt she couldn't lavish presents on her because of the other children. When she gave something to her, she had to give something to the rest of the children. As Leslie got older he could sense it. She gave them a hobbyhorse. That should have been a gift for the two of them, but Mother resented it when Leslie played with it.

Marjorie would say, "That's my horse, and you can't play with it." She was a child. Leslie was still too young to understand. Mother always gave Christmas presents to all the children. She would not show favoritism any more than she could help. But it was there, and Leslie was sensitive enough that he picked it up.

I had always thought that the relationship between Leslie and Judy was so special as brother and sister. They were so very close. I wanted that to happen between Leslie and Marjorie and there was no way. Deep down he resented her. Today I can understand that.

I feel so guilty about that, because I should have stepped in. I should have talked to my mother more and I didn't do it. When Marjorie was born my mother bought the crib, my baby coach, and baby clothes. When Skip was born she bought the smaller crib. I wouldn't have had any of that if it hadn't been for her.

The fact that Raymond had the first divorce in the Ballinger family and he was the first-born son was a terrible blight on the Ballinger name. Then Ginny got married when she was three months pregnant. Raymond had married Clara when she was pregnant as well. I'm sure his family knew or at least guessed. They could have said the same thing about me because it was very close. We were the only ones that really knew although other people thought they could put two and two together. It took me years to realize that Raymond was born seven months after Pop and Alice were married.

In a marriage each individual has their faults and it's up to the other person in the marriage to determine what faults they're going to live with, and what faults they can't live with. It's their decision not their parents'. My parents saw things in Raymond that they did not like and did not want any part of, and didn't want me to have any part of it. But, they knew that there wasn't anything they could do about it.

After we had gone to live up at the Homestead, Raymond was still having a difficult time with Mother and Daddy and Bud. He finally consented to have Bud work up there. Why, I will never know. Pappy had begged him to do it, and the fact is that he didn't have to.

I don't know what it was that set Raymond off, but on one occasion after Bud started working at the farm, Raymond wouldn't even sit down with him at the Thanksgiving table. Mother and Daddy were there. What could I do? Here I am with a new marriage with a new husband. How do you explain that to your parents? I was constantly warning everybody to tread softly around Raymond. I never knew when his temper was going to appear.

He didn't blow up. He just refused to come to the table. If I had persisted, there would have been an explosion. Then there were other times that were better. Daddy would come over to help us and he would climb up to put the chain on that stupid silo pipe. Raymond couldn't do it. He was afraid of heights.

Much later it just came to a head. Raymond wouldn't have anything to do with Daddy and Bud and Mother until she died. I just couldn't accept it because he used the words 'white trash' and I said "Well, if they' are 'white trash' then what am I?"

Pop was always up in the morning before Raymond and I can remember him standing out there in the back at the Homestead calling for him, because he was still in bed. I used to be so embarrassed, because here Pop was, such an older man, and all crippled up, and he was up and out and his son was still in bed. There was no reason to be in bed, not when there was milking to be done!

All the trouble started over Judy. It was brought to a head one Sunday morning, and Alice came storming into the kitchen hysterically and yelling that Judy had done something. This time Judy had cut up a dress. Alice was standing in the kitchen yelling and screaming and Raymond forced her out the back door. I was trying to make him stop because I was afraid she'd fall. He wouldn't listen to anybody and she wasn't going to quit either. He got a bucket of water and dumped it all over her and said, "Maybe that will cool you off."

Ginny hit Raymond with a clothes pole, we were all watching, it really was awful. Granddad was standing on the porch where the wisteria was. Ginny had no right, but she was a determined woman. It had taken a long while for things to build up and then to go back down to some degree of normality. After they moved from the Homestead to their house in Marlton, relations became very pleasant again. We would go to their house for dinner and they would come out to the farm. Larry was out in the barn all the time. I had six kids and was twenty-four years of age. How was I? Really?

Alice had some weird ideas. She got it into her head that Pappy and Mom wanted the farm. You could go down in the cellar and walk underneath their part of the house and you could hear everything they were saying when they were in their den. I never told anybody that I did that. I remember hearing Alice say that my mother and father were trying to get that farm. Poor Mom and Dad. That was the last thing in the world they ever wanted.

Things got back onto a more even keel after Alice and Pop left the Homestead and moved into Marlton. Pop would come out every Sunday morning while we were milking. Alice also came occasionally.

Lois and Don got married. Our son Skip was born in February, and their son was born in April. We would all have dinner at their home in town.

Ruth could go in the city and look at little dresses and come home and make them. I was so envious, and I tried so hard. I made one dress for Judy, a red plaid one. She and Marjorie had the same plaid. When Judy graduated from eighth grade in 1952, I actually made her graduation dress. Unfortunately, it looked it.

I think that Daddy never really made Mother happy. Opposites attract. They loved one another but they were exact opposites. Mother was very sentimental. Daddy was not. He did not enjoy the movies. Mom loved them and she would coax him into going once a year. She used to go every week when she had the money, and especially on Mondays when they gave you the pink Depression glass.

Pappy built a boat in the garage, and when we were living with Aunt Beulah, he built a racecar in her basement. My parents had nothing in common except for their children.

I didn't drive. Raymond would take me to Haddon Heights to visit Mother and Dad. I tried to take a sewing course but that was during deer season and Raymond had to be out in the woods, not driving me to a sewing class. When he wouldn't take me, I was extremely upset. But, for the most part, he did take me everywhere else. I was totally dependent on him. He would even take me to the A & P for grocery shopping.

Then Raymond came up with this new plan. He had heard about a farm in Milford Neck,

Delaware with lots of land. First there was always the excitement of going to a new house, and second there was the horror of it. Can you imagine that we did this with livestock and who knows how many children at the time, not to mention the fact that I was usually pregnant.

Raymond had a way of making it sound really, really, terrific. He could romanticize a skunk into a mink.

Of course we moved to Milford Neck. A moving van took the household furniture. He had to have flat beds move the machinery and cattle trucks for the livestock.

My mother told him that she hated him for taking me away. Later he did everything to find them a farm near us. There was one place that they liked and Mother absolutely loved the house. They came very close to buying it which would have been another disaster, because we left two years later. They stayed in Jersey while we were in Delaware.

I had loved the house up at Marlton. We had lived at the Homestead the first years of our marriage, and Skippy was born there. I had ambiguous feelings about moving. We were leaving the Homestead and that house down there was nothing. Raymond had to do a whole lot to it.

When we moved to Milford Neck in 1952 I became pregnant with Nancy. Parts of Milford Neck I liked and parts I didn't. There was no electricity or plumbing in the house. You never knew if the house was going to be warm or cold in the morning. We got Sears to put in the heating and Raymond built a nice kitchen. The other rooms were small and there was no upstairs. I don't think there was even any downstairs.

The mosquitoes were a menace. I had seven children, four of Clara's and three of mine. I had been married six years. Raymond loved the boys, but he wasn't as responsive to the girls. He adored Skippy with his long curls. He would call him little old man.

Skip had the best disposition of all of the babies, always laughing or smiling. The mosquitoes and the flies ate the cows alive. The six kids were all together in an upstairs room and they were eaten up by mosquitoes.

Pop died while we were there at Milford Neck and Mother Alice came down for a visit. I was so embarrassed about the conditions in which we were living. The children were all bitten up. She was appalled. I really had my hands full.

Nancy, our second daughter and third child, was born that May. Each time I had had a child I was put to sleep and this was the first time I came awake. Nancy didn't cry at first and I was panicked. I thought afterwards that they had given me too many drugs and that they had a hard time bringing her to life. I wanted to see her immediately, but they didn't give her to me until she was all wrapped up. All I could see was her little face and her nose. I was only in the hospital for four days with Nancy.

After Dr. Monroe had delivered Skippy in Marlton, his comment to me was, "What's Raymond Ballinger trying to do? Have his own baseball team?"

Shortly after giving birth we had strawberries that were ripe and I went out and picked them and Alice near about had a fit. I don't think we'd even gotten the house painted yet, and that also appalled her. She visited two or three times.

That same week Skippy ran off into the woods. I was mortified. My three-year-old child had disappeared. The final straw was that twelve-year-old Raymie had run over Beauty, his beloved dog, with the old Chevy pickup and had locked himself in a room.

As a kid, I had no way of learning to drive, because the only car that Daddy had was one of those great big Rios. Pappy was a mechanic but he couldn't afford a car. The Rio was a huge, heavy old car, more like a bus. Just the thought of driving that thing petrified me. As always, Daddy lacked patience with me.

Subsequently I first learned to drive when I was twenty-nine with seven children. Raymond showed me the basics on a dirt road at the farm and that's where I learned to drive. Next I tried to drive a truck in the middle of one of his hay fields. Unfortunately, it had hay on it. Daddy was there, and he wanted me to stop. He kept yelling, "Both feet! Both feet!" Well, I could have put them out the window for all I knew what to do with my feet. Raymond didn't have a whole lot of patience teaching me either. I didn't take to it right away. Of course we had a stick shift and it certainly wasn't up on the steering wheel. Until I got my license, I was totally at Raymond's mercy! Me and all the children! I couldn't even go to the store. It was Raymond's choice not mine.

Breakfast at the farm was a challenge with a large family. I would make oatmeal in a double boiler because Raymond always had to have it creamy. I made a big pot of cocoa and then we would have bacon or ham or sausage and eggs and fried potatoes. That was standard.

Larry would come in and start with a bowl of oatmeal. Then he'd sit down with his eggs and his bacon and his fried potatoes and a couple of pieces of bread and his cup of cocoa. Then everybody else would eat. When they were all done there was usually oatmeal left over, and Larry would clean up the whole pot full of oatmeal and finish up the rest of the cocoa.

Larry could put it away, that was for sure. Larry wasn't big and he wasn't very tall, but man, he could put food away at dinnertime. We would have enough meat for a small army and it would be gone before I could eat any of it. Where he put it I will never know, but he did eat, believe me.

Raymie would take a quart jar full of milk when he came home from school and squeeze in an orange and add some vanilla. He would carry it out with a couple of sandwiches and put the milking equipment together, drinking that quart of milk and eating the two sandwiches. I don't know what we would have done if we hadn't had our own milk. Raymond would make milk shakes in the quart jars, with an egg and sugar and vanilla.

On the Homestead in the summertime when they were haying I went out in the afternoon with a big jar of iced tea, and a cake or cookies I had made. Everyone will tell you that you should not drink ice-cold water when it is so hot. It surely didn't apply to Raymond because he drank it no matter what. We'd sit under that big old buttonwood tree with the horses.

Leslie acted with Skip the same way Larry acted with Raymie. Raymie and Skip would spend as much time trying to get out of doing something as it would have taken them to do it in the first place. Leslie and Larry were the exact opposite. You never saw Leslie walk. He was always on the run, and he wanted to get things done.

Doc Grey, our Vet, brought his spotted Chincoteague stallion over and bred him to my buckskin mare. She threw a spotted colt which Raymond asked me to give to Marjorie and Nancy. Doc Grey also brought the unbroken Chincoteague ponies to us and Raymond lassoed them and helped Larry and Raymie break them. The boys each got to keep a pony.

Larry finished the eighth grade and he didn't go back to school. He had had such a dreadful time in school and I thought that it wouldn't do him any good if he did stay in. I don't feel that way now. He should have gone to vocational school.

We went to the Delaware State Fair in Harrington and we saw this horse that could have been Chief all over again. We looked up the owner, and it proved to be Cal Hollis. Raymond and Cal's friendship progressed, and I met his wife, Mary, who was a lovely person. Cal was a representative for International Harvester. He travelled, and he told Raymond that he was going down into Virginia. He asked him to go along, and that's when it all happened, once again.

First they went to Charlottesville, Virginia. Land there was more expensive and I think Raymond saw some beautiful places, but certainly not within our means. He met Mr. Wheeler, who had a motel he wanted us to manage. Wheeler also had racehorses and when Raymond didn't see anything that was affordable, Mr. Wheeler sent him to the Wahl's in Culpeper. Mr. Wahl eventually sold us the Sullivan farm in Culpeper.

PART VII

Larry Ballinger

RAYMIE (9) DAD (33) PAPPY (51) BUD (22) LARRY (12)
AT THE HOMESTEAD, 1947

Larry Ballinger

I WAS BORN AT HOME in 1935 in Marlton, New Jersey, at that first little bungalow on the Marlton Pike. They had a midwife deliver me.

I can remember back to when we lived at the bungalow when Raymie was born. I've got a lot of good memories there.

I used to get on my little scooter and ride it all over the place, headin' on down the road over to Grandpop's, in the first daylight of the morning, before anybody else got up. Of course I got whipped a couple of times for that, but it didn't stop me from going. My Grandpop had chickens over at Cousin Jesse Evans', across the street from our bungalow. He would feed his chickens 'bout five o'clock in the morning. I'd get up, eat a bowl of cereal, and crawl in his truck and go back over to the Homestead with him. I'd stay with Grandpop all day long while they were planting, working in the fields and just following along behind watching him plowing with a team of horses.

Dad was working at the shipyard on the day shift. Dad went off to work at eight o'clock in the morning and I had to be gone before he came back. I'd have to leave the homestead before he'd get back home. A couple times he'd come over and get me but usually Grandmother Alice would call and tell him where I was and that I got there alright. I was three or four years old.

That's when I first starting milking cows. My first cow was an old half-Jersey, half- Holstein whose name was Seal. They gave me one of these little ol' half-gallon buckets and an ol' wooden keg to sit on. I tried to hold that thing between my legs and I never could do that because it always hurt my legs.

Ginny and I used to play house together. There is four years difference between us.

There was a big buttonwood tree in front of the woodshed. Grandpop had a huge white Holstein bull. When they brought the cows in to milk, we'd get down inside of the old buggy and hide from that bull, trying to keep him from seeing us. We didn't figure he could see us through that vertical board fence. We didn't know any better. Ginny was always superstitious. She said to be sure not to wear any red out there because if that bull saw red he would attack us and kill us.

I had one of these big red handkerchiefs. It was Granddad's and I always wore it around my neck because he always wore one. His was a blue one, but I liked the pretty red one. She'd make me take it off and put it in my pocket so that bull couldn't see it.

We played house in the buggy, and going to the doctor, and then going to get groceries and see friends. We had make-believe friends and everything playing in that ol' buggy.

We used to follow the big timbered wagons and hay loaders while they were making hay. This was about the same time of day that Ginny wanted me to play with her, but I preferred to be out with the men, making hay. I'd follow them along and when I must have been about four, Granddad gave me a small two-pronged pitchfork, with a little short handle on it and he paid me for walking along behind that hay loader and picking up any bunches of hay that were missed. He'd give me a quarter a week. I was so proud to get that quarter. I thought I was making big money back then.

Granddad got to where he couldn't walk. With his asthma so bad, I got to drive the team. I started just pulling the rope block, and soon I was driving the team that levitated the hay fork to pull the hay up into the barn. My brother Raymie graduated into pulling the rope block. Dad would work on the back end of the wagon and fork the hay over and I had to pack the two front corners until we got to the barn.

Granddad always had a bunch of Jamaicans that picked the tomatoes and they would load 'em up on the wagon. They'd take their machetes over a head of cabbage and cut the head from the roots. Raymie's job was to grab the cabbage. He always thought they were going to cut off his head! He'd just shove the baskets and run.

The men would plant about twelve to fourteen rows and then skip a row for the wagons to run on. We'd go through and pick up the tomatoes. I'd just be sitting on the wagon holding the reins and telling the horses "Whoa." I was between five and six.

Occasionally I used to go at night with Grandfather down to Campbell's Soup to take a load of tomatoes or a load of cabbage. He hauled most of the tomatoes into Campbell's. The rest of the produce he took across the ferry into the Philadelphia market. We'd leave there 'bout six o'clock, six-thirty in the evening and sometimes we didn't get back until three or three-thirty in the morning. We'd go in that old Rio truck... with the canvas top on the cab. The doorpost was all wood.

We went into Campbell's Soup one night and we had to wait, and there was a great big long line. I wanted to see them make the soup so Grandpop took me down and showed me where they were making tomato soup. We walked up where they had this colored girl working. She was supposed to be sorting the tomatoes as they were going into this great big kettle. It must have held four or five hundred gallons of tomatoes, all stewed up. There was a mouse floating up on top of it. She pulled that mouse out and just flipped it and threw it in the corner. That fixed my tomato soup. It was years, before I could eat it again. I would just imagine that mouse. I had loved tomato soup.

I liked to go with Grandpop and we'd sit in the truck and he'd buy me a pack of Nabs, little Nabisco crackers, and a half pint of milk to drink. Sometimes I would just put my head right over in his lap and go to sleep. He'd take little naps too. He always took a blanket with him to cover up with if it got chilly. Then we'd drive back and I'd go into the house and go to bed.

Granddad couldn't even go to bed. He got to where he couldn't lie down in bed, so he'd sit up in a Morris chair. He slept for the last thirty years of his life like that, the asthma was so bad.

Dad always had some chickens and hogs at the bungalow, but I stayed over at the farm with Grandpa and Ginny. We would go skating together on the pond. One time I fell through and she wrapped me up in a big blanket. She took my clothes, put em' on the radiator and got em' dry. We had a time!

Aunt Lois was working and she'd catch the bus and come home at night. Aunt Ruth worked as a secretary in Camden. (Aunt) Ginny and I caught the school bus together and we used to ride bicycles together all the time.

I always liked Grandmother's cooking more than anything else. She was one of the best cooks I ever knew and she always called me "Larry Boy."

I never did have much interest in school. It was hard for me to adjust to being inside. When I was in first grade, I had an abscessed ear and I missed half the year so they held me back. When I was in the third grade, I had the same thing and missed half the year again and was held back another year.

Dad always liked fox hunting. He wasn't a family man. We never did anything as a family. Never did. I was enough like him that I liked fox hunting and I would go with him a lot. Clara belonged to the Grange and the church and she took us with her. The Grange did public works, more or less like the Rotary Club today. They did good deeds for people whose house had burnt down or suffered some other tragedy. Then they got to where they offered group insurance.

They met at the old Community House building behind the school. Once a month, they had a pot luck dinner. After the dinner they'd have their meeting and talk about what they were going to do for the next thirty days. A lot of people belonged, especially farmers, men and women both.

Then there was the Baptist church in Marlton. We would go on Sunday school picnics down to Sunshine Lake or on hay rides. Mom and I were close until she left. She called me Larry. I used to help her pick berries. I would take my wagon along the roadside and we'd pick blackberries and put them in a bucket. Clara would cut the berries with a pair of scissors and pack em' in my wagon and I'd hook the wagon behind my little scooter. I rode that scooter everywhere I went. I could fly with that thing. I'd get going and just cruise on down the road. I had a little bell on the handlebar. Grandmother always said she could know I was a 'coming, She could see my head bobbin' up and down coming down that road. When I got to the gravel road where it was too rough to ride I'd just run with it. I never would walk.

Raymie and Judy were closer in age and played together a lot back then. They were always gettin' in trouble. I always got out of it because I was never around.

When they started school that really bothered me, because I was left alone and I would sit out by the side of the house. I had nobody to play with anymore with Judy and Raymie gone. About that time Dad got a little beagle dog. He had traded for a hound and he ended up with that beagle. It stayed in the yard and we used to play with him. He was a good little rabbit dog. Dad finally gave it to Grandfather because he always had a couple of beagles around.

I was only seven years old when we moved to Barrington, because Clara left when I was nine. I heard Clara and Dad fussin' and arguing a lot at the bungalow. They would never let us stay around when they were doing it, but it was always in the background. I wasn't old enough to understand what was really happening. Then, it got to the point where she'd start going to town at nights. Dad got that horse, Chief, and then Pappy Shuster got to comin' over there. Ginny would come over to the bungalow and babysit.

Clara used to wash in the tub out in the back porch or in the kitchen when it was cold. When we went to church I remember she used to wash us in that basin in the kitchen and it would be as cold as hell. We finally got forced hot air heat in the house. Pappy came and put in ducting and a new furnace.

It was early spring when we moved to Barrington. It was before Easter because I remember she took us to church on Easter Sunday. We came back home and Dad was out plowing the garden alongside of the house. I loved to smell that fresh dirt.

I liked the school in Barrington. It was a little far, and Dad got those bicycles for us. He traded for them. That was on a dog trade too. We got them two bicycles. Mine was a green one with a big sprocket called the American Flyer. I could fly with that thing. I had mine until I got my horse. Leslie had it after I did and then Ashley inherited it.

Clara took us with her to the Grange meetings. Once in a while she'd go somewhere, maybe shopping, or over to Philadelphia. Then she'd leave us with Ginny.

One time I just kind of had the devil in me. Ginny said I was supposed to get ready for bed and I wouldn't do it. She locked me out of the house. I went into the garage and I got a screwdriver and I took the door right off its hinges and climbed in. Then I got scared she was going to tell on me and I went and hid underneath the porch. I didn't come out till way after dark. Mom came back and she called and called and called and looked all over for me. Finally, I got so scared that I answered her from underneath the back porch.

Another time Judy got her thumb caught in the washing machine. I pulled the plug and hollered for Mom. She has a big scar across her whole hand.

Raymie wanted to drive and he started up the ol' Model A and ran it into the pigeon house and upset a whole wheel barrel full of pigeon manure. Dad swatted him with the broomstick and then took his belt off to him. It was his famous punishment, his belt.

I had to help milk by hand. We didn't have the Delavals when we first moved to Barrington. After two or three months, Dad bought the milkers at a sale. We started with fourteen cows every night and morning. Then he got about thirty-five head, and he and I done all the milking. The barn didn't hold all of them and he kept some in another barn and he'd bring them over to milk. I was nine and ten years old.

He also had that big ol 'white bull that he bought from Tallman. Raymie's job was to pump water. He'd get tired and after I got done milking, I'd have to go pump. Those cows stayed in the barn and drank tons of water. We had a big concrete trough that probably held one hundred fifty gallons of water. A group of six cows could clean that out in ten minutes.

We had to take the milk to an old bathtub that was full of ice. Dad would set the milk cans in it. After we were living there a while, he started to have ice delivered.

He put fences up the whole time he was there. There was only one field that was fenced when we started. Most of the fences he put up were electric.

We'd get up at four thirty in the morning before school. We'd milk the cows. There was a wire running down behind the cows and we hung a lantern on that wire. As we milked each cow, we'd slide that lantern down to the next cow.

Pappy came to help the second year. Dad had two high school boys working for him, Marshall Simmons and Bob Remus. They helped him do all that barn work and make hay. Marshall Simmons had brought Pappy over. Pappy had a horse, Sheba, which belonged to Jean, and he came to buy some hay and corn for her horse.

We were at Barrington for two seasons. That first spring, school was still going on and I had to stay home to help make hay. Back that early, I stayed home sometimes three or four days at a time. The first season we made all the hay by hand and the second season we had this fellow come in that didn't have any legs or nothin' and he baled the hay. I rode on the baler and you had to put the blocks in. It was wire bales. I had to stick the wire through the hay and the paddle in through each bale. I rode on one side and that fella' with no legs rode on the other side. I was only nine and could have been chopped up in that bailer.

The no-legged fellow did the tying. I had to pass it through to him, then push the blocks through my side and then he had to pull them out as they went through. By the time I was finished I figured out why the man had no legs.

Dad leased some of that back land and planted soy beans. We had to load by hand with a pitchfork. I was up on top of the wagon with Pappy Shuster. The load turned over and I was buried in there! They had to dig me out! I couldn't even holler. If it wasn't for that little beagle Suzy coming in after me, I would have been lost forever. It took us two and a half trips to load that wagon back up and to get it into the barn.

The fights between Dad and Clara just kept getting worse all the time. It got to the point where Clara was gone every night, and Dad was gone every night. Dad would go meet Jean or she would come over on her horse. They would be out riding until midnight.

Lots of times we were left alone. Granddad came over one Saturday and picked us up and took us all home with him. He was really upset. Leslie was only a little newborn baby in the crib and he had dirty diapers. He had never been changed or nothing and Judy was tending to him. She wasn't but nine. I would drag Judy and Raymie around in a burlap sack. Raymie was a mean little rascal. He'd aggravate me to death and I was supposed to be in charge and sometimes I'd get pretty mean myself. We had fun. We'd laugh and play and carry on. We'd play under the table a good bit back then. Probably we were too afraid to come out in the open.

Clara and Dad left us alone frequently and Judy did most of the cooking with that old kerosene stove. That was when Judy put gas in the kerosene stove and like to have blown the house up and us with it.

Judy had to fill up the stove with kerosene. She would peel potatoes, put the meat in the oven, set the table, and be ready for us when we came in from milking. Clara had already taken off for the evening. Dad would come in, wash up, and change, and then he would take off.

Jean used to come over and help Dad get up hay. I can remember him and her being up in the barn loft. She and Pappy would come over in the evenings

Clara and Edith used to go to some kind of a woman's club. That's where Clara met George, her second husband. It was a singles club over in Philadelphia. Clara would leave at five or six at night and walk down to Barrington and catch the bus. Then she'd come back around ten or eleven o'clock. She'd be gone all evening.

Jean, Pappy, and some of Jean's cowboy buddies from Haddon Heights would come over. Jean brought a record player a couple times and played some old cowboy songs. Dad would get out his cowboy gear. They didn't think we knew what was going on and the little kids didn't really. I was the oldest and I knew what was going on. I actually caught them in the act in the barn loft one time up there in Barrington, up over on top of the horse stalls one Saturday afternoon.

Raymie and I were out playing, riding bicycles, and I was supposed to have the calves watered and we had to go to the pump. There was an electric wired gate across the driveway then. I waited till about dark and figured Dad was coming home and I took my bicycle and two buckets to go down and get some water from the old hand pump. I thought that gate was open. It usually was, but Dad had shut it and it was dark enough that I couldn't see. The bicycle and the buckets went underneath of the electric fence and I went over the top. That wire caught me right across the chest. It knocked me out. I seen stars. I didn't know nothing for a few minutes. When I woke up, Dad was standing over me. He sure was nasty and I got whipped and then I had to go feed my calves in the dark. I was still a little bit scared of the dark. I was only nine years old. I still have a scar all the way across my chest from hitting that wire.

Dad wasn't real rough. He was strict though. I was his favorite but I always had to work. If I got my cows milked before he got done, he'd make me stay out there and wait until he got done milking. He wouldn't let me feed the calves. I don't know what it was. I wanted to go play ball or something and I couldn't go, I had to stay there and work. Maybe he wanted the company, but he wanted the work done too.

Farming was the only thing I wanted to do, from the time I was two or three, ever since I can remember. I knew right then what I wanted to be for life. I wanted to be a dairy farmer. I wanted to milk cows. It was rough at times and especially when I had an abscessed ear and had to go out and milk fourteen cows. It hurt so bad that I'd just sit there crying, trying to milk. I had no business being out there.

I never missed a milking, not one single milking, from the time I was nine years old until the time that I went down deer hunting and met Maxine. I never missed a milking. I missed plenty of school.

Clara finally just left and took Leslie and Judy with her. She was pregnant at the time with Sandy. We stayed at the farm in Barrington after she left until the auction. It wasn't very long after Clara left that Jean used to come over and get us and take us to her parents' house and feed us and bath us. We used to sleep in her bed upstairs.

I can remember the sale. It was a hard time for me. I didn't want to see it and Mom was gone. I remember Dad asking me what I wanted to do. Did I want to stay with him or go with her? I actually had a choice? I wanted to stay. He gave me that choice. I wanted to stay with him. He had the horses, of course. He did just like he always did - he baited me.

He had Dolly and Molly, the iron grays, and Doc and Gerry, who he bought when he went to Barrington. Doc balked all the time. One night he left him on a load of wheat, hooked to the wagon. He wouldn't pull it up the hill and Dad left him hooked to it all night. He unhooked the other one and took him to the barn. He just lay down, he wouldn't get up. Later he reared up in the barn and hit his head and died.

Dad had Chief and he brought Sundown just before he sold. After he sold he took both of them to Pappy's garage in that snow storm. Dad would tighten up the girth and Chief would hold his breath. One time Dad yanked it tighter to make Chief stop holding his breath and he turned the horse upside down in the stall.

After Clara left, it was thirty or forty days before we moved off the property. After we had the auction, we were there only a week or two. We walked the horses to Haddon Heights in the rain and sleet. We got soaking wet. We had to walk them down through Barrington. It was Chief and that palomino. It was raining and Jean took us over to her house and gave us a real hot bath so we wouldn't catch cold. The reason why I can remember so well is because she put me in a pair of her breeches. I had to wear a pair of her breeches and they didn't have a zipper in the front. I thought I was the biggest sissy that ever was. I wore her breeches quite a bit back then. They were too big and I had to roll them way up, and then had to double them up under my belt. Raymie was kind of lagging along behind and fussing. He was cold and crying and Jean got him to put his hands between the horses' thighs to keep warm.

After they got the horses up there, Jean took us in the house and Dad stayed out there with Pappy. It was sleeting. Dad had to cut down some barbed wire fences to get us through.

There was a walking path but it was too small for the horses, so we had to go down around through town. I can remember the rain because I was frozen to death. I just had a little pair of cotton gloves on. We went back the next day and got my bantam hens and put them in a little corn crib on the top of Pappy's garage. All we had to do is go down the street and across through the woods and it was right there. We done a whole lot of things you wouldn't let your kids do.

A few days later Dad took us up to Grandmother's. It was probably a week or so. Pappy had taken our old green Chevy over to the school where he was teaching. They overhauled the motor in it before Dad went out West. The students did the work because he was teaching them.

Jean's brother Bud went out West with Dad. Jean was supposed to join them later. We had to start school in January over in Marlton. I dreaded that worse than anything.

We had just celebrated New Years in Haddon Heights. Clara came and visited us there over Christmas. She came alone and only stayed for an hour. She was very uncomfortable. I don't remember Dad or Jean being there.

Someone had given me this big wooden walking Basset Hound on a string. When Dad took us down to the Homestead, Granddad still had their Christmas tree up. They had these glass candles with lights and bubbles rising inside of them. We had Christmas there and Dad was out West.

Dad was gone from January into May, about four months. He sent me a postcard. It had a saddle on it.

We were in Barrington two years and seven months till they split up in October and we moved out late November. After we sold out at Barrington Raymie and I went up and stayed with Grandmother and Grandfather.

I was glad to be at the Homestead, but it just wasn't right. Our mother had left and our father was divorced and people made fun of us. The Coopers and some of them Italians made fun of us. Ginny beat a couple of them up because of it. She took our part.

Clara came to visit the Homestead on Raymie's birthday in May. She called before she came. I had gotten used to staying there. I really didn't want to leave. I just felt cold. I was really angry at both of them because they had done what they had done. They wrecked our lives. I've never gotten over it. It hurts. I mean it's just done something to me.

Dad returned from Reno. He said that he and Jean were married and Jean was our new mother. I didn't like it at all. I was very bitter about that. Jean was good to us. She'd give us ice cream, but this was a different story. I don't see how she put up with us or done as good as she did really, in a way. But she brought it on herself.

They brought Judy back within thirty days. It's no wonder that Judy's in the shape she's in now. That's all we had. It was just us three together. Leslie was just a little baby. Together we could make it, but apart we got torn to shreds. I can see it just as plain as day.

In the beginning I can remember some discussion about Clara taking Raymie with Judy and Leslie. I couldn't decide if I wanted to go with her or stay. I never did know why they separated. I knew they weren't getting along. I didn't know that she knew about Jean and I knew that he was runnin' with her and I was old enough to realize that he had no business doing it. I saw him doing the things that he was doing and that hurt me that he would do something like that and drive my mother away, which is what I thought. That feeling stayed with me up until this day. I never could forgive him for that.

Dad came back and took us to Lyndell, Pennsylvania, to manage the Bruno place and we lived there in that big ol' farm house except for Leslie. We had to go over to the Bruno farm and milk, or at least I did, but he did have milkers. I was ten and a half and was doing most of the milking. I thought that barn was the best there ever was. It had a manure pit and a big carriage bucket for manure that ran on a track around the barn. Raymie used to hang on that thing and I'd push him up and down that track round through that barn. We had moved there in the spring after school was out and we left there before school started back.

Jean's parents, Pappy and Mrs. Shuster, brought Leslie out for a visit, and he sat on a nail out by the chicken house.

We would roll tires down a hill into the Brandywine Creek with ourselves in them, right across the traffic into a black top road, and no one stopped us.

Dad wasn't gettin' along up there with Bruno's wife. They were having a big argument about the Holsteins that Dad had put in there. The Bruno's had had Guernsey's before Dad was hired. Bruno's wife didn't like the Holsteins. She told him that he had to get rid of them. Dad was furious. He had a man pick up the Holsteins the next Sunday. Then Dad told Mrs. Bruno that if she only wanted Guernsey's, she had to get 'em herself because he was leaving.

Dad found a new job in Lancaster, managing a farm with a registered Holstein herd. He worked at Kraph's for a month while we were still living in Bruno's old farm house. I went with him. We didn't move. Kraph didn't have a house for us to live in, just a small apartment.

Granddad came up and asked Dad if he would come back and take over the Homestead.

We moved back to Haddon Heights to the Shuster's house just before school started. It was hot and I rode in the back of the moving truck going once again across the Delaware Bridge, from Pennsylvania into New Jersey. I was in the fourth grade. I had just turned eleven.

Raymie was eight years old and in the second grade at Haddon Heights. I continued to go back and forth with Dad to milk. I slept in Haddon Heights, but I ate my meals at the Homestead. Judy and Leslie slept with Dad and Jean. There was just one bathroom right in front of the stairway. We slept on the sun porch. Raymie used to stutter pretty bad then. I got up at four o'clock in the morning and wasn't back until seven or eight o'clock at night to eat supper. Then I had to do homework.

I remember Dad screaming at me one night, in Haddon Heights in front of the fireplace. He grabbed me by my hair and kept asking why I couldn't remember a piece of spelling. I was tired and I just couldn't..... I couldn't learn. He'd have me go over and over and over and over it again and try to spell them words. I just couldn't. I never was taught how to pronounce syllables and letters and words. To this day I still have trouble. And spelling, I can't spell worth a nickel right to this day. I can read pretty well. But right to this day, I can't spell worth a nickel.

We had gotten pretty settled down back in Marlton. We used to go to those 4-H Club meetings in Medford. They had barn dances and hay rides. The only real problem was that the Italian guys from Pine Grove would try to beat us up. Then Dad said that the Coopers had stolen one of our pigs and they were terrible people. Raymie beat up little Janet Cooper, Hognose's daughter, and he told Dad he did it because Dad had told him she was no good and they had stolen our pig. Dad whipped him for it.

From the time Dad traded in those Delavals, and got those four surge milkers, he quit milking. Raymie and I milked. He was ten and I was twelve. We had some cows that would fill that bucket up twice in one morning, and twice at night. While we were living with Granddad we stayed home from school. Dad kept us out so we could stay there and milk.

Dad put the Homestead up for sale. He only took part of the herd. He culled out the poorer cows and took them down to the Cowtown sale. We kept the rest of them, and bought some new ones from Jake Greenberg. Greenberg moved them all to Delaware. They had to take them across on the ferryboat, because they hadn't built the bridge yet.

We moved to Milford Neck in the spring of 1951 but Raymie and I stayed in Marlton and milked while Dad was in Milford working on the house. Granddad would come back and forth and we stayed with him and Grandmom at their house in town. That was when Raymie stuck the pitchfork in his foot.

Dad bought a blue '49 Chevy just before we moved to Delaware, and an Allis Chalmers tractor. He sold all the old horse equipment. The rest we took on the truck to Delaware. It wasn't much, just an old mower, disk, a tractor, and some tools. One truckload, that's all. The fellow we bought the Allis Chalmers from hauled it down for us, and the plow that went with it. Dad also hired moving vans, one for the furniture and one for the machinery. Greenberg hauled the cows.

In the beginning that house was one big mess. Dad had to remodel the whole place while we were living there. There was a big dorm space on the second floor that became a large bedroom for Raymie, Leslie and me. Man, it was terrible! That roof came right down on you. We had our two border collies, Beauty and Penny. Penny died of distemper after we gave her to Pappy. Raymie ran over Beauty with the pickup.

The school authorities had sent our papers down to Milford and didn't want us to start school until the papers came. That way we got to put up new silos and put in new stanchions. I helped Dad and Raymie watched. Dad had the skill to build almost anything from scratch. He knew how to mix the mortar just right, how to lay his blocks. It never ceased to amaze me how perfect his buildings were.

I had to carry all the concrete blocks to him. We had stacked them clear over by the wagon barn, and I had to carry those damn things. After fifteen or twenty they got heavy. I know we complained a lot but we sure did learn how to build.

There was no bathroom in the house before we moved in. There was a privy. That old colored fellow that lived there, John Townsend, called it the 'sitting room'. He was the heir of slaves who had lived there. John's family's graveyard was in the back field. His wife's name was Viola. We thought that was the funniest thing there was, that John called the privy a 'sitting room'. John and Viola came with the farm. They had a lifelong tenancy.

In the west front field there was a vineyard, and underneath the two big potato barns were the wine cellars with a few kegs of red wine in them. We didn't know they existed until we couldn't find old John but we heard him singing through the trap door of the cellar. John was sitting down there with a lantern, singing old slave songs, and drunk out of his mind. We had trouble getting him up that ladder. It took us almost an hour. Dad was mad until he realized he had two wine cellars!

We used to get eggs from John. Viola raised herbs. She'd have them hanging on the side porch in wire racks. She taught me every herb and what she used them for. When John came down to the barns every morning I'd ask him how he felt. John had a different saying every day of the year.

"Oh, I'm about like an old Model T, spittin' and sputterin'."

"I is about as dry as a young beaver without a dam."

"I feel as empty today as a tree without fruit."

Milford was alright. That was a pretty good time. We made good friends and we had a lot of fun there. We went to 4-H Club and that's where I graduated from the eighth grade. We had our Chincoteague ponies and our colts. We made harnesses with the rivet machine. Riding those bucking ponies almost got us killed.

We had a pretty good life there.

PART VIII

Sandra Wilkins

SANDY AND WILL WILKINS, 1988

William James Wilkins, Sandy's Adoptive Father

——————

I WAS BORN IN 1912 in Mount Holly, New Jersey on King Street. We moved to Camden when I was six and stayed until I was about nine years old. We just didn't have a bathroom. We had an outhouse. Every day you threw a cup full of lime down there. It killed the odor. When it got to a certain height, you hired somebody to come and clean it out. They would put it in barrels and haul it away.

When we moved back to Mount Holly, there were no cars and no electricity. We used oil lamps. All your little country stores carried kerosene. You took the can down and bought two or five gallons to fill your oil lamps.

We moved to Main Street and now we had a bathroom! I used to work at the butcher shop. I was only a little kid but I used to ride with the guy who delivered the meat. He would let me drive the horse.

My Dad was a carpenter. He had been a farmer. During the First World War he went to Fort Dix as a carpenter. After the war he joined the Union. He was a Union carpenter right up until he died. At that time, a Union Carpenter made one dollar twenty-five an hour. That was big money in those days.

We used to buy milk. Ozac made ice cream, and he had a horse and wagon. He went around selling and delivering his ice cream. He skimmed off the cream to make his ice cream but there was still plenty left in the milk. We bought the skimmed off milk for twenty-five cents for a big five gallon pail.

In the winter when it snowed, we wallowed through it to school. The horses and carriages would change to a sleigh.

My dad went to work for Fennimore Feed Company. From the back of the wagon he'd drop a hundred pound bag of corn on his shoulder and take another hundred pound bag under his arm on the other side. It was a wonder that he could do it. He was small like me.

My mother, Caroline, had three children with Schluter, her first husband. Only the youngest child lived. After Schluter died, she married my father, William Wilkins. They had my older sister, Anna, who is nineteen months older than me. Then she had me and gave me the same name, William, as my Dad. Then my brother Alex came along in 1916. Alex married Clara's sister, Edith. Their kids were the same age as Larry and Raymie. Before my younger sister Cathy was born, they used to come over to Marlton to Pop Ballinger's.

When we moved from Mount Holly to Camden we got electricity in 1924, but there were still a lot of houses that didn't have it. The middle class had plumbing by that time, but not the poor. Up until I was about ten years old we still had a pump in the kitchen.

I went to high school in Philadelphia, North East High School. One of the first jobs I had was working at Twitchell during the summers in Philadelphia. They made paper products and wove automobile seat covers and stuff. When I first came out of school, I worked in Snellenburgh, a big department store like Sears. I banked for the members of the firm and I made out expense checks for the buyers. I worked there for about three or four years, and then I left. I wasn't cut out to be an office worker.

My next job was at the Peerless Silk Dyeing Company, blocking felt hats on hot blocks. I worked on that until I went back to work for Twitchell. I worked there for quite a few years until they went on strike.

I was in Philadelphia during Prohibition and I was only eighteen years old. Well, if you knew where to go, you could buy booze, bathtub booze. They mixed it in the bathtub and bottled it. When the Revenue officers moved in, they pulled the plug and let it go down the drain.

In Philadelphia they put out near beer. It was a special malt beer with hardly any alcohol in it. Then they started putting out beer in New Jersey that had more alcohol than the regular beer. We used to go to Jersey to drink.

The Depression really started in 1914 with the First World War and went through the stock crash and up until the mid 1930's. The Stock Market crashed in 1929. I remember all the guys that had dough. The banks closed, and boy they were jumping off bridges, committing suicide and everything else. You know how those rich guys were when their dough got all tied up.

It didn't affect me because we never had no money anyways. We were just a poor class of people. It didn't affect us any. We struggled to get along practically all our life. We were still struggling. We didn't notice too much difference.

Then I went to Brunel and Haskell, the paper products company. I was twenty years old. My family had a store up on the branch of Mill Street, and I didn't like tending store.

I got a job at Scheibels' Knitting Mill. I worked where they knitted the sweaters. Downstairs there was a hosiery mill. I ran the machines. I worked up from $3 a week to $15 a week. If they had let me make the chains that controlled the designs, I could have become a mechanic, and I would have gotten $125 a week, and I could go anywhere and work, with expenses paid.

I told them, I said, "I want to learn to make chains." They told me they didn't need another mechanic so I went back to Twichell where they took paper and twisted it and made millions and millions of yards of what they called fleece yarn. After they sheared the sheep, they put the fleece in bundles and they tied it with this yarn. When they threw it in the machines to wash the fleece the paper would disintegrate in the water, so it wasn't hooked in with the wool. They also made carpet filler. They made seat covers for cars out of those.

I worked for them for quite a few years, until they went on strike. I made good money there, until the NRA came in. You know what the NRA was? National Recovery Administration. It cut my pay over half. There were so many people out of work in the Depression. It was supposed to help give more people work. The idea was that because they didn't have to pay as much to one person, they could hire more people.

That was Roosevelt's idea.

In other words I was making good money, and I was doing the same work, and I couldn't even make half of what I had been making before that came in. I didn't go picketing or nothing. I just quit.

I came to Mount Holly and I got a job with the Slunk Construction Company, which built the high school. I went to work as a laborer and then they put me to work as a carpenter. I knew the foreman. That's that big school up there with the big dome with the silver leaf on it.

I framed all that. Laminated that stuff together, and cut it and made that dome. I worked for them till the high school was done. They wanted me to go to North Jersey to build another school up there, but I didn't want to travel.

I went back to Twitchell a second time. That's when everything was shot all up. Now, for the work that I had always done where I could make $120 a week, I couldn't make $40. They finally offered to make me a foreman and pay me $50 a week.

I said, "$50 a week don't pay me to travel to Philadelphia, and I don't want the responsibility for $50 a week. I have done that work, and could have earned $125 a week for years here. Now you expect me to do the same work for $50? I can't do it."

So, I left and came back to work at the knitting mill. I knew the money was nothing, but I wanted to learn the trade. I knew once I could make chains, I could go anywhere. That's what I was figuring on. But it didn't work out. They wouldn't let me progress.

I left and I went to the Delaware Ordinance Depot.

It was a civil service job, deboosting 75 mm shells.

During the First World War, we didn't have TNT. They made a product called Amatol that was a by-product of TNT. They poured the shells and they put these boosters in them. The arsenals were full of them, 75 mm shells that weren't being used. The boosters were filled with what you called Tetra. That's one of the highest explosives there is. It burns with a real brilliant heat. When that shell would go off it would light that Tetra. It would burn so bright, and so hot, that it would melt the Amatol, or the TNT, and the gas would explode. The whole projectile would split into millions of pieces. That's your shrapnel.

This country zoned all their shells. They could fire the shell and they knew the exact distance it would go before it would explode. They were all zoned by weight. Every shell was weighed, right to the exact amount. All the powder that went into the casing that pushed that projectile was put in there according to the weight that would take that shell so far.

We used to have to lay them gently in a box and then strap that box up. Then they took them and dumped them into the ocean. They were dangerous. Once in a while when they were deboosting, one of them shells would go off. Now the stuff that was in them wasn't dangerous once that booster was out. They had pipes sticking up and they had live steam. They used to set them on these pipes and turn the live steam on and it would melt everything out of them. It would run down a tray and go in boxes and harden.

I worked there two years at the Civil Service. It was the year I got married, 1935. I was still working in Civil Service at the Delaware Ordinance Depot. One time I asked for a relief. I had to go to the bathroom and I walked out. There were two men working deboosting. One would go back to the barricade and put the shell in the vise and then carry the shell that was deboosting out and put it in a rack. While he was doing that, the other guy would turn the wheel and deboost the shell. He'd pick up another shell, and go back and take the one out of the vise and put the next one in.

This guy named Pierce who I was working with never wanted to do it that way. He wanted to carry two shells back, deboost one, take it out and put that one in, and carry two more shells out. That way he had to make only half as many trips. Him and me used to argue. I told him, "I'm gonna turn the wheels while you are back there."

Pierce was married, and had about four children. I wanted to go have a smoke, you know. The bathroom was the only place you could smoke.

I asked for a relief and he was turning the wheel as I went out. Pierce carried two shells back there and I had just got my pants down and went to sit down on the toilet when I heard "Whooom !!!!"

I went to look out the window and the roof of the building I was working in was gone! Sides were blown off and the whistles were blowing. By the time I got to the window, everybody was running to the bomb proof shelters. I was on the four to twelve shift. We were in the bomb proof shelters for two hours.

The fire company came and they started counting noses. The guy who had relieved me had gotten knocked down and had a broken leg so they had taken him to the hospital. They counted everybody else, and there was only one guy missing, Pierce. They couldn't even find enough of him to put in a match box. It had ripped him all to pieces. The only thing that was left standing was the barricade.

Nobody went to work anymore that night. The twelve to eight shift was knocked off. They sent our shift home. I went in at eight o'clock the next morning. They said, "Well, you ain't supposed to come in until four."

I said, "I ain't on the next shift. I want a release right now, that's all, period." So they gave me a release and I went to work at Campbell's Soup the next day.

I went to work for Campbell's Soup, June of '42, in the tomato section. They made me a foreman in the tomato shed. Then I went to the cooked chicken section.

They brought the tomatoes in through the washing machine and the women sorted them. Then they went upstairs to the vats where they were cooked. They took the seeds and the skins off and then just the pulp came down. Then it went into the plant, and it was made into tomato paste and stuff like that which was used for baked beans. When tomato season was over, I went into the cooked chicken department.

I weighed the cooked chicken after it was all sorted. There were fifty to seventy-five women there. Some of the women had breasts, some had legs, and some had necks and wings. They pulled the meat off the bones and it was all weighed. Then it came down and they dumped it in on the table, and diced it up in little square pieces. When it came out of the dicing machine, it was weighed again and sent to the department where they made the chicken soup. They dumped it in and a wheel turned, and the cans came and so much dropped in every can.

I worked days for quite a while and got made a foreman in cooked chicken for pretty near a year. Then they started making their own noodles. They made their own dough with eggs and flour.

They took me out of chicken and put me in the noodle department. I worked there and put that on production. Once I got on production, they cut out the other noodle department. They told me they were going to take me off the noodle job, and I'd have to go back into chicken.

I said, "No way. I put this job on production. I got seniority on this job. It's a new operation, and I've been on it for a year."

I ended up making my case to Mr. Durance, the President of the company. He told me that he had promised the job to someone else.

"I'm too big a man to go back on my word. So, Mr. Wilkins, you'll have to go back to cooked chicken."

I went to the shipyard and got a job.

First I had to go to the War Manpower Commission and put in writing what Campbell's Soup had done. They had to give me permission to leave.

I worked one day in the shipyard, and the next morning I was told that they couldn't let me work there because Campbell's Soup wouldn't release me. I went down to Campbell's Soup and argued for another week. Finally, I went to the War Manpower Commission, and I told them I refused to go to work. They still wouldn't give me my job back without permission from Washington. I finally got the job because it was defense work.

I worked in the cleaning department for a few weeks until they found out I could read blue prints and build templates. Then they put me in the ship fitting department. After six months I was made a leader.

I worked at the shipyard in the ship's engine and boiler rooms. I knew Raymond before I began working at the shipyard. I had met him with Clara and Edith because of Edith being married to Alex, my brother. That's why I knew the Williams long before Raymond knew them. I knew Clara's Dad, Bill Williams. He was a loom fixer in the textile mill at Twitchell. Alex married Edith, Clara's sister, in '33 when he was around twenty. I married my wife Helen in '35 when I was twenty-three.

I knew Raymond and Clara and I knew Pop Ballinger too. I used to go out to the farm in Marlton with Helen about then.

This is the way the government spent money. The boats had to be built according to the blue prints. They knew when they built those boats, that parts of the boats weren't going to be accepted, but they had to be built according to the blue prints, right or wrong. After they were launched and they went to the Navy Yard and were ready to be commissioned, the Navy would send them back to make all the changes. That's what I worked on, Navy changes and alterations. I was the foreman with two first-class fitters and four second-class fitters and four linemen.

I worked on a premium system. I lifted the templates, and sent them to the plate and angle shop, and when they came back, I had the fitters working on them. Some of the boats were hit with torpedoes, and collapsed and sunk. They needed to put extra ribs in them so they could get hit with torpedoes but wouldn't sink.

I had premium piece work tickets and I could turn them into two-hundred percent profit. I was making my paycheck but my premium check was larger than my paycheck every week. They would give you a ticket for $400. Well, you would knock that ticket out with maybe a couple of other tickets in a week. So, you'd take your week's pay and then that ticket on top.

I was ashamed to turn them in. I had a stack of tickets in my pocket. I must have had $5,000 worth of tickets on jobs that were done and I hadn't turned them in. I was ashamed to turn them in.

Then they put on the bulletin board that Germany had surrendered, and that anybody who wanted relief from the shipyard could get it. I took the tickets and divided them up among all the men working for me. Then I went to the office and told them I wanted out.

They said, "You are on Navy changes and alterations!" I said, "I don't care what I'm on. I want out. The war is over. It says on the bulletin board I can get a release."

They didn't want to give it to me.

I said, "I want out."

They said, "Why?"

"The war is practically over. Pretty soon this place is going to be laying off twenty thousand men out on the street, looking for a job, and I'll be one of them! I want to go get a job now."

They didn't want to let me go but they released me to the War Manpower Commission. I couldn't take a job. I had been offered a job at Twitchell. I had quit there years ago, and now they had a plant in Maple Shade. The commission told me I couldn't go to that job. They wanted to send me to Pearl Harbor to work as a ship fitter.

I said, "Bullshit! You ain't sending me to no Pearl Harbor!"

Then they told me to go back to the Navy Yard. I told them I had just quit the shipyard because I didn't want to be out of work when the other men hit the street. I had a job, and I wanted to take it. They refused, but they offered me one more alternative.

"I said, "What's that?"

"Campbell's Soup wants you back."

"I don't want to work for Campbell's Soup."

"Well," he said to me, "You go down there to Campbell's Soup, and you talk to them. If you take a job down there, it's alright. If you don't, you have to come back here and take whatever we have to offer."

I became an Inspector. I worked there until V-J Day. That's when Japan surrendered. Then the War Manpower Commission no longer had the power to tell anyone where they could work, so everybody in the plant walked out.

I went back to work at Twitchell as a night superintendent.

The first time I met Raymond was not too long after the war started in Europe, around March of 1941. I think he was in the tin shop at the shipyard. I think that's where he worked, and if I'm not mistaken, I was working there with him when Clara and him broke up. That was right before Sandy was born. Leslie was only a baby. Raymond had told me they had broken up, and Clara had gone to live with Edith and Alex in Merchantville.

Raymond had told her to get out. He throwed her out. He told me that he told her if she ever got pregnant again, that he'd kick her out, because it wasn't his. I didn't say nothing because I knew he had a girl friend on the side at the time.

Jean was working in the shipyard's electrical department, Jean Shuster. I knew that they were having an affair, but it was none of my business. I never mentioned it to nobody outside of what Raymond told me. The whole time he worked at the shipyard he was having an affair with her. I don't know for how long. I do know that he was having an affair before he and Clara broke up.

I didn't know if what I heard is true or not, but I heard that she was pregnant, and her father said that he had to marry her. Jean didn't have a child. The daughter that she had was later. She might have had an abortion at that time. It wasn't hard to get an abortion in those days. Clara mentioned this to me.

Clara left with Leslie and Judy and she tried to work. It was pretty tough with two children. Judy wanted to go back to be with her brothers. Clara was also pregnant and she didn't think that she could take care of the three of them. Raymond had said that if she was pregnant it wasn't his. He claimed it wasn't his child. Clara said she would have to adopt the baby out.

I told her if she was gonna adopt the baby out, we'd be glad to take the baby. We didn't know whether it was gonna be a boy or a girl at that time. And then just a week or two before she went to the hospital she asked me,

"Did you mean it, when you said you would like to adopt the baby if I had it?"

I said, "I meant every word of it."

Helen and I adopted Sandy as soon as she was born. We went through the legal proceedings for adoption. It takes about a year. We adopted Sandy and Clara signed the paper and Raymond had to sign. I took my wife and Sandy, and I drove to Marlton. Raymond was out in the field plowing. I pulled up, blew the horn, and waved to him. He stopped the tractor, and walked over. I said, "Raymond, I'd like you to sign the papers for adoption. We're adopting the baby, and you have to sign the papers."

He said, "Sure, I'll be glad to sign."

I gave him the papers and he signed. And he said, "Could I see the baby?"

I said, "Sure, why not?"

So, I stepped on one strand of fence, and held the other one up while he stepped through. He went over to the car, and he looked at the baby.

Helen asked, "You want to hold her?"

She opened the door and handed Sandy out to him. He held her, and tears run right down his cheeks. He cried like a son-of-a-gun. He got himself straightened out, and he stood right there and he told me, he said,

"I accused Clara of having this child and it wasn't mine. But there is no doubt in my mind, that she is mine."

Sandy was the spitting image of her sister, Judy.

He asked, "Would you bring her up to the house so that Mom and my sister could see her?"

I said, "Sure."

I drove up to the farmhouse and Helen took the baby and went in, and Mrs. Ballinger and Ruth were all crying. They all said there is no doubt about who she belonged to. He told me afterward, he said, "There is nobody I'd rather have her, than you and your wife."

I don't rightly know what happened with Clara and Raymond. It was one of those things. I guess nobody is to blame. I think it was just on his mind that they had too many children.

I can remember when he first married Clara. Boy, he was jealous as hell! He wasn't the type of fellow to go to a lot of places. When Raymond was out in public with Clara, he didn't want anybody to look at her. He was that way, you know. He was always jealous. I don't know what happened in later years. I believe Clara was faithful to him to be truthful. I know Clara was highly sexed. That whole Williams family was that way. I'm not saying anything against Clara. I don't think she ever went with anybody, 'cause I don't recall her ever running around.

I think as far as Clara being highly sexed, she was sexually satisfied. I think he kept her well satisfied. That's why I could never understand what could have happened. I think more or less, it was so many children, and she had them fairly close, one right after the other. I imagine one blamed the other one, because they kept having them.

Clara spent a lot of time with her sister Edith. Edith didn't drive. Her husband, Alex, had a little Ford. Clara didn't take no furniture.

I never knew her to want to go back. She never mentioned it, certainly not in my presence. When she went back to Alex and Edith's, that's when she met George Mahaffey. That was after Sandy was born.

Alex belonged to the fire company across the street from where they lived in Merchantville. They had a dance and a supper at the firehouse. Helen and I went with Alex and Edith and Clara. George belonged to the fire company and he played on the softball team. He worked for the Pennsylvania Railroad. That night he came over to the table we were all setting around.

Alex introduced George to Clara and after that I heard that George had started dating Clara. He had never been married. He was a nice man. He was very good to Clara and she was good to him too. She took care of him till the day he died. He suffered for a good many years. George had to carry an oxygen tank with him all the time. I used to laugh, you know. She would get on his back and bawl him out because he would sneak a smoke! He'd crave a cigarette, and she'd catch him. The irony was that Clara smoked as well.

I understood about Clara giving up her kids. There was no way she could take care of them. She took Leslie and Judy and she was having another one. That would have been three. Judy wanted to come back to be with her brothers. She got homesick for the boys. Leslie needed a lot of care. I don't think she had any choice. I don't think she disowned her children but I think she just realized that it was impossible for her to go on and take care of them.

She was trapped. I feel she was. Now I might be wrong. Some people say they were her children, and regardless of whether he wanted her to leave or not, she should have stayed. But, it could be a pretty hectic and unhappy life for everyone of them. It could have been worse for the children if she had stayed.

I think it took guts. Clara always spoke very highly of the children. She loved her children. I was practically an outsider. Alex and Edith knew more. She was very fair. When Sandy was growing up, I refused not to tell Sandy, as soon as she was old enough to know. I told her from the time she was a baby that she was adopted. I told her who her mother was and her father. Sandy was never in the dark about her adoption or nothin', because I'd never kept it from her. We never took Sandy away from her Grandmother and Grandfather Williams. We took her up there for them to see her the whole time she was growing up.

Clara stayed away. If we were up at my sister's to visit and she happened to be over at her mother and father's she would call up and ask if she could come over. She never said nothing, but she just wanted to see Sandy. She checked on Sandy as she grew up. Sandy knew she was her mother, when she got old enough to realize it.

We couldn't have children. Helen lost three. She had an ectopic pregnancy twice. One time they took one tube out, and the last time, they took the other tube out. Helen wanted children so bad.

All I heard of Raymond was that he had married Jean and he had three or four more children. When Grandma Stacey Budden Williams died, Judy was over at the Williams' house, and I remember Raymie being there. That was in 1956. Raymie was in the service or just out of it.

Sandy, Sandra Wilkins

MY FATHER IS WILLIAM JAMES WILKINS and my mother is Helen Marian Strabel. I grew up and spent most of my life in Moorestown New Jersey. We lived in a small bungalow. It wasn't even a Cape Cod. The earliest memory I have is of my mom doing hair in her shop at home. Mom was very old fashioned. She grew up on a farm and was very quiet, sweet, and tolerant. I never heard her say an unkind word about anybody. Dad worked a lot. He was very loving, but I remember him either working or when we went on vacation down on the shore each year.

My mom was home all the time. I was happy, but lonely as a child. Everybody else in the family had brothers and sisters and a lot of family. I didn't.

Dad was thirty-four and Mom was thirty-two when I was adopted. I didn't find out that I was adopted until I was seventeen years old and a junior in high school. My father told me, but my mom didn't know that I knew. To the day she died, she talked about how she had me.

I was an average student and very quiet. When I was very young I was terribly thin. Because of my asthma, I was sick a lot until I was about twelve. Then I became a chubby kid.

I grew up with Edith, Clara's sister. She was married to Pa's brother so she was always my aunt. There was a lot of conflict inside of that family but I always got along well with them. Edith was close with me. I don't remember having known Clara.

I had suspected that I was adopted and had heard rumors from my cousins, but nobody was sure. The kids my age had heard their parents talk. I wasn't surprised. It was good knowing for sure, because growing up I didn't fit in. There was always something that wasn't right. I knew the Williams, Clara's and Aunt Edith's parents, as Grandma and Grandpa. I got birthday and Christmas cards from them and they were always signed Grandma and Grandpa Williams.

The first time I saw Clara was when Grandma Williams died. I didn't know who she was. When my father told me that I was adopted, I didn't understand how I was connected to the family. I didn't know who my natural parents were. When I met Clara at the funeral, I just thought she was Aunt Edith's sister. I was always aware of this undercurrent of my being adopted. The secrecy from not telling me and of living that lie and carrying the secret was so hurtful to me and my parents as well. Once I knew, I was fine. People talk. They think you're a kid and you can't hear, but you hear things, and then you make up stories in your mind. I think it's worse than knowing. If they had been open and honest it would have been a lot easier.

That's what Leslie felt with Jean. They never told him that he was not Jean's child until he was seventeen. Leslie knew they were lying to him. That's what has continued to make him so angry.

My half-sister, Penny, had a hard time with my looking so much like Clara. I see a lot of Clara in myself. In just the short time I knew her, between Mother's death and Clara's, I could see that she was so different from my mother. I see a lot of my mother in me as well.

Clara was a very strong woman. I got a lot of my strength from her. I can't imagine how she coped.

Clara loved Raymond until she died. She told me that.

I started dating Don when I was fifteen. We met at a dance. I fell in love with him, and we married when I was eighteen. We were married for two and a half years. He went to Vietnam and it was hard. My father hated him,

I don't know why. Don had a very hard time dealing with Vietnam, and came home on emergency leave because his father died. He went totally berserk and he couldn't go back. The only way he could stay home was if he was the sole son living at home with his mother. I didn't handle that well. I was too young. We divorced.

Then I met Win Jones. I had actually gone to high school with him and knew him by name only. He had been married to one of my girl friends, and they had split up. Win had two children. I was not quite twenty two. We dated about two years and got married in Hawaii when he was on leave from Vietnam.

I had my first child at twenty four. We were only together a few days before he went back to Vietnam. He was home when Donna was born. Vicky and Debbie were born three years apart. When he came back we had the kids and we started a normal life.

Win had a car accident when Debbie was a year old. He was alone and on his way to work. He slid on ice, and lost control of the car. He was thirty-two years old and broke his neck and severed his spinal cord. He was paralyzed from the neck down.

We don't see him. He called the girls every couple of weeks. He had five girls and he has nothing to do with any of them. I asked Win for a divorce because I was on the verge of a nervous breakdown, and the doctor said it was me or him. I had three young children to raise. We sued the county for the car accident. We settled for one hundred thousand and the lawyer took the biggest part. Luckily the house was paid for.

I moved to Orlando, and we were there for eight years. Clara had moved to Fort Myers after her husband had died to be closer to her sister, Edith, who had also retired there. Her younger daughter Bonnie, my half sister, had also moved there. I got to know them better and we became close. I worked for a car dealership in Fort Myers and just survived. At age forty five, I met my future husband, Jim.

Leslie was ordained by then, and he married Jim and me at our house in Orlando. I think it was the first wedding that Leslie performed. He was so nervous, he couldn't talk. He was crying. Leslie's wife Marge made the wedding cake.

I couldn't talk to my father .Will Wilkins was a very chauvinistic person and worse than most. Once Jim got up after dinner to do the dishes and man, he about had a fit. When he was sitting on the stoop and he'd see Jim in the kitchen, he'd ask me "Why are you making Jim do them dishes?" Will was wonderful to the kids but you couldn't go to him for help or to just to talk with him.

Then in 1990 we found out Will had cancer and was dying. Jim and I decided to leave Orlando and come back to Marlton to be with him.

PART IX

Raymond Evans Ballinger: 1948–1953

RAYMIE (12) 1950

Raymie, Raymond Evans Ballinger

BEFORE WE MOVED TO THE HOMESTEAD, the family would gather there every weekend. The women would play croquet in the yard with the big picket fence.

My Aunt Ruth started dating Uncle Bob when I was around five. He was probably home on leave and he gave me a sailor hat.

Don, Lois's boyfriend, came over with a little chess game which they played.

Within two or three years Ginny started dating Frank Davenport who was quite a bit older than her. Granddad disapproved of him.

The winter that Larry and I stayed on the Homestead while Dad was out West, Bobby Moore was dating my Aunt Ginny. It was 1946 and the war was over. Bobby had been in the Army Corps of Engineers and stationed in Alaska where he worked on the pipeline. Bobby hung around the Homestead and occasionally helped out Granddad. He was playful and still wore pieces of his army uniform. Bobby had been known to be quite wild and the women liked him. He could get himself in a lot of trouble very quickly, but with his boyish smile you couldn't help liking him. Larry and I saw him as a big brother.

The first season at the Homestead we had a huge amount of snow. That winter they had taken the old sleigh from up in the wagon barn and hooked it up to our iron grey. Bobby took old Silver and harnessed him to the sleigh with bells on, and took us all sleigh riding and then they turned over the sleigh! It was really exciting! Ginny was very impressed and ready to do anything that Bobby asked. He taught her how to drive a car that winter.

That next spring they married. I believe that Ginny was pregnant with Frank Davenport's child. Years later, after Ginny and Bobby were divorced, Ginny married Frank Davenport.

When we came back from Lyndell to live with Grandmother and Granddad, it wasn't as exciting as it was when we were there with my mother. The uncles didn't come any more. There was tension in the atmosphere at the Homestead. Ruth lived next door, but she knew she was going to have to move. Lois's husband, Don, was a pilot during the war and they were gone. The war had dispersed a lot of the family. But we, Dad, Jean, Larry, Judy, Leslie, Marjorie, and me, were back at the Homestead. I had finally come home.

After Granddad asked my father to leave Pennsylvania and come back and run the Homestead, Ginny persuaded my father to hire Bobby to work for him.

The following winter, we had just finished eating lunch and Dad and Bobby decided to arm wrestle. At first my father beat him. Bobby didn't want to quit, not when he was losing. They ended up wrestling in the middle of the dining room floor. It went on forever. Even though my father had always been the cowboy and the family hero, Bobby was quick and agile. During the wrestling match he ended up throwing my father to the floor, and held down his shoulders. My father finally asked to be released, which leaked a stark silence into the room. As my father climbed up from the floor we knew it was the first time he had ever been beaten in his whole life. It was evident from the blank stare of disbelief on his face. Bobby continued working for us, but it was never quite the same.

When we moved to Milford Neck we lost touch with him. The rumor was that Bobby had gotten fed up with the Ballinger perfectionism, including that of his own wife. He was an orphaned child and had an insatiable need for love. We heard that he had run off with a 16 year-old baby sitter, leaving Ginny alone with her three children, two of which were Bobby's and one who was Frank's.

I never believed that Ginny was an easy person to live with. She seemed to have more of the Welsh temperament from her mother's side. At times she could be loud and demanding and a little on the rough side. I recall a number of occasions during which Bobby and Ginny would actually get into real fistfights.

WE USED THE HORSES for just one year at the farm in Barrington. Dad kept them at the rental farm until he sold them. During the summer we made hay and made hay and made hay. Dad almost worked Larry to death trying to pack that hay in that big loft by himself. My job was coiling the rope by the block and following the hay loader. Pappy Shuster drove the team for the hay, and Dad used the harpoon fork and unloaded it.

When we moved into the Homestead, Dad had a fellow come in and bale the hay. He pulled the baler with an old jeep. Sometimes Jean drove the truck and often she almost dumped it over. We all loaded the hay and brought it up into the barn and stacked it in the loft. We had no elevator and Bobby had to throw the bales up there. Larry was up in that loft stacking four and five bales high. He couldn't throw them up that high. He had to carry them up, and he built steps going up. It was so hot up in that loft. Jesus, God Almighty! Sometimes we had to carry them clear across the barn and then walk up with them. Stack em' up!!!

We made tunnels through the hay as we stacked and eventually we had tunnels ten feet below the top bale. Larry and I would dare each other to go in through the maze. Then we'd block off the openings. Larry thought he had killed me after he blocked it. He got scared and took the bale from the opening, and yelled "Raymie, Raymie, where are you? I'm really sorry. Please come out."

I was playing possum in the tunnels. I scared the hell out of him. It was thirty feet back into that hay, and ten feet deep. Larry scared the hell out of me too. We used to use the flashlights, until he dared me to go without one.

Jean was only twenty-four years old, with four of us and two new children of her own. Jean's priority was her own blood. Larry and I were just so damn lonely, and forced to do so much work.

I was back in Marlton School in a lower grade, with kids I didn't know. I would put my head on my desk and cry all the time. Beulah, Jean's aunt, had given me a book, *Beautiful Joe*, to read. The dog gets his ears cut off and then nobody wants him. He wanders around the village looking for an owner. Finally, this young boy keeps him in his playhouse, and doesn't tell anyone about Joe because he wasn't supposed to have a dog.

That whole year in school, all I would do is lift up my desk top and read that book and cry. I don't remember if I felt like the little dog or the boy or both.

The kids would poke fun at me, because they didn't know why I was crying.

WINTER'S END, LOFT EMPTY, only one small spot of misty moldy hay in the barn where the rain and snow blow through the cupola. Spring finally comes, sweet meadow lark. Spring of my youth.

Through the field I go, where my father is mowing and raking with teams. I smell the sweat of working draft horses.

Dad raises his cap and wipes his brow with a paisley handkerchief.

"Gee - up" he says.

Around they go like some carnival machine. Side-delivery rake rakes and turns the newly-mown hay. Dust rises. Under the morning sun the horses become important, a married team of sorrels with gold flaxen manes, wafting in the morning sun. Locusts put their sounds on a china plate, like coins chattering to one another, announcing the scorching heat. Around the men go, as they cut and mow, hacking down tall grasses, Indian grass, timothy, and clover. It falls, giving away, relinquishing, to a greater need, bowing down with the wind.

The wind row piles before the rake, stirring a bouquet of cured hay. Squeaking sounds of the rake, teeth and tines scraping along the bow-guide, chiming against random stones. Like the master spring of a clock, toiling time into seconds, and seconds into minutes, and minutes into hours, hours into days, and days into seasons.

Over and over through the wind-rows it rakes, making us aware, acutely aware, and keenly aware of time.

Morning time, sun disk intensifying, heating the earth, curing hay, emanating a potpourri of timothy and clover. Microcosms of the season become the salt on your lips, the sweat from my father's brow. Horses' lather profusely foaming, slippery froth, caught between harness and primal energies.

One with nature, the team corresponds with a snort, or the simple swish of their tails, wiping off greenheads, or blue winged flies. In the distance you could hear a rooster crow.

Cars pass by, watching the teams cradle life's harvest, sustenance for their winter, stacked away high in the loft, salted and stacked till icicles drop, till snow folds across the fields, and sleigh bells tell us that winter is face to face.

We heartily work to fill the great timbered wagon, a team of sorrels and grays pulling, pulling a caravan of wagon and loader. Raking and lifting, conveying it to the top, above the wagon stakes, floating, descending, questioning until it lands. Wagon, full to the sky, reaching with tongs to the top, topping it off, grabs it, stacks it higher, higher.

The overloaded wagon squeaks, grinds and crawls over the sandy soil as we load and load. Bolsters creak, horses strain with colossal strength pulled to the test, veins protruding.

"Gee - up there, hey, Gee-u-u-u-p" he screams to the team.

The first two dig in, each to each, over the swingle tree. Going with the lead, traces sap the sweat, taut as a razor strap, slithering across leg muscles.

Jerry and Doc slack.

"G-e-e-t up there, you red devils. Molly and Dolly are putting you to shame. Gee - up."

Onward they go. Doc curses his master. Jerry rubs his collar.

"It's alright," Doc reassures them. "It's okay. It's only a wagon of newly mowed hay."

Up to the barn we go. Marching. Ecstatic they are. Entering the driveway right into the loft, over the back ramp, above the dairy. Hooves echo from percussion planks.

"Whoa there, e-a-s-s-y Dolly. Unhitch the grays, bring them around, and drive them to the block. Larry, you drive. Raymie, retrieve the rope from the block. Alright, men, are you ready up there?"

Harpoon forks thrust deep into the load. God's piece of pie, rise, high, high. Here she comes, boys, watch for the trip rope. Salt her down, she's plenty green. Rising, like some phantom out of a heated underground, floating across the track on its trolley, traversing with tonnage to the back of the loft.

"There she blows!"

Like a great storm cloud, she parachutes, wind falling, vibrating, shaking the beams to their trunnels, clear to the peak. Right through the cupola she blows.

"Spread it around, boys, spread. Put her in her proper place. Larry, teams back from the tackle. Bring them back, son, bring them back."

Little boy, Raymie, wraps the rope around and around, coiling it like a sailor.

"Pull it back, till the block is empty."

Again the harpoon dives, as deep as God's eye, into the loaded wagon. Lifting, rising, pulling it onto the track, down to the far end, tripping dropping, heaving, twisting, turning, packing it.

"Don't slack, men. Don't slack."

Finally the wagon is empty. The Percherons are re-hitched.

"Back with you, Dolly, back. Out of here, Doc. Out."

Anticipation of fresh cool lemonade under a great buttonwood, reposing into a frozen image, like a grand painting. Under that shaded tree, the teams stand on one foot, like ballet dancers, suspended in time, tails stopped in motion from swatting flies.

Pitcher's empty, Grandmom's fresh orange cake devoured.

With one single stomp from the Belgian sorrel, and a high pitched squeal from the hog pens, stillness dissolves. Teams rise on all fours, as Jake spits black tobacco juice toward an amorous rooster. Down to the field we go, bouncing.

"Gee-up, girls. Come on Doc. Wake up. H-a-a-a, H-a-a! Move on there, you lazy devil!"

From a trot to an open gallop, teams float across the landscape. We bounce over culvert bridges and into the open meadow, where crickets warn us of the rising heat.

"Load the wagon, stack it tight, till the sun goes down and the day is night."

I WAS EIGHT OR NINE when Jake Greenberg came to the Homestead with a huge freight truck full of cattle, for my father to stock his dairy. They had brought the cows out of Wisconsin. There were some pure-bred Holsteins which included a set of twins. They had freighted them to Jake's farm in Woodstown and trailored them over to our place. Those twins had twins

as well, and one of the calves had gotten stomped on in the freight cars. The other twin had a bull calf that we butchered and a little black calf with a white star on her head, like a rose. Some of the cows belonged to my Granddad and Granddad gave me that calf, Rosie, for the start of my own herd.

Now I had my first cow and I raised her and showed her in the 4-H Club. She had milk veins the size of my wrist. Eventually I had calves from her and raised those

until I ended up with seven or eight cows when I went into the Navy.

We stocked the farm in Marlton with Holsteins. I watched Jake make a deal with my father. He had a white pad with a wire spiral on it. He took a pencil out of his pocket and he wet the pencil with his tongue, and he slowly wrote down $130,000. Then he slapped his palm against my father's. He carried my father for around $70,000 with just a handshake. My father put the paper in his top pocket and they walked away. They trusted each other and had done so through three generations of Greenbergs and Ballingers - Jews and rebellious Quakers. My father paid him money from the milk check every month until he had paid for all those cows.

Later, when we moved to Culpeper, Virginia, we bought our whole herd from the Greenbergs, a hundred and twenty head, but when we got down there we found they had Bang's disease, commonly called foot and mouth disease. You had to get rid of them all. We had to bulldoze a space in the back of the dairy farm. We limed it all down and we put the cows in there and shot them. God! It was a horrible sight to shoot those cows and run them into the pit. Good cows. I'm talking about cows that produced ninety thousand pounds of milk a year. My father called Jake up right away and Jake said, "Well, Raymond, what the hell are you going to do?"

Dad said, "God! I don't know. I still owe you about $60,000 on those cows."

He said, "That's alright, Raymond. When will you be ready for some more?"

Jake came back down and made good for all of those cows. My Dad picked another forty or fifty head to make up the difference and he kept paying the old payment.

THE ROCK GARDENS, the herb garden, the hydrangeas and the grapes and the fruit trees were my Grandmother's. Granddad had planted them for her and it was her yard and it was exactly how she wanted it. She'd cultivated and nursed those plants throughout the years, the perennials and the annuals. She did not want Jean or anyone else coming in there, and certainly Jean didn't know anything about planting.

Jean planted like a bull in a china shop. She went into Grandma's garden and decided to redecorate. She naively ripped out flowers that were practically ancient. They had made their homes for close to half a century in the rock gardens and in the flowerbeds. Jean started putting in her own more common marigolds and other mundane annual flowers and she destroyed those wonderful old perennials.

Grandmom was furious, and this time she had a good reason to be angry. She never forgave Jean until Jean had made her own garden many years later.

Grandmother had the power because she was the wife and the mother, and she was still living in the power side of the house. Granddad had always lived at the Homestead, except for the few years when he was in Philadelphia. Grandmother had raised her family there and made the Homestead hers. All of a sudden a new family was present with a new wife and new ideas. Their history was being ripped apart. There was so much change. The transition was very painful and very violating. My Grandmother did not want Jean telling her how to plant her flowers or how to use her cellar. All her canning and her pickling had been stored in the cellar, and now Jean wanted to put her eggs in there! They didn't have room for the eggs because the pickle barrels were down there and Jean wanted to throw the old aged barrels out. She didn't know what they were or understand the intrinsic value of aged objects. As with most new brides, she saw them as being in her way. The pickling barrels had been there for a century on the clay floors.

Granddad raised chickens in coops with his hens laying by the hundreds. They would line up on the fence. He had had them for years.

Jean bought eggs and chicks from an incubator and stuck them in and raised them heavy-handedly in a massive production line. She tried to get the laying hens to give her all the eggs they could in order to make her more money. She stored their eggs in the cellar because it was cool.

Within a year Jean had lost almost all of her chickens because they were so over bred that they became too delicate and couldn't take the cold weather. The white leghorns didn't have the stamina of Grandfather's old breeds.

It was a shock to move from Grandmother's world to Jean's.

"She could at least have waited till I moved out of here to plant those marigolds in my garden. What is the matter with that girl? Does she not have a head at all?"

Grandmother fought with Jean. She was harping on about bills to pay and drains that were going to be clogged and about cooking and canning, and every real and imagined infraction ending with,

"At least Clara knew how to do this. At least Clara could do that."

This of course was the same Clara who couldn't do a thing right for all those years. She had instantaneously forgotten her disappointment with Clara once Jean was standing there.

In frustration Dad threw a bucket of water on her. Ginny, not to be left out, took a clothing pole from the line and smacked Dad in the behind and on the back. I squatted down behind the lilac bush, watching everything and staying out of the way. They went on and on and on for about an hour and a half.

Both my father and my grandmother had that black Welsh temper. Ginny was just as bad. Granddad sat back under the wisteria porch and just watched the whole thing. He was too smart to get involved. It bothered him deeply. I think this is really why he had his second stroke.

They took him to the hospital and they brought him home in one of those crank beds. They put it in the den so that he could sleep on the first floor. Eventually they had to return the bed and he got a Morris chair where he could sleep sitting up. I would visit with him and we would lie down and listen to the radio. There was his big deer head in the den. Eventually he moved to Marlton and I could ride my red bike over to visit with him.

Every Sunday, after they moved out, he'd come over and he would be with us. He'd go into the barns and he'd talk to Jean. Grandpop was a peaceful man. It broke his heart to see his family breaking up and fighting. He was the one who had asked my father and Jean to come back to the Homestead. My father thought that Granddad should have been the one to manage Alice and govern the whole situation. Instead he accepted the role of a bystander.

When Dad had taken over the Homestead in 1948, it was not an easy transition for anyone. Grandmother Alice and Granddad had lived there since 1913. We had our first Christmas there in 1949. In 1950 the Shusters bought the adjacent Roberts farm. When Dad moved into the Homestead and was running the farm without his father there was no balance. A dairy farm has a different balance from a vegetable farm. When you truck farm you work seasonally, and you only earn money six months of the year. With dairy farming you work hard all year long, every day, but you also have income all year long. My grandfather had ten cows. My father had sixty.

The Homestead was too small for that size of a herd. Dad started renting additional farm land for feed. He put Ginny and Bobby at the Hemaline Farm, a fifty-five acre property. He also rented a few other hay fields. He was running himself ragged and constantly moving equipment around. That's when he decided to sell the Homestead. He had heard about another place in Milford Neck, Delaware with 900 acres including 400 acres of timber and a lot of swampland. He bought the place.

On March 18, 1952, Dad sold the Homestead. It had been in the Ballinger-Evans family for 281 years. During this time the Homestead was ripped apart. Everything in the attic, the perambulators, parasols, gowns, Quaker suits, children's toys from four generations, sleighs, carriages, antique family furniture, farm equipment and draft horses were disposed of in one week.

That spring our family moved to Milford Neck, Delaware. The house at Milford Neck looked like an Australian outback house with a porch running on three sides. However the Milford Neck house was even worse than the one in Lindell, and the one in Barrington. It had been used as slave quarters seventy-five years before, and it was a serious mess. The main farmhouse which we finally tore down was in worse condition than the slave quarters that we rebuilt.

Dad helped Jean fix it up. He built shelves and cabinets and he put in a partition between the dining room and the kitchen. He had bathrooms put in. At Milford Neck we had some sheep for a while and the Chincoteague ponies. We inherited an elderly black couple, John and Viola Townsend, who had once been slaves and who had worked for Mr. Carlyle, the previous owner. Their family graveyard was out beyond the horse barns.

There was a wine cellar below both of the potato barns that went down 12 feet into the ground. Carlyle had had vineyards in that whole front 100 acres. He had barreled red wine at the turn of the century. Old John Townsend would climb down into the cellar through the trap door and he would draw wine from the barrels. He would get so drunk he couldn't climb up the ladder. He would be down there for hours chanting slave songs that he had learned from his parents. Larry and I would hoist him out with a rope.

Viola raised herbs. I had thought they were just wild flowers that she was growing in all these pots. She would make tea, lineaments and salves. She kept an old stone pestle on the fireplace mantel, which she used to grind up the herbs and introduced me to the power of herbal medicine.

She told me "You have to keep the motion going from right to left and not reverse it because it won't work."

That's when I started doing the lawns. I could fool with a lawn all day long. I'd look in the window and see Jean watching the soaps, or hear her listening to them on the radio. I would sneak in and listen and then of course I would forget about mowing the lawn. Dad would say "Boy, you've been out here all afternoon, and you haven't mowed that lawn. What's wrong with you?" I'd be daydreaming.

Judy had her first date. The next year I had my first date with Wanda. I was fourteen. Jean took me to the roller skating rink. She told Dad that I had a right to go out with my friends. I needed that. Jean was really good about it. She told Dad that it was not fair not to let me out and then she asked me what I wanted to do. No one had ever given me a choice before. I wanted to go roller-skating and I went during milking time, and Dad didn't like that at all. Jean took me, and she had an argument with Dad about it. She picked up Wanda and she dropped us off. This was right after she started driving. I was ecstatic! I was out and I wasn't milking! I did that three or four times, and Jean did that with me, just with me.

After we moved into Milford Neck was the first time I actually helped Dad build. He taught me how to mix the mortar. I would carry it across in a bucket and load it on to his trowel while he mortared it between the cinder blocks. I felt like I was accomplishing something, watching those blocks rise. The building was big enough to push the feed carts down the aisle for the cows to get their silage.

Then he cut the rafters for the roof. This is when I learned what a bevel square was. He was just amazing. He could do everything in his head. Now I build the same way. With Dad we had an apprenticeship in farming, building, masonry, landscaping, cattle breeding and judging. I know we complained a lot, but now I think that we were lucky to have a father to teach us all of this. I just wish I could have learned in a kinder way.

Shortly after we bought Milford Neck, the lumber jacks descended, cutting out those 400 acres of timber which paid for the rest of the property. Dad ended up with over 550 tillable acres, where he had less than 150 acres from the Marlton place.

He had hired the lumberjacks to cut the timber off and load huge tractor trailers and big logging trucks. They brought in timber mules and they had lead horses, probably Percherons. They were big and white and the loggers rode them. Sometimes they'd pull too, but they would use the horses to lead the mules that were pulling the logs. They were hauling trees out of that wilderness for probably six or seven months.

Harry, the boy that was living in the other house on the farm in Milford Neck, and I became friends. Harry's family raised peanuts but I never saw them. Then I learned they are roots, like potatoes, and grow underground. Harry and I would play together, and we could really get into trouble.

We went down to the lumber camp and we told the men that we'd like to ride their two big white horses. They said, "Boys, if you pump water for all the mules every day, you can ride the white horses any time you like." They had about 12 or 15 big mules. Harry and I went back and we pumped water, and then we'd ride those big white horses.

My father had told us to stay away from the camp. The men were rough and they're drinkers, and they gambled. "You don't belong next to those people. If I catch you there, I'll whip you." Of course we went anyway, all the time. It was way back in the woods, and we'd hear them singing and rough housing and gambling and joking, and carrying on, and smoking. We thought that was really exciting and a real man's world. Then we would pump their water and ride their horses.

One night we forgot to put the pole up on the fence in the corral. We turned around about ten minutes later and looked back and all the mules were out following us as we rode the Percherons. We had about sixty or seventy acres of soybeans, and corn planted for the silos. Out those mules came and ran right into the soybean field and rolled all over the soybeans, forty whole acres of soybeans. They just destroyed them. Fifteen or twenty mules rolling around - let me tell you, that's a mess. They were rolling and eating and tearing them up and fighting with each other and carrying on. We couldn't get them in. Nothing we did worked. We just couldn't get them in. They were wild and they were glad to get the hell out. They'd probably been locked up every day and worked hard for months. Mules are ornery creatures anyway.

Quickly and quietly we put the horses back and put the bar up, and ran like hell back to our houses, like we hadn't even been out there. I went to bed quickly, and I heard my father screaming and yelling through the bedroom window, "What! What the hell are you talking about? Where's he now? "

Jean said "Quiet, Raymond, he's sleeping, he's in bed. He's got school tomorrow."

"Well, he'll have more than school when I get a-hold of him."

I was looking out of the window, listening to him.

The next morning I came down, and right after breakfast he said, "I think you know where you've got to go, boy." So I had to go to the woodshed. I took my pants down and I waited, and he whipped me so many lashes for lying to him and telling him that I didn't do anything. It hurt. I cried for hours and had sores on my back and my behind until I couldn't sit down.

Harry's father got on his ass as well.

But the lumberjacks were exciting, and they were fascinating. The trucks came in and out of there every day loaded full of huge logs, fifty or sixty feet long.

Dad was still a pretty good roper when we got those Chincoteague ponies in Milford Neck. Those ponies were wild. Their mothers had never been touched by human hands. Man, they would kick and bite. We drove the ponies into a corral down by the apple orchard. Dad told us we were going to break them. We figured that that old man was just talking and we waited to see if he could do it.

Dad pulled his hat down tightly down on his head and told us to herd the ponies around a couple of times in front of him. The dark one ran away from the rope bucking and kicking up her heels. Dad dropped the rope and then went for a second throw as we made the ponies pass by one more time. He knew what those horses were gonna do. He threw the rope right around that dark one's neck, just like he was back in the rodeo.

Larry and I were impressed when he wrapped the rope around the snubbing post and pulled the crazy pony in, until it was snubbed tight against the pole. My heart was pounding so hard that I could hardly breathe. The sun was hot and pouring down on us. The mare's baby foal kept calling to her. I didn't know whether to laugh or cry. We had these hard cavalry saddles then and Dad told Larry to put the saddle on her and then to hit the stirrup and jump into the saddle. I thought Larry was going to have a heart attack.

We had hackamores that we used to tighten the bridle around the nose instead of a bit. Larry was backing up. He was pretty sure he didn't want to do this. As soon as he put his foot in the stirrup Dad loosened the snubbing rope and that pony started bucking, and away she went around the corral. The other ponies had run under the shed. They didn't want any part of it.

Larry rode her around the ring, two or three times before she threw him. Dad caught her and mounted her, just like in those old cowboy movies, as quickly as she was moving. She finally bucked him off, but he had stayed on

271

her until she got pretty tired and rubbed him off against the fence post. He still had the reins in his hand. Then he asked me if I wanted to try. I was ready to pee my pants, and I said "No, I'll do it my way."

I tried riding a buckskin mare and I went a couple of rounds. She threw me off on top of a two by six at the corner of the barn. That beam caught me right in the ribs and took my breath away. I thought that I was going to die. I yelled, "Larry, I'm dying! Get a doctor!" I was sure I was really gonna die. I swear.

Dad thought this was the way to break a horse. It was how the cowboys out west used to do it with wild horses right off the prairie. These little Chincoteague ponies were worse than any wild prairie mustang. That brown mare continued to jump in the air all the time. She'd go three or four feet in the air and just knock you right over. Dad thought he lost his touch. After the iron stirrup hit him in the head, he decided it wasn't worth it. He had too many kids.

We got some more unbroken ponies from our vet, ol' Doc Grey. We would work with them two or three days, trying to calm them down. The young colts you could tame but the mares were too old. One of the mares had a beautiful red filly. I called her Rusty. I told Dad that I didn't want to break her spirit. He said I was just trying to be smart. I think I had a special affinity for her because we both had the same color red hair.

I kept her in the orchard and I used to give her apples on the way to the barn until she started to come to me when I whistled. I rode her without having to tie her up. Dad finally admitted that I did have my own way with horses. I didn't break her. I just schooled her pretty decently. Dad never had the patience. She was the best-trained pony we had.

I was in the seventh grade, and very good at sports. My teacher came over to see my father. He looked at the Chincoteague ponies and at our farm. He told Dad I was an extremely fast runner and talented in sports. He wanted me to be part of the sports team and told Dad again that it would be very good for me to do it. My Dad said, "There's just no way possible. I need him to help milk." So I couldn't do it.

The year that we sold the property I was in the eighth grade, and I was also failing math. If I didn't pass math I would be put back a year. My math teacher was the Principal, Mr. Grady. Mr. Grady came out to the farm and saw how I could build and how I did things, and said, "I don't understand how a boy like you, who's so logical, and so constructive, would have trouble with math." Then he started talking to me and found out that I had been moved from school to school. When you get behind in math, you can't get caught up. If you miss the fundamentals of math, you lose math forever. Mr. Grady tutored me on the side. Here was the Principal, on his own time, teaching me geometry.

He asked, "You love art, don't you?"

I said, "Yes."

He said, "Do these drawings. Now, if you're going to measure from here to here, and go from here to here on this cone or this diamond, how far is it from there?"

I said, "I don't know."

"Well, this is how we do it," He showed me the Pi square, the square root, and the basics of geometry. I loved it because it was art.

Dad should have learned some lessons from Clara, but that house in Milford Lake was still a wreck, and he was still having children. The difference was that this time he had a willing partner. Jean had already proven to him that she would work along with him. I remember her re-finishing old chairs and tables for the dining room. From the time that she married him, all she wanted to do was be with him. When she wasn't working in the house or taking care of us children, she would work in the fields late in the evening when we were trying to get in the last of the hay. She'd drive the tractor while my father was hauling hay.

Jean was twenty-three-years-old with someone else's kids. When she met my father she didn't know how to boil water. I don't think it was so much a sense of adventure as it was very important to Jean to make her marriage work and to build her own life from the start. For Clara, that just wasn't her priority.

Clara was a selfish, self-centered person and her biggest priority was herself.

GRANDDAD WAS VERY POPULAR and well liked in the town. When he died at the age of 61, we went to the viewing in Medford. I couldn't figure out why all those cars were lined up throughout Medford or why everybody wanted to see my Grandfather lying in his coffin. We could hardly get into the funeral parlor. He had established friendships with so many people and had done so much community service. I was emotional and upset anticipating what it was going to be like. Larry and I were the only ones allowed to go to the viewing.

I tried to crawl into the coffin. I couldn't help it. This was the first time I'd ever seen a dead person. I couldn't imagine him dying. My father was embarrassed and tried to comfort me and pull me away from the coffin. I kicked and screamed, and told my father it was his fault. Larry tried to help my father pull me away.

Larry and I were not allowed to go to the funeral because we had to milk the next day. I loved my Granddad. He had been my savior. After my mother left I felt that I had no one except for him. He'd take his engraved penknife out of his pocket and break a grain of corn off of an ear and with the knife he would open up that single grain of corn in the palm of his hand and hold it up to the sun. Lowering his hand, he would show me that it pulsed like a Mexican jumping bean. Looking me straight in the face, he would say,

"This is the secret of life, son, here in my palm. Your heart beats the same way, as does mine, and all humans on earth, all animals, birds, fish, every living thing. It all has a right to be here. It's all part of the design of our universe."

My grandfather loved me and nurtured me. When he died, it broke my heart.

I HAD BECOME A SHILL FOR OUR RACING SCAM. I had Rusty, my pony, and Larry had Dusty, a brown bay mare. Larry harnessed his colt and was driving him all over the place with a little express wagon. I tried it with Rusty, but she didn't want to cross the cornfield with the damn thing. As soon as she heard it behind her, she flew into the air, and I flew into the cornfield. They all laughed at me driving across the cornfield with that wagon going two or three feet off the ground. I almost killed myself.

Dusty ate the dirt from the grass roots and that bogged him down and it killed her. Dad let Larry buy a retired black racehorse. The neighborhood boys would come over with their horses and we would ride together and make bets. They would start on Larry and ask him where he got that scraggy ugly old horse. Larry would answer,

"Well, she used to be a racehorse, but she's not really very good right now."

The boys would study her. "She doesn't look like she runs very fast to me."

"Well, listen, if you want to put your money where your mouth is, that's fine with me."

Often, I would do the talking." That horse can beat you! She'll beat any horse in the county!"

"Bullshit." Then the kid would offer ten dollars on his horse and say he could whip us.

Larry would go across the cornfield and of course the minute he would get the horse lined up in the field she would think she was back at the gate at the race track. By God, she'd break out of that line as soon as you said 'Go" and slapped your hands. That horse would bury the competition!! She'd come across those cornfields that were rough and plowed, and man, she'd just bury them! She'd be gone down the road half a mile, while the other horse was just starting out!

We'd go around the neighborhood looking for any fool who had a horse. We'd do a whole show! We'd come on real slow and easy and say, "She's really an old horse. She really isn't that good, you know" and we'd make bets.

I'd plead to give her a little head start and of course they'd say sure. Then Larry would pitifully cut in, "No, we don't need a head start. I'll be okay." The horse would just be hanging out, as calm and sway backed and lazy and easy going as can be, like an old retired fighter. We'd make a line in the dirt. Soon as you slapped your hand, that horse wouldn't let anybody get ahead of her. She'd run like a son-of-a-gun. The only thing that stopped us was that word got around that the horse was better than she looked. We had made a heap of money by that time.

Late July, Larry and I were putting in fence posts. I was just learning how to drive the truck. My collie, Beauty, used to lie under the wheels to keep cool. I had raced Larry to get there first so I could drive and pull the truck up. I wasn't looking, and I ran over her. I was devastated. She didn't die right away. She ran out in that south field, where the Sedan grass was, and I laid there with her as she was dying, petting her and telling her how sorry I was. She was really my dog. I had taught her how to herd the cows for me. Grandmom was visiting, and I left the field and locked myself in my hot bedroom crying the rest of the day. Grandmom came up and tried to comfort me. It felt like the old days when Larry and I were living with her at the Homestead. She would comfort me when I had bad dreams to calm me down. I didn't want to drive after that.

While we were living in Milford Neck, I was raped. A guy, Tracy, who was living and working on the property, cornered me in the hay loft.

I think that somehow I was vulnerable. This guy saw in me some vulnerability. I think he recognized in me that I was ready to let go of something. I felt, I think that if I did bad things and I let bad things be done to me, that I would be one of the armored bad people. I would be free of the burden of protecting Paradise.

This was a turning point for me.

"See how bad I am. I let that son of a bitch rape me. I didn't even fight him."

I didn't. I didn't fight him. I let him do it. Then I went out behind the barn. I bled and I cried. "You see. Now I'm bad like you are. Now I'm like all of you."

I cried in the tub for hours, and only Judy asked me if I was alright. I just stayed in the tub and cried, and washed and washed and washed.

I could never wash it off.

It was the dirtiest thing, the ugliest thing.

I was very confused. I didn't really want to be bad. I didn't want to be like them. I didn't want to be part of that world.

I receded to get back into myself again.

After I lay in the tub for hours and hours I finally came out dressed in all white clothing. Nobody even noticed.

Although it was never mentioned, I often wonder if Dad knew. Tracy just disappeared. Immediately afterwards, Dad encouraged us get our Tennessee Walkers.

When Larry and I bought our Tennessee Walkers I was in the eighth grade. We paid for them with most of our own money. We had been breaking the Chincoteague ponies and had been paid fairly well. After about a year and a half, Dad asked us if we would like to sell our ponies. He knew a man in Pennsylvania who dealt in Tennessee Walkers. If we got a decent price for our ponies, we could buy a couple of Walkers. We were very excited about the idea because we loved Dad's Tennessee Walker, Chief Allen, that everybody was so impressed with.

One day in late August a large tractor trailer came driving up our road. Dad went out and greeted the man who had about ten or eleven Tennessee Walking Horses in his truck. This is where the fun began. Larry and I brought our saddles and bridles out while the man unloaded two of the horses. One was a strawberry roan with a white bald face. She was about sixteen hands high and real pretty, but she had a mind of her own. Larry threw a saddle on her. He liked her because she was the color of Chief. He got on her, rode around the orchard a bit and when he came back to the truck with her, he was very pleased.

Then, it was my turn. The man had brought out a young black gelding, satin black with a thick mane and tail. I was really impressed with him. He reminded me of the Island Stallion from Walter Farley's book. I girthed up my old army saddle, put a bridle on him and mounted. He handled very gently. I hadn't ridden a Walker very much, only my father's stallion when I was very young. The gelding had a large over-stride. For some reason, I felt he was more like a merry-go-round horse and not much of a challenge.

Throughout that afternoon, I think we tried all ten horses. Larry was set on the strawberry roan with the bald face. The last horse I took out was a fancy little chestnut mare with a white mane and tail and a couple of white socks. She had a white star in the center of her forehead. When I tried to put the saddle on her, she became very spirited.

I loved the life in her, but I was a little bit awkward because I wasn't used to her. Dad mounted and lifted me up in front of him. The mare was neck reined and she stepped out real fancy lifting her feet high in the air. She arched her neck tucking her chin in and raised her tail like a peacock. Dad and I sailed down that half-mile driveway like we were on air. When she got to the end, she didn't want to turn around and come back.

Dad just heeled her a little bit and we went back down the driveway to the truck. I was in love! Dad dismounted. The man laughed and said, "She's a nice little mare. She's your horse." After a little horse dealing and that's how I bought Stardust.

Larry's strawberry roan never seemed controllable. She wouldn't cross the bridge off the property. That next week, she jumped clear over a puddle of water and threw Larry to the ground. Larry was a great rider, but he just didn't get on with her. The following Monday, another horse dealer came with an empty truck to pick up our four Chincoteague ponies. It was so painful to part with my little sorrel mare, Rusty. I had trained her and ridden her by myself. She whined to me on the way down the driveway to the truck and then I decided I didn't want the Tennessee Walker. I wanted Rusty back. It was too late, I had agreed to it.

As for Larry, after two or three more throws into the mud puddles, Dad was convinced that he needed another horse. He called the horse dealer back, and again he appeared with five or six horses on a late Sunday afternoon. Larry tried three of them. The one he liked the most was a large dark liver-colored chestnut with a white blaze, two white socks and a black mane and tail. She was huge. Her name was Lady Chance. For Larry, she was a fine horse. She was quiet and sound, but had a lot of spirit, and man, she could run.

My horse's name became Stardust, from the star on her forehead. Larry and I rode our horses for hours, most evenings, weekends, and moonlit nights. We rode them over the entire countryside, all over Delaware and later from Culpeper and Brandy Station, to the beginnings of the Blue Ridge Mountains.

I kissed my first girl on Stardust. We'd take girls to the drive-in movies on our horses. Leaning back on our saddles and watching the movie, usually a Western, our horses pastured on the drive-in grass. When the horses on the silver screen whinnied, our two horses whinnied back. You could hear the people in their cars, laughing.

After we moved to the farm in Culpeper, Virginia, during the summer of those two high school years, and up until I enlisted in the US Navy, I herded cattle on Stardust on those 200 acre hay fields in the back of the barn. She was my best friend.

That whole winter of 1953 we didn't have to milk, because Dad had sold Milford Neck. Our cows were sold with the farm. We stayed in Milford Neck for a while until we went to Culpeper. I played sports for the first time and Larry and I rode horseback almost every day. We left Milford when I was in the eighth grade and I was just getting ready to graduate. I finished the eighth grade in Culpeper and failed because I couldn't make the transition. I never graduated from high school because I went into the Navy. I finished high school when I got out of the service and took an equivalency test. I never graduated from anywhere.

I LOVE THE SMELL OF THE ANIMALS, the smell of the cattle, the smell of the feed and the hay from the loft, the smell of fresh milk, and the smell of lime and manure in the gutters. These smells are all encapsulated for me in the barn. The sounds come back to me very easily and I think of those days and those times and those moments. The birds and the rooster crowing, the cattle calling to each other, the men talking to the animals while graining down the chickens, feeding the sheep or taking care of the geese and the ducks. These sounds were integrated into the symphony of farm life. It was what life was, and how it was going to be. There was a satisfaction. There was just something very pleasurable about fitting into the harmony of things.

In the evening, as I would walk toward the barns from the house, I could hear the chugging hollow hum that reverberated from the boiler room through the milk house door. The vacuum compressor (milking machine) was a very recent luxury for most farmers. It had eliminated most of the hand milking, and was cleaner and a lot more efficient. Before leaving the milk house it was a common practice for everyone who passed for the first time that day to taste at least one cupful of fresh milk as it flowed down out of the pouring trough and over the rippled frozen surface of the aerator.

You could catch it with your empty cup after it had saturated the icy coils, transforming the body heat of the milk into an almost freezing temperature.

I can still taste and feel the un-separated cream, as the ice cold milk passed through my lips and down into my throat. If you drank it too fast, it would make your head ache from the cold.

I would enter the barn through the milk house and smell the freshly cut corn silage that my father was so carefully measuring out to each cow. When I walked through the barn toward my father the cows would simultaneously turn their heads in the stanchion and stare, as though they were being operated as one single puppet from a string. If you were familiar and they recognized you, they would immediately go back to chewing their food, or blowing hot air over it in order to sniff out the full grains of corn. If the feed cart had not yet reached them, they would stomp their feet in anticipation, leaning and rocking with the full weight of their shoulders against the stanchion.

It's very hard to imagine just how much food and liquid a dairy cow can consume. Our Friesian Holsteins after calving and during their first three months of lactation could produce an average of 80 to 90 pounds of milk per day. If their body weight was between 1400 and 1600 pounds, they could consume at least 50 to 60 pounds of dry food or grass in a single day and drink an average of 10 to 11 gallons of water.

I knew that the water consumption figure was correct. I had spent many hours hand pumping water for our dry cows, heifers, and breeding bulls. They came up from the pasture to an adjoining field. The only available water was from a large hand pump that fed into a hundred and ten gallon cement trough built alongside of an old well. I could fill this trough up multiple times a day.

DAD AND LARRY WENT DOWN TO CULPEPER in the beginning of March, 1953, to set things up and to buy a new herd of cows. Shortly after the new cows were delivered, Dad left Larry to milk. Larry slept in our new home, an old stately mansion with no heat turned on. Dad had also forgotten to buy groceries for Larry. The next day, Mr. Wahl came by and took Larry into town and bought him some food.

Two days later, we packed a large moving van full of our furniture and belongings from Milford Neck. Leslie and I rode in the back of the moving van. Six hours later, we arrived at our new Culpeper farm.

Brandy station, used in the Civil War, now belonged to the Ballingers, Mr. Wahl so kindly stated. He did not mention snow. When Leslie and I climbed out of the back of the van all we could see was white. "I thought it wasn't supposed to snow in Virginia," our driver said. He was a cowboy from West Virginia and had played Hank Williams country songs on the truck radio all the way down there.

My Dad had driven back up to Milford Neck to get Jean and the younger kids. Larry had never been so happy to see Leslie and me. The first thing he asked was "Have you eaten yet?" Then he took Leslie and me and showed us the barn. It was an amazing building. We had never seen anything like it. It was a hundred and twenty feet long and forty feet wide, with a tall hip roof built like a church on the inside of the loft.

"My God," I thought. "Are we really going to have to fill this with hay?"

"Sixty thousand bales," Larry said.

Larry hadn't started the daily milking yet. There was another young man there helping Larry, Earl Bailey.

In two months I would be fifteen. Larry had just turned seventeen and Leslie was nine.

By the time Dad had arrived with Jean and the rest of the kids, the moving van was completely unloaded.

On April 1, 1953, hurricane Hazel hit. She began about four o'clock in the afternoon with a rain storm. By the next morning, she had lifted a large four-foot- wide willow tree trunk right out of our backyard and torn a part of our machine shed roof off where our Tennessee Walking Horses had been stabled.

Stardust had gotten hysterical in the night. I could hear her above the wind in my bedroom. As the hurricane progressed she kicked at the door and the sides of the stall. I took a flashlight and checked on her, climbing over debris from the storm. Larry's mare, Lady Chance, was a little calmer.

The following day, Dad kept us out of school to help clean up. We cut, split and hauled as many cords of wood as we could carry to the porch and the rest we stacked along the archway that went from the summer kitchen to the main house. At the end of the day we had thirty-five feet of wood, stacked three feet high. This was just the beginning of what our life was going to be like at this farm.

In Culpeper, Larry and I would go out into the barn to throw in the hay. The cows would nuzzle the hay and push it out of the manger in order to get to the seeds and the head of the timothy or the alfalfa grain. They would then throw the bulk part and the stem into the walkway. When you're throwing in the hay for one hundred twenty cows, it's a lot of hay!

It was not the work that Larry and I liked, but it was the excuse that it afforded us to get out and sit on a couple of bales in the back where it was warm. We often had to open the windows because of the body heat of those cows, even when it was only ten degrees outside.

There could be a frost on the windows. Sometimes we would take a buffalo nickel and make buffalos all along the window with the frost on the windowpane. You could smell the cattle moving in their stanchions. At nighttime there was a peaceful quietness about the barn, with the jingling of the stanchions and the cows moving their feet from side to side. Sometimes you'd hear a cow peeing, like a leaking faucet. You knew you were in a large embodiment of life.

Larry and I would call back and forth from each aisle to one other and talk. By the time we'd got to the end we'd sit on a couple of bales and lean against the cool back wall. We would talk about our deepest and most vulnerable feelings, our girl friends, our grades, and our futures.

When I think back of my best times spent with Larry, it's always in the barn.

My father would come out and say, "What the hell are you boys doing out here?"

Then he would join us and start talking with us. We'd three end up sitting and sharing. In the comfort of the cows we would confess to each other the things that we felt about life, surrounded by the sounds of life. You didn't feel obligated to be doing anything more.

At the dining room table we were required to report on our day. In the barn we could say what we really felt. We would speculate on getting married and who we would become. I asked Larry if I would ever be famous.

"Sure," he replied.

"How famous?"

"About as famous as Arthur Godfrey!"

Larry and I worked like full-grown men the whole time we lived in Culpeper. We each did the work of two men, working in the fields and milking that hundred and twenty head of Holsteins. School days, I had to milk my sixty head of cows each morning, clean up and shave, have my breakfast, go to school, fall asleep in classes, come home at three, throw down silage and milk my sixty head again before dinner. Then I would attempt to do my homework. The only easy thing I did was fall asleep. This continued seven days a week, 365 days a year. I was never as happy as the day I left for the Navy.

PART X

Larry Ballinger 1951–1957

LARRY WITH FOX HOUND PUPS

Larry Ballinger

GRANDDAD WAS SIXTY-ONE when he died in 1952. Grandmother Alice was sixty-six when she passed in 1959.

Granddad's tool room was behind the house, set off from the driveway. He kept his tool trunk and the woodworking tools and all of his leather working equipment, including a big old sewing machine. He had a two foot tall coffee grinder that sat at the west end. We used it to grind corn for the horses and make chick mash for our banties.

The shop was built for our farmhand Jake and he lived there the entire time. He had a bed, a hand pump, and a pot-bellied stove. He had his main meals at the house in the kitchen where Grandmom used to keep her pies.

The night that Granddad died we were in Delaware and we had milked real early, about one or two o'clock. Dad wouldn't let us go to the funeral that next day. I went out and got stuck with the tractor and I threw a fit when I got back.

From that time on, we milked all of the cows. That's when Dad had the big herd. After Bobby quit, from that time on, Raymie and I did all the milking, seven days a week, three hundred sixty five days a year, clear up until we both left Culpeper. Raymie carried the milk and stripped the cows and washed them off and put the belts on them. I ran the milkers.

Bobby used to call Dad at seven o'clock to wake him up. One time they were hand wrestling and Bobby wanted to show Dad karate. Dad said it didn't matter, he could handle him anyway. Bobby swung with a karate movement and Dad grabbed him solidly, after which Bobby stuck his leg between my father's and twisted Dad to the floor. Then he climbed on top of him and held him down at the shoulders like the wrestlers did on TV at that time. Dad got a little bit hot. Bobby had gotten the best of him. He was a wiry little devil.

After Granddad died, Grandma took her money from that Medford bank and put it in a bank near where she lived. When she came back from visiting us in Culpeper she decided to sell her house in Marlton. She moved to Collingswood near Aunt Ruth, to a second floor apartment.

Grandmother Alice died a horrible death. Her blood would thicken. They said it was something that they would see in other states, but not in New Jersey. They wanted to know if she had traveled to other countries, but she never had. She probably never went out of Jersey more than a few times. When they took her to Cooper Hospital, they said they couldn't admit her because she didn't have insurance. She had the money to pay, but the hospital still didn't want her without insurance. Finally they took her to Our Lady of the Woods Hospital. Of course, Grandmom was dead set against Catholics, and that's a Catholic hospital, but they accepted her and treated her well and they did everything they could.

They treated her best they knew how, but she had multiple blood clots and she was bedridden. She just looked like a cow that was ready to have a calf. She had internal bleeding and they kept pouring blood into her. Then she would be bled once a month. She was in the hospital for a long time before she died.

The doctors had said they could operate and take one of those clots out to save her life except her heart was damaged and she wouldn't survive the operation. She just laid there and died inch by inch. She lost her hearing and she lost her speech. It was terrible. Today she would have lived with simple blood thinners.

We stayed in Marlton until we moved to Milford Neck. I went through the last half of the sixth grade, the seventh, and half of the eighth grade before we moved to Culpeper. I had missed so much school working, that my little sister Judy and I ended up in the same sixth grade.

Living in Milford Neck was very special. Those months between selling Milford Neck and buying Culpeper were the only time I didn't work. I had a girl friend, Janet. I had Mr. Grady as my math teacher. He got me straightened out. For the first time in my life I got to learn.

When I finished the eighth grade in Milford, I was sixteen. I had to quit school. Dad said I didn't need an education if I was going to milk cows. I regret worse than anything that I didn't go back to school. I should have run away and gone.

I wanted to farm and I took Dad at his word. He promised to pay me this, that, and the other thing which he never did. Dad could wiggle his way around and get me to do just about anything he wanted me to do.

When I got married all that changed.

Dad sold our herd to the man who bought Milford Neck. He sold everything. He didn't take nothin' but his tools. I went with him to Culpeper and to a sale at Leesburg, Virginia, where he bought six Guernsey cows and some surge bucket milkers.

I didn't know that he had already made arrangements with Greenberg about more cows, and certainly not about another sixty head.

The next day when Greenberg brought the cows down they were stopped at the state line by the weigh station across the Potomac River and kept there all day. They claimed the papers weren't right. Finally they had to release them. Greenberg threatened to turn them in to the SPCA. They finally got things straightened out and brought the sixty head into Culpeper.

There wasn't anybody there but me, by myself, for three days milking the cows. Dad had left me with a brand new John Deere tractor that I had never been on in my life and a barn full of sixty cows and I had to stay there and milk those cows and clean the barn by hand with a shovel behind the cows, because I couldn't turn them out and get them back in by myself.

Raymie stayed in Milford Neck and played basketball.

Dad had left me to go back to get the family and the furniture. When he left me there for those three days, Mr. Wahl, the realtor, was supposed to come and get me, but he forgot I was there and he didn't get me for breakfast or nothing.

I was just sixteen with a brand new herd of cows and a new tractor with nothing to eat but I had a hell of a lot of fresh milk to drink. Doc Anchors came over and took me to his house for breakfast. I hadn't had supper the night before and hadn't had any breakfast that morning. It was almost dinner time and I was about starved to death.

I stayed there in that big old house by myself. There was no heat and I slept on the floor on an old horse blanket.

It was along about two o'clock that next day that Mr. Wahl finally showed up.

"Boy, I forgot about you."

He wanted to take me then. I was so mad I wouldn't go with him. Doc Anchors started bringing food over for me to eat. He lived on the hill next to Brandy Station. Doc finally wound up buying that old confederate camp and the Brandy Station Battlefield where General Lee had made his encampment with his troops.

Earl Bailey helped out a little on the farm. He carried milk but he helped very little with the milking. Raymie threw the silage down, a lot of it, and I fed it to the cows. At first Dad would come out and give the cows grain once in a while. He'd come out at seven o'clock when we were finishing up and then go back and eat breakfast. Then it got to the point where he didn't come out at all.

In the evenings I did it all. During the day, Dad did the plowing, disking, harrowing, harvesting and field chopping. Mornings, Raymie would go in and shave, wash, and have his breakfast and go to school. I had to go back out there and work. I usually had to shovel that barn out by myself.

Raymie and I had our Tennessee Walking Horses, Chance and Stardust. We would take them out in the fields and watch the cows chew on the alfalfa. We would make the horses rear up and take off like they done in the Westerns. We were jumping on them from the back and running and jumping on them from the sides. Once my horse wheeled around and there was a cow where she shouldn't be and she threw me off backwards and I sprained my wrist. Judy had to come out and dump the milkers for me, because we didn't want Dad to know. We just went because we had to get the hell out. We'd take our horses and go, Raymie and I, without any supper. We'd ride until one o'clock at night, just to get out.

Dad went up to New Jersey with Jean to Pappy's. We had to get a whole field of hay up while he was gone. He'd cut it down and it rained there a little bit and I had to rake it and we were supposed to bale it. We got part of it baled and it started raining again and we never did get it up. He raised hell about that. Of course, he was gone the whole time.

Then I had the mess with Earl. We went to the movies, and Knut Lindsey's sister was there, and Earl Bailey, he wanted to follow her. I didn't actually do anything. I was just riding with him. When we come out of the movies, she came out too. All we did was just follow her home and she got scared. She had his license number and turned it into the police. The police came and got Bailey, and then of course Bailey's Daddy came and told Dad. Dad didn't stop to ask whether Bailey did it or I did it. He just blamed me. I didn't lie to him. I sure didn't. He just got angry 'cause I was in it. I was part of it, you know. He beat me for it.

I stayed away that night and all the next day. I slept in that old barn over at Doc Anchor's. If I could have gotten my money and had a way to leave I would have. That Bailey chickened out on me. We were going to take off. He didn't have the backbone to go. I would have too, then. I was fed up with the whole mess.

Dad never liked anybody we were with. He didn't like our best friends, the Peters. He said they weren't nothing but common trash. Mary, the sister, came down there one time for dinner and said something innocently. He said it was disrespectful. "If you couldn't find any better friends than that, you'd be better off without any." They were fine people.

He didn't like Frank Peters. He said he was a "gigolo." Can you imagine? That's exactly what he called him. I don't know what was wrong with Dad, but nobody was good enough. I went to Tennessee with Morris and Frank Peters. At nineteen years old, it was the first and only vacation I ever had in my life. I went deer hunting for three days. We left late on a Friday night and hunting season opened on Monday. We came back on Tuesday.

While I was there I met Maxine. She was staying with Morris Peter's aunt. Her daddy had died when she was little. After meeting Maxine and coming home I told Morris I was going to marry her. Maxine thought I was the ugliest thing that ever was. Before I left I asked her, "Would you mind if I wrote to you?" She answered my letters.

That next Christmas Maxine wanted me to come down to visit. She was in a Christmas play at their church in Dungannon, Scott County, Virginia, right down at the Tennessee and Kentucky border, just a little country town. She was still staying with Morris's aunt. She wanted me to come down to the Christmas play and Dad wouldn't let me go. At Easter I was supposed to have visited and he wouldn't let me go again. I packed my clothes to leave.

He said, "If you leave boy, you're not coming back. Just forget anything you've got here. Just don't come back."

So, I didn't go. And she quit writing to me. She got mad.

I worked like a dog. One night I was out there plowing, back there in that field towards the inlet, at twelve o'clock at night. I fell asleep on the tractor. I just happened to run up between two cedars and their brushes hit me in the face and woke me up. The front end of the tractor went clear through the fence.

Occasionally I got to go off with Morris and double date. I saw Betsy Figgins. Dad didn't like her either. He never did like anybody I was with. I don't know what was wrong with him.

PART XI

Culpeper 1953–1957

RAYMOND AND JEAN BALLINGER, 1953

Dad, Raymond Ballinger

I THINK THAT SELLING MILFORD NECK was my biggest mistake. Soybeans were first coming into their own. We could have been very profitable just growing soy beans and a little corn. The profits wouldn't have been all used up for new cows, machinery, and new buildings. We could have had a house elsewhere and just used the land.

I did well and went down to Culpeper and paid $80,000 for that farm. I didn't have to do any rebuilding. Washington DC was the best milk market in the United States.

I also made money when I sold Culpeper, but not that much.

I got a lot of kick out of buying those other two places, especially Kenton. I did a mess of work up there. I rebuilt it and put up silos and augers and the house. I had made a little money out of those later moves. They were all nice farms. Every farm I've ever owned became a nice farm.

I sold Culpeper right after Raymie left for the Navy thinking that Larry was going to leave as soon as he got married. It was going to be too much for me to handle.

I had my own dreams and I wanted my sons to have my dreams too. That was my mistake. I had no right to dream their dreams.

Raymie, Raymond Evans Ballinger

WE MOVED TO CULPEPER when I was fourteen. Larry was eighteen and Judy was sixteen and becoming a young woman. Marjorie was seven and Skippy was four and Nancy was around six months old. My father was in his prime in his late thirties. My stepmother had reached her prime as a woman and had gotten used to living with Dad and had learned how to move around and get what she needed in life. Culpeper was big and beautiful. There was an ice house next to the tool shop with wild grapes growing overhead. We had

a horse barn and an old dairy barn that my father converted to a kennel for his fox hounds. A huge irrigation pond was where the cows waded, and the driveway was about half a mile long with split rail fences on both sides.

It snowed heavily that March when we arrived. We had everything we owned, including ourselves, in the back of a huge eighteen wheeler. Gray and misty snow was covering the ground. The echo of the snow blowing and reverberating against the Blue Ridge Mountains was all we could hear.

When we arrived we saw Larry who had been left there waiting and then my father appeared. Our first night was spent at the Wahl's home. The next day we unpacked and our horses arrived. The house was really big and you could easily get lost on the property.

We already had so many cows and then Dad bought another herd from Jake Greenberg with Bang's disease. The following summer we had a hurricane that created another mess.

That summer, we had a dry season that made the farm like a desert. It was a hundred and ten degrees in the shade. The cows wouldn't eat grass so they didn't give much milk and our milk production went way down. Larry had to quit school and my father was worried. The baler broke because the hay was so dry and dusty. Then Dad lost his puppies. They just ran off. Next the water ran low and now we were worried about running out of water.

I started milking as soon as I arrived. I was getting very tall and equally skinny. I wasn't doing well in school and was failing almost everything until the girls started helping me and doing my homework. I was falling asleep in classes. After milking a hundred twenty head in the morning and at night with Larry while I was supposed to be doing homework, I'd fall asleep at the dinner table. Then we would go to bed and I'd get up and fall asleep in classes after milking. It went on and on and it never stopped.

We were laborers and poor ones at that, because we were always tired and rundown. My father was under so much financial pressure that he kept pushing us all.

I had bought Stardust only six months before we moved from Milford. We didn't even know that she was pregnant. She came out of Tennessee where they breed their jack donkeys to horses. They cut a lot of timber down there, and they used these mules to drag the logs out of the woods. There was always a shortage of mules and they loved the Tennessee Walking Horse mixes, because they were well-tempered and moved smoothly. In April, Stardust started bagging up and she had the colt a month later.

I was so excited that she was having a foal right around my birthday. Dad woke me up that May morning and said, "You'd better get up, boy. You've got yourself a Tennessee Walking mule colt."

There in the corral was the cutest foal. I refused to believe that it was a mule. I was just so happy to have it.

"Why did you tell me it was a mule? That's not a mule! It's just a long-eared horse."

The colt was about two months old and I used to let him run alongside while I rode his mother. I got to visiting friends that lived on the other side of the highway and I was afraid of the colt getting hit by a car. Even though he stayed pretty close to Stardust, he was getting old enough and more confident on his own and he would stray. I decided it would be best to lock him in the box stall while I rode. One day I came back from hard riding and I put the colt out in the corral with his mother while she was still a little overheated. I had walked her to cool her down, but too much exercise heats and curdles the milk. This was something that I didn't know and neither did Dad.

The colt drank the milk, and it twisted his intestines and he died. I cried my eyes out. Two of my girlfriends drew me a card, and sent it to me, of a little mule kicking a bucket. It said, *We are so sorry, and hope you feel better in your hours of distress, Love, Linda and Mary.*

Culpeper was the turning point in my life. We were given all the work to do and left alone to do it. Earl and Larry would clean out the barns during the week. On weekends when Earl was off, Dad made me do it. We used to come out fighting and yelling." Don't splash that shit on me!" Larry and I did a ton of work on that farm.

Dad began having a lot of trouble with Jean. Once Jean got in the car and locked herself in. She had packed her suitcases and was going to leave. Dad talked her out of it. He threatened to bust a window in the car and everything else.

Because of the drought that summer of 1953, the corn tasseled out before it reached two feet. The rye and wheat didn't grow more than a foot from the ground. We had spent a lot of money planting soybeans in the south field for extra profit. By August there were just sprinkles of soybeans here and there in that desert-like field. That big irrigation pond where the cows used to drink was nothing but mud. We had to lock them out to keep them from drinking the muck. The front fields had only two to four inches of hay, nowhere near enough for the winter feeding.

Dad kept telling Larry and me, "By God, we're going to go bankrupt if we're not careful."

He said that he didn't have any money to pay the bills that month. I was worried and I was looking out through the stairway watching him sitting at that roll-top desk through the whole night trying to figure out how he could make ends meet.

Dad finally got a loan from the Culpeper National Bank, paid off his debts, and when he got halfway straightened out he up and sold out.

We worked hard there and we didn't have any time for play. We hadn't had a break since we left New Jersey except for those few months between Medford and Culpeper.

JEAN'S CHILDREN WERE GOING TO SCHOOL with all this fancy clothing and their lunches packed. She would kiss them goodbye as I stood there watching.

One day Jean sat down on the lawn and had Marjorie read to me. As a young boy my mother had always read to me and I would read to her and I read very well. When she left, I stopped reading. I refused to read. When I got a little bit older I had a teacher, Mrs. Melvin, who read to us The *Last of the Mohicans*. She would give me other stories to enjoy. I loved *Robinson Crusoe* and so I started reading again, bit by bit.

By my second year in Culpeper, my English teacher, Mrs. Richards, got me into reading once again. She liked me a lot, and she said, "You have a wonderful sense of drama in you. You should be reading more." She'd give me short stories from various literature books. All of a sudden I loved books! I loved the different colored book bindings with their special textures, and the smell of printer's ink.

Books' faces, like peoples' faces, are designed to show what's on the inside. Sometimes they were deceiving, but the ones with exotic colors, or great photographs and engravings excited me. I liked the wholesome embodiment of words bound together with a good exterior. I think this is why I was a printer for a short time.

Books were meant to be read, used, worn, torn, and digested so that when they regurgitate in your brain they fuse and become part of you, and you become part of them.

I would carry the books around with me. Jean noticed and said, "You know, you've been carrying that book now for three weeks, have you read any of it? Can you open it up and read it to me."

I read and I still read poorly. She compared Marjorie's and my reading, and it showed me how Marjorie could read. That made me angry and hurt me. Marjorie had gotten to go to school. She didn't milk sixty head of cows daily, and she didn't have to struggle to stay awake.

IT WAS THE MIDDLE OF MARCH on a Saturday afternoon. Dad had asked me to move some grain into the granary. There were four bins. One had seed grain in it, two were empty. The bin at the far end had grain that was to be taken out to the mill and mixed with the cow feed. We did all of this to help keep the feed budget down.

The feed man was coming Monday morning. I hated to do extra work on Sundays other than the milking. Dad had asked me to move the grain from the far bin to the one nearest the door. This enabled the feed man to be able to reach and vacuum it into his truck.

I had a habit of not totally listening to my father. I had half heard the request.

Larry told me that I had better get up there and move.

I was young and in good shape from the farm work and confident that I could shovel that ton of grain within a couple of hours.

Larry said, "You're fooling' yourself boy," and he bet me five dollars I couldn't do it. I took off my shirt and went to work. I had it done in less than two hours, although I was feeling the crunch. No matter what kind of shape you're in, a ton of grain is a ton of grain. No sooner had I shoveled in the last shovel that I felt the presence of my father standing in the doorway. "Now, what the hell have you done boy? You shoveled it in the wrong bin. That grain man's hose will never reach. You're gonna have to move it again, to the one near the door. "

"What?" I screamed.

"Don't use that tone on me, boy. If you'd listen to what I'd told you, you'd be done and on the way to the movies with that girlfriend of yours. "

I kept silent throughout the whole thing. Grabbing the shovel, I continued. There were tears coming down my face. Reaching for my t-shirt from the staircase, I pretended I was wiping the sweat from my brow.

This was the last straw on my back. To top it all off Larry decided that he wouldn't pay me the five because I really hadn't shoveled the grain into the right place, and therefore I wasn't done. I smashed the shovel against the grain bin and knocked one of the top boards off so that I could reach in more easily. It wasn't this just this particular situation but everything. I felt more than ever I was always being told to do this and to do that and it was becoming unbearable.

I was expected to finish the morning chores before school since Jean was waiting in the car with her children who got up at seven thirty and were fed, dressed and put comfortably into the car. I was always threatened that if I couldn't finish the barn work, take my shower, put on fresh clothes and have my breakfast and be ready to get into the car along with Jean's children, then I shouldn't be going to school. Dad and Jean agreed that if I couldn't do this, I should quit school like Larry had in the eighth grade.

Obviously, my grades weren't good. How could they be? I usually fell asleep by the second morning class. It was just too much for a fourteen or fifteen year old child. Everything had melded into an inexplicable mess. With so many unresolved issues, only anger prevails. It was impossible for me to express myself to Dad, especially when he was feeling his own stress.

I had a friend who lived across the inlet on a road between the train tracks and our farm. We shared a fence line. Often my friend Marshall and I would meet on our fence with flashlights, and we would read maps and plan how to make our great escape.

Marshall's father was an undertaker and usually there were a number of corpses in the basement of the house where Marshall lived. He told me he couldn't stand the smell and that he didn't want to be living anymore with a bunch of dead people.

I had also made another friend from the time that we were living in Jersey. He had moved to Lexington, Kentucky and his father had a barn near there. I called him and said we were going to visit a friend down near there and asked could if we stay in his barn.

At the age of fifteen, I was still a lean small-framed kid, standing about five foot six inches and weighing less than one hundred twenty pounds. I was also an expert horseman and could ride like the wind. I had spent two full summers herding cattle with Stardust and I was fearless. I knew I could have a big career as a jockey in Lexington, if I could only get there.

All the injustice accumulated. Marshall and I decided that March morning we would take the school bus and walk away before classes began. The freight train was only about a quarter of a mile away at the edge of town. No sooner had Marshall and I arrived then we saw a train moving out and heading for Richmond. It moved less than five miles an hour, with the freight doors wide open. We jumped the train.

They were hauling furniture. Some were boxed while other pieces were just sitting there in packing straw. Marshall and I each took a chair and in comfort we sat back and watched the world go by as we escaped. All we had to eat were a few boxes of candy that we had bought the night before. After a couple hours of traveling, some of the excitement and cockiness wore off and as the trip progressed it diminished to two young boys running away from home.

The train ride was pretty indirect and we knew we would have to hitch some. We decided that when we got to Raleigh we would jump out before the train pulled into the station.

Eventually we found ourselves in Raleigh at a bowling alley drinking coffee like grown-ups and eating hotdogs and a half a dozen donuts. No sooner had we gotten off the stools then we saw two cops coming in for their coffee. The tall officer was young, probably in his early twenties. The short heavy one had a big voice and talked from his throat and looked over at us and smiled. We smiled back. We paid our tab but the fat cop was mumbling something to his partner. We knew it was about us. We ran. We hadn't even reached the door when the throaty cop called to us to hold up, and asked us where we were from. We told him Richmond. They didn't believe us.

They took us down to the police station and turned us over to a desk officer and told him that they didn't know where we lived, but we sure didn't belong there. They decided to "book" us for the night. We wouldn't tell them our last names so they left us in a cell to see if we would remember them. Marshall couldn't decide if he wanted to laugh or cry so instead he asked to go the bathroom. I said I had to go as well.

We went down the hall and when we got to the bathroom we saw our escape hatch. The window was wide open and only one story up. We locked the door and took off and thumbed a ride in a pickup truck that took us into Charlottesville. I tried to fall asleep, but I could only catnap. I kept thinking about where we had come from and where we were going. What was my Dad thinking? Were they worrying about me? Larry must be finished milking by now.

I had left my sister Judy a note on the school bus. It stated my feelings about Dad and the futility of my life, and I said that I was going to try to make it on my own. I had told Judy not to give him the note until later on that evening. I figured he must have it by now.

The next morning we were in Charlottesville. Wanting to get our bearings, we sat on a small bench in the center of town. There was the usual armed soldier statue from the Second World War commemorating courage and loss of life. Marshall and I just sat there staring at it. The soldier did not seem courageous. He seemed to be as frightened as we were. I became very emotional and started to cry. I wanted my grandfather and my grandmother. At that moment, I felt I was the only person left on earth.

The early morning passed and we had a half an hour before the bus to Lexington was to depart. Marshall and I wandered back half a block and purchased a scrambled egg sandwich. Then we got on the bus. This time we sat as far from the driver as possible. The trip was long. We arrived in Lexington starved and broke.

I called my friend and he met us. He looked shocked to see us and a little frightened. He never thought we would make it. I introduced him to Marshall. Then a tall round-faced black man greeted us. He told us we could sleep in the barn for one night.

He wouldn't let me ride anything, but he did let us lead some horses onto the track and clean up a bit, and he paid us a little money.

We hung around that barn for two days and slept in the hay and used the bathroom and washed and combed our hair in the sinks. We had no place to eat, but by this time we had about $12 each, which was a lot of money for us.

We didn't know what we were going to do, so we went to the edge of town to a pool hall. You would think that Marshall hadn't eaten for a week. We bought hot dogs and started to shoot. I had never been in a pool hall. I had this full thick head of red hair, and was tall and skinny, and young. We looked too home grown to be out wandering around a pool hall.

While we were shooting, some cops came in to get a cup of coffee. This time these two were older and much more suspicious. The one with the mustache came forward and asked if we had an ID and where we were from. Then they took us with them.

We knew we were in trouble again, and this time we wouldn't get out of it so easily. The station was a three story building. Their office was on the second floor. As we climbed the stairs, I could hear chains rattling from the floor below. My heart was skipping beats. Marshall was right behind me.

"What shall we tell them?" he asked.

"Tell them nothing," I replied.

"Now to save you boys some time," the desk officer said, "We know who you are. We've received calls that you've escaped from Raleigh. I got to say one thing," he continued. "You boys got guts. What could have been so bad, to make you leave home? I'm going to put you on the second floor in the women's cells, because I can't put you down here with these men. They're all chain gang men."

Marshall was about three cells down from me, and I could talk to him loudly, but I couldn't see him. I was in that cell for two and a half days. It brought my whole life in front of me, the loneliness and the pain. I started to feel sorry about running away from my father. I missed my girl friends, and Judy, and Larry. I cried nights. It rained all the time I was there, and I could hear the church bells outside and the rain on the roof at night.

There was a cot and a sink that was also used as a toilet. They brought me corn bread and cabbage for breakfast, and I hated cabbage. It was cooked cabbage and the corn bread had fallen into the cabbage broth and the cabbage was cold. I took the whole thing and threw it back out through the bars, on the floor. They told me to clean it up and handed me a broom. I took the broom and put it between the bars and broke it, and threw it back out.

By this time Marshall had told them his last name, and they had called Marshall's father, and he said he'd be down to get him, but it would take him about two and a half days to get there. They didn't call my father.

That evening, before dinner, the officers had asked me if I wanted to go home or go to reform school. Without thinking, I blurted, "I'll take the reform school." I don't know what possessed me to say that. I just wanted to change my life. Seven days a week milking cows is not what I wanted my life to be. The officer told me that he didn't think I meant that, and the following morning he would take me over to the boys correctional center, just to show me how they live.

We walked in there, and I saw metal trays, and people waiting in line. They were all lost kids, some of them shaving, some weren't, but it was like a prison. I started crying.

He said "You don't want to be here, do you?"

All of a sudden things started to add up. I had a home and a family.

Marshall's father didn't arrive until the next morning. He had had a funeral to perform. It was a very long drive from Culpeper. That meant we would have to spend one more night in the cell. I had already decided to ride back with Marshall and his father.

Our breakfast was a serving of hominy grits and toast.

Finally, Marshall's father appeared. He seemed to take the whole thing humorously interpreting it as though this is what young boys do when they're feeling their oats. For me, this was not the case. I was devastated. I wanted my mother who had left me. I wanted my grandmother who had held and comforted me. I wanted my grandfather who had died.

My father had given a note to Marshall's father, to say that I was big enough to make a decision for myself. If I didn't want to come home I didn't have to. It'd be up to me.

"Jean and I have thought about this very carefully. Raymie, you have been a very hard child to understand. For some reason you are not like the rest of the children. You do not belong in a large family. You've always required special atten-tion which we have never been able to give you. We know that it's been hard for you Raymie, but we've done the best we could. If, at this point in your life, you feel you have the courage to live in that outside world we wish you luck. But, if you

decide that you would like to return home, it will be okay. You will not be punished. Nevertheless, if you're going to live with us, you must follow the family rules and do what you are told. Jean and I both believe that you are a very bright young man, and have a lot to look forward to. I hope you choose the right decision."

I read the letter with jerks and angry tears.

These were the things running through my mind when we were released and climbed into the back of Marshall's father's hearse. You couldn't even sit up in the hearse or you would hit your head. His father had thrown a couple of pillows and blankets into the back for us to rest on. The return trip went smoothly. I must have slept four or five hours. Marshall's father had persuaded his son to ride in the cab so they could talk.

When I awoke and realized that I was alone where coffins were placed, I panicked. I remembered this mad dog in Marlton that was roaming down Elmwood road by the Homestead. The town game warden had been tracking it. He captured it with a noose on a long stick and then put a small netted mask tight around the dog's face. They controlled him like a criminal puppet on a string, lifting him like a hangman into the hearse, a van similar to the one that I was riding in. I started hyperventilating. I had to get out. Screaming, I scratched on the glass between the cab and the back of the hearse.

Marshall's father quickly became concerned and opened the sliding window. Pulling the hearse out of traffic, he came to a complete stop at the side of the road. The doors at the back hearse would only open from the outside.

"Why?" I thought. "Were the dead people trying to escape?"

"What's a matter with you boy? Have you lost your senses? Climb into the cab. You'll be home soon."

Shortly thereafter we found ourselves driving down the inlet between my father's fields and the train track. Larry was in the barn milking. Earl was milking my side. Strangely enough, it felt good to be home. Larry really missed me. I felt as though I had taken a ten thousand mile journey. Earl and Larry both wanted to know the details of my great adventure.

"I don't want to talk about it," I said, picking up two buckets of milk. I loved being back with Larry. I loved racing down the barn milking cows on each side, and I loved drinking the milk off the aerator. I liked learning country-western songs with Earl Bailey. I loved my horse. I loved my girl friends.

But, I was still very empty and lonely. Something wasn't right. Something was missing, deep inside me.

After I came home, I was emotional all the time. I'd sit at the table over dinner and start crying. I was trying to find out who I was. I was trying to become a man at fifteen.

I remember wearing a piece of jewelry round my neck, and my Dad said to me, "What the hell is that crap you've got on your neck?" I insisted upon wearing it. I wouldn't let him touch it. Some girl gave it to me.

My father let me have some space. He never whipped me for running away. He just didn't talk to me for two or three days. I worked in the barn. I kept waiting to be whipped. I almost wanted to be whipped, just to get it over with, but he wouldn't whip me.

He said "You're too big for that, son. You have to find your own way now. I can't do any more for you."

I let my hair grow long. I rode my horse and I got cocky and mouthy with Dad a lot, and he began accepting it more. This was the time when I became an individual. I had done something that nobody in the whole family had done. Jean had wanted to do it at times. Larry had wanted to do it. Judy wanted to do it. But I actually got out and did it.

My father recently told me that "Of all the kids, you had the most courage. You would confront anything and do anything. That was a nice quality to have in a man."

After returning to Culpeper, Morris Peters and I became best friends. We drove around and we dated girls. I would tell them about my life and my dreams. I would ride my Tennessee Walker. We drove to the Blue Ridge Mountains and the Luray Caverns. I began to seek new adventures. I started seeing girls more seriously. I had a relationship with a teacher. I would do anything to get the love I needed without the hate and without the anger. Gradually, the armor swelled, and cracked, and splintered, because my individuality and my soul was coming out. I felt that I was becoming a whole person.

IT WAS CAROL ANN SEAL. When Larry moved from Delaware to Virginia, he decided that he would quit school and just dairy farm. When we finally got settled in Culpeper, Larry was seventeen and had no way to meet girls. I used to get him dates from our school.

This particular time I decided to give him one of my very own girlfriends. I actually thought that I could have the choice to make a decision for another person to date my brother. For Larry, I would've done almost anything, except give him Carol Ann Seal. Carol Ann didn't mind being friends with Larry, but I was in love with her and we wanted to go steady.

Larry and I had a huge fight over her. I offered him Ellen. She liked Larry a lot. Larry didn't want Ellen. He wanted Carol Ann. I refused. We were in the middle of the barn milking at the time. He called me a lying son-of-a bitch.

"Don't call me that" I screamed as I came down the ramp of the milk house toward him.

He was standing below alongside one of the cows. Then Larry let loose with the proverbial, "What are you gonna do about it?"

Up to this point he could always beat me in a fight. He was taller and stronger and older than I was. He shoved me as I came down with an empty bucket from the milk house. I dropped the bucket and hit him with a right hook under the chin and knocked him clear across the barn floor. As soon as I hit him and saw his face I regretted it. This was his last chance to be in charge and to have something over me. When he got up, he was pale, his mouth hung open, and he was in total shock. His little brother had grown bigger than he was and had knocked him across the floor.

Larry never hit me again and he never hit anybody. I think that he lost his nerve. He felt that God had come down and told him he was the last man, the last for everything. I tried talking to him. He would just squat down alongside the cow and pretend that he was fixing the milking machine. The rest of the evening he wouldn't talk. I told him he could have Carol Ann.

I loved Larry a lot. I had never meant to hurt him. To this day, I think that Larry and I both knew that this was a standoff, and that our love for each other was greater than anything else, including Carol Ann Seal.

Earl Bailey and I used to drink coffee in the morning before milking. This was at five-thirty AM, and it would help wake me up. We would go into the boiler room with our cups filled with milk, and add a teaspoon of instant coffee, and then go to the boiler tank that we used for steaming the equipment. We would open the overflow valve into that powdered coffee and milk and we had our version of cappuccino. Of course, we had never heard that word. We just thought we were clever.

Larry didn't drink coffee. He used to get mad because when we took water from the valve it lowered the pressure in the boiler, making it harder for him to steam the equipment. He got so fed up with Earl and me about the boiler that he decided to throw our coffee out.

The next day when Earl came to work, he brought a new jar of coffee. Earl and I were in the boiler room fooling around, and laughing about Larry never drinking coffee. Larry came in there just as I opened the valve to fill my cup. Larry grabbed my arm to make me turn it off not knowing that the cup already had some scalding water in it and the boiling water went all over his bare back. He ran out of there screaming that I had done it on purpose.

We had this huge concrete silo and there weren't any ladders to climb with, just steps to shimmy up. Anytime I ever got in an argument with Dad, or if he was after me about something, I'd run up one of the silos, not the cement one but the sixty footer with that little narrow ladder on the outside. Dad would never come after me because he was afraid of heights. He'd stand at the bottom of the silo and demand that I come down that very minute. I would sit up there at the top and tell him that if he would go away and leave me alone, I'd come down.

Then he'd say, "Boy you'd better get down here before I whip your behind."

I'd say, "You go away and I will." Finally, he would walk away. Then if I saw him a half an hour later, he'd look at me and kind of smile, and say,

"You're pleased with yourself aren't you?"

I'd think, "No I just don't want you to hit me."

That was the only way that I could defend myself with him. The other children thought I had guts.

Each summer I had to watch the cows in the two large two hundred acre hay fields behind the barn. I did this for three summers. As soon as I got out of school the first week of June, Dad would send me out there by myself for seven days a week, until September. After the first couple of weeks, I got so bored I thought I'd go out of my mind. That was when I started to train Stardust. They call it high schooling. I would take the saddle and blanket off, and throw the reins over her neck. I'd be lying there on the ground with a blanket, leaning against a saddle, and I got her so that I could just give her an oral command.

When I saw a cow out of place, or wandering, I could just point to it and that horse was like a sheep dog. She would run out there and bring that stray cow back into the herd. Then she would come back to me, bow down her head, and I'd give her a lump of sugar and tell her she was fantastic. I had her so trained, that she would lie down for me, pull the blanket out from under me, count, and shake her head yes or no.

I could run and jump on her from the back, and she would rear up and paw the air. She would whinny when she wanted something. She was almost human.

I couldn't play football because I had to milk, and Dad wouldn't let me run track. Instead I used to do half-time tricks at the football games with Stardust. I later told my wife, Babette, about Stardust and I'm sure she thought I exaggerated. When I took Babette down to see Culpeper, I thought that maybe there would be some people down there who would remember me. Instead they would see my distinctive red hair and they would stop me everywhere and ask,

"Aren't you the kid who had that trick horse?"

They all remembered the horse, but not me!

We had parked the old tractor in the long wagon shed. I was fed up with it. I thought maybe it just needed a good cleaning. One Sunday I laid a couple of the horse blankets down on the frozen ground, put a piece of plastic over them, and I took that tractor totally apart. I had almost every piece of that tractor lying on the two horse blankets. Dad came out there and demanded,

"What the hell are you doing boy? You mess that tractor up and I'll whip your hide."

I said to myself, "It's already messed up, what more can it hurt?"

Earl Bailey came by, took one look, and started laughing. He had been a part-time mechanic in town and knew quite a lot about engines. He said, "You can do this Raymie, you're just going to need a couple of new gaskets, a new oil filter, and some spark plugs, and about four quarts of oil."

This tractor had a governor on it with a special spring to the valve on the fuel line. Somehow, taking it apart, I lost it. Fortunately, Earl had one in his car that was very similar. He gave that to me, and he went and got my supplies over at the garage where he had worked. By the time Earl returned, I had pretty much scraped, cleaned, oiled and prepared every part before putting it back in its place, praying that I wouldn't have some stray part left over at the end. I was really sweating it.

Earl helped me put the gasket onto the block and bolt everything back into place. I filled it with gas and oil and gave the starter a push. The battery was a little bit low, but she started up. I adjusted the throttle, and she purred like a kitten. Just as Earl was about to slap me on the back, I heard a voice behind me saying, "I'll be damned if you didn't do it."

"Of course," I said "I told you I could do it, and you owe Earl for a set of plugs and an oil filter. If you think it's worth it, you ought to be able to come up with that!!" Dad reached down in his front pocket, squeezed his lips together, and handed Earl the money. Then Dad turned to me, looked me straight in the face, and said,

"That's pretty decent, boy."

That felt good.

At sixteen, I mostly unloaded the hay on the elevator. Dad, at forty, drove the bailer and Larry, at nineteen, loaded the hay out in the field. Earl and I stacked the hay in the loft. On one hundred ten degree day we were out hauling and bailing. We were on this rough front field and Dad was driving in third gear.

I yelled, "Slow Down!"

Dad answered "I can't slow down, it's gonna rain."

"Well, you've got to slow down."

"No, I'm not going to slow down."

"Well, I'm not gonna haul any more hay!"

But the bales kept coming up. I had stacked about half a load at the back.

I repeated, "You slow down or I'm not going to take them anymore."

One fell off under the wheel and turned the whole load over. It knocked everything off on to the ground. Dad stopped the tractor, and I took off across the field. This was typical of Dad and me. He ran after me and yelled,

"You get back on the wagon!"

"No. When you get back on the tractor, I'll get back on the wagon," I yelled.

Dad and I were standing out there in the middle of the field, just like two rams, horn to horn. I wouldn't get back on the wagon and he wouldn't get back on the tractor. We must have been there for half an hour. Finally, I reloaded the wagon and he got back on the tractor. He dropped it down into second gear after that.

That's the only time I ever got my way with him. I never forgot that. It's like yesterday. It is a very vivid memory. We hauled in the rest of the hay.

Larry and I had decided to leave Culpeper. I was almost eighteen and wanted to join the Navy. Larry wanted to marry Maxine, and Dad and Jean were so against it.

Dad was beside himself. I was filling the silo and Larry was in Tennessee with Maxine. My father agreed to sign my papers if I filled three silos. I filled those silos so fast you couldn't believe it. I had tractors going back and forth full of silage and had them emptied in the silo and leveled off before he got to the next field.

He said, "Boy, why don't you work like this all the time?"

I left. Dad let me go and he wished me luck. He didn't know what to do with me most times. I was a misfit kid. They should have had a psychiatrist for all of us. They certainly didn't know how to handle me.

At the Homestead we lived together, but we were independent. We were so intertwined with our family that we wanted more than we should have. Dad was particularly guilty. He couldn't delineate where he stopped and we started. We couldn't stand apart from him and develop as men. I think while that is part of the pain of growing up, it was excessive in our family.

When you cut grass, it's violent. It's an amputation. When you milk a cow, you are stealing milk from the cow. First you take her calf and then you convince her that it is okay for you to take her milk. With plants, we separate the roots and put them in different pots. We do a lot of things with various degrees of separation and often with cruelty.

I've watched baby birds shoved out of their nest. The mother pigeon would shove her baby squab out of a forty foot high nest. The fledgling pigeon would start flying or die. Most learned to fly very quickly but some did die.

Should we do that with our children?

From the cradle to the barn or from the barn to the world, you love your mother and you leave. Parents cry at weddings. They fear the loss of their children. It's like a limb being amputated. It's a cut that has to happen.

My father should have given us the confidence and encouragement to go out in the world and be on our own. He was aware of the world and his perceptions were keen. He just didn't know how to teach us and how to share the outside world with us.

Perhaps Clara did not have difficulty adjusting to farm life. She learned to cook and to can. Instead, after eleven years of marriage, perhaps she just didn't want to be controlled. That may have fueled her discontent and her anger more than being a farmer's wife.

I saw him in Pine Grove as a man who had a great sense of humor and cockiness and bravado about himself. I saw a man who was very loving with my mother, Clara. I never saw that kind of light in his personality with Jean. Perhaps it was my perception but I felt he had lost some of his air of confidence in his own omnipotence and instead replaced the confidence with mistrust, anger, and introspection.

I did see him happy and mellow with Jean. Maybe it was age, but I think what I recognized was his loss of dreams. When things were going well for him, he was a great person to be around but when he was angry or hurt you didn't want to be near him. He was like a volcano. He had an extreme personality and I have that in me, but I have worked to curb it. I've learned how to channel it into my work and my life so the temper dissipates into a level of balance. Dad didn't know what to do with the temper. He'd contain it inside of himself. He'd go out and work in the fields and pound fence posts into the ground, but he still couldn't contain it.

He loved his sons. He loved his children.

It's very difficult to watch your children fail or trip or make mistakes. You want them to succeed. It's a reflection of your training and how you raised them. It's hard to step back and let them live their own lives. That's what I felt with my son, Thomas. He didn't want my help. He wanted space and time to find himself and go off on his own, and be successful, and be able to fail without being mourned over by me.

My father was always comparing me to my mother, and how she was a tramp and lazy. She didn't know how to adapt and I was just like her. I would speak up and answer back and say what I felt, and in that I was just like my mother. My mother defended herself. Jean, however, took it all inside of her and at the end seemingly lived a life with a lot of regret. Clara at age thirty-one made a very hard decision to leave my father and her children, rationalizing that we children would be cared for.

Dad and Jean had a good life together. I heard Jean making love to my father in the other room continually, and saw her playing with Larry. She would be rolling in the grass and chasing us with a fly swatter, or having her girl friends over and watching soaps. She would cook meals and go out with her friends or my father. Jean and Dad would be out in the yard or riding. She could step out of her front door and look at the Blue Ridge Mountains every night. She had children that she loved and a husband that she loved and respected and a challenging and often successful business.

They were partners in a business that was difficult with huge uncontrollable challenges. Most often they succeeded. They weren't wealthy, but they supported a large family and lived well. They always had nice cars to drive, good clothing to wear, electricity and heat and abundant food. They owned beautiful rich pieces of land and lived in large homes they had renovated.

Dad kept selling out when he thought he was losing a son and would have no one to work with. He never realized that he was in fact driving his sons away. His sons weren't leaving.

All the guilt Jean carries for not having nurtured us children the way she thought we should have been nurtured is really a hair shirt for her. No one is blaming her, and most of the issues are the norm for children and their parents. Jean continually judges herself as relentlessly as she often judged those around her. None of it is necessary or legitimate. Life twists and turns and all in all she raised a large family that has done very well in life.

Jean also blames Dad relentlessly, especially now that he can't answer back.

Why did they not just own up to their unrealistic expectations, or lack of capabilities in themselves and accept their own inadequacies? Why not just look back on all they accomplished? The man did the best he could. He worked seven days a week, fifteen hours a day. Was he a failure as a father? All his children are strong and capable, with excellent values.

Jean's life was only amiss in her later perception. In reality her life was both rich and rewarding.

Part XII

Jean 1955–1985

CULPEPER FARM

Jean Shuster

JEANNIE, OUR YOUNGEST DAUGHTER, was born in Culpeper. We had to buy all the school books. We'd never had to do that before and we both had a fit. It was a lot of books for seven children.

The children caught the bus at Brandy Station for school. Raymie was in the eighth grade and Judy was in high school and dating Earl Bailey. Dad found out she was meeting him out in the field and he kicked Earl out. Raymie ran away from home and was caught and put in jail.

Raymie joined the US Naval Air Force during high school, and Judy went into the US Air Force right after her graduation. Larry was still milking. I hated to see them go, especially Judy, but at the same time I felt that it would be the best thing in the world for her. She was dating Frank Peters at the time, and he joined the Air Force. He was madly in love with her and wanted to marry her. When she didn't, he joined the paratroopers and went over to Germany.

My mother-in-law Alice came to visit.

My perception of my husband Raymond changed over the years. I don't know how he felt about me. In the very beginning there were times when he would get really angry and I had no idea why he was angry. I can remember begging him to tell me what I had done or said, but he would just push me away and not say anything and go. Maybe he was just angry with himself.

Then there were other times when I was afraid of him, not physically, but I was afraid of his mouth because he could make me feel like nothing.

There was only one time that he ever raised his hand, and that was at Kenton. It was because I did it first.

Raymond was from the old school where you didn't go to the dentist until you had a tooth pulled. I don't think the condition of Raymie's teeth were as bad as Larry's or Judy's. I was so ashamed when I finally took them to the dentist in Culpeper, and the dentist took one look at their mouth and said "Where in the name of heaven have they been?"

I don't know who it was there at Kenton, but I had taken some child to the dentist, and I'd gotten the bill and Raymond near about had a fit. He wasn't going to pay it and told me that I was all kinds of a fool and that I had no business doing anything like that. I think that time, I swear to goodness, that I would have left him if I'd had a place to go. I picked up something and I was going to throw it at him. He never changed.

Another time at Kenton we had three shelves and behind the shelves was a door. The door went up to the bedrooms above the kitchen, and we had a table in the center. There was another counter that separated the stove from the sink and the table and I had some knick-knacks.

It wasn't cluttered but Raymond told me that it was, time and time again. One day I just had enough. I took my arm, and I swept everything off onto the floor. Yes I did! I broke every bit of it. It was stupid because I was the one that paid, not him. They were my things. My temper didn't come out very often in the early days, but it progressed.

We always had money problems. There were times when we lived from one milk check to the other with nine children. I understood that. Raymond did all the books. Never, never, me. I used to hate doing the income taxes, because he would save each little thing. The check register used to be the little checks stubs and he would save every receipt and every bill, and we would have to go back over all of it, and then we would have to make lists. In Culpeper we wrote checks for thousands of dollars, and there was no way that I could have done it on my own.

Raymond did not know how to balance a check book. Neither did I at that time and I never learned until we moved to Tennessee. But, I could count on my one hand in all those years the times that we were overdrawn, even with handling all of that money. Well, I had to help, and I had to sit there. I had to smile. I did. I had to sit there and wait while he thought and then he would tell me what to put down. I can remember sitting there at that roll top desk. It was torture.

We didn't have a calculator. Are you kidding? There weren't any!

At thirty eight I got pregnant with Ashley. Afterwards, Dr. Pritchard gave me the birth control pill. I never asked for anything before. I should have stopped having children after Skip, but I never thought about that. With any common sense and with four other children, two should have been the limit.

Raymond enjoyed the children before the work got in between. The boys were always outside helping him. It was only through his knowledge and expertise and good management that we kept our heads above water. In Culpeper, with the drought and diseases that we had with the cows, it was especially difficult. That made it hard on the boys because he couldn't have made ends meet if he'd had to hire men to take their place. That was the inequality.

It took twenty years but my heroic view of Raymond began to dissolve. There were still many good times. Sometimes when you look back you only see that one bad time instead of the twenty good ones. We had each other. We would talk and we would do things. Kids make their way into life. You put kids in a room together and believe me, they'll have themselves a good time, whether you like it or not.

When we came to Kenton we made friends and we had barbecues. We used to play ball with all the kids. When the children were all at home and we lived on the farm, we didn't have time to think of anything else. Once the children were gone we didn't have anything to talk about. Nothing. There was absolutely nothing there.

Raymond had never changed. He was absolutely content with his fox hunting and his television. Then he got to reading books, and that's all he wanted.

We never went to the movies. First of all they became too expensive, and secondly a lot of them to our mind weren't worth going to see anyway. We did go out for dinner once in a while. Then I began teaching remedial reading. Raymond wasn't interested. He did not want to hear anything about my school and about my work. I don't think he said it in so many words, but you could tell. We didn't even eat together. He would sit at the kitchen counter and watch the news. I sat in my chair and because I had no other choice, I watched the news.

Raymond used to tell stories, but he didn't talk about his life and his feelings intimately.

I would get him Westerns to read from the library. Soon, it got to the point that he had read all of them.

We had a relationship, simply because we were two people that had lived together all these many years, but I wanted us to grow, to occasionally go to the theatre, and maybe travel.

I could never get him to go to anything or to go anywhere with me. The only exception was that once I did get him to go with me to see "Annie Get Your Gun." He did like that.

Raymond was an earth person. Farming was his life. He wasn't interested in anything else nor did he try to be.

PART XIII

Leslie Ballinger

SENIOR PROM: MARGIE FORD BALLINGER
AND LESLIE BALLINGER, 1962

Leslie Ballinger

———————

CLARA AND DAD HAD JUST MOVED TO BARRINGTON in 1944, so I was born in Pemberton Hospital that November. I lived with Clara the first year and a half of my life, and then I was brought back to Haddon Heights to Mrs. Shuster and Jean.

As an infant I had terrible asthma and almost died. When we left with my mother Clara, my big sister Judy took care of me. Judy was so homesick for Larry and Raymie and she continually asked our mother if she could go back home. When Clara said no, she would have a tantrum. She would lie on the floor and kick and hold her breath until she turned blue. She continued this for weeks until finally Clara asked the doctor what she could do about it. The doctor said to let her go back to live with her brothers. Dad told me that Clara had said if he paid a $25 dental bill, she would allow him to pick up Judy and myself.

The only thing I can remember about Marlton is that my brothers would get up hay with a big deep wagon and a team of horses hooked up to it. They would pull up under this hayfork driveway and drop the load in.

I was six years younger than Raymie and two years older than Marjorie. I was in the third grade when we left Milford.

I was around nine when we moved to Culpeper. Marjorie and I wanted to paint a little metal wagon and Pop said no, we'd get paint all over us. We decided we were gonna paint it anyway. We took that thing on to the front porch and we were going to hide underneath the lattice trim and use the John Deere green paint .We had paint in our hair and everywhere else. Marjorie's blond hair was so full of it! We snuck in the house and got a pair of scissors and I started cutting that green paint out of her hair and she did the same for me. Finally Jean caught up with us. She took gasoline and washed my head and it burnt. I mean it burnt like fire! That was my payback for doing something I wasn't supposed to be doing. I got a big-time whipping on top of that when pop got back. Marjorie's hair was chopped up looking for a long time.

There was a little hole in the bottom of the door of the smokehouse, and Marjorie wanted to get in there and Dad told her to stay out. He had always told us kids to stay out of there. That was his private tool room. Marjorie crawled through the hole in the door and there was a nest of bumblebees in there. All I could hear was her screaming. Of course she got a whipping plus a stinging. She got eaten up with those bees. That might have been the reason why Dad didn't want us in there.

Pop and Jean had gone away and left us kids home alone. We were milking the cows and finishing up. I had gone up into the loft to throw down some hay and straw. It got dark and then we saw the barn was all lit up at midnight. We thought somebody was up there. We got together, holding hands, scared to death, afraid someone was up in that loft doing something they weren't supposed to be. We walked down to the barn and Larry opened the door to the barn, and said,

"If there's anybody up in there, you'd better come down or we're gonna shoot!"

We were all shaking in our boots. We could hardly move, all four of us, Larry, Judy, Leslie and Marjorie. Raymie was in the Navy by then and we sure did need him. Finally we got enough guts to climb the ladder and of course there was just the four of us. I had left the light on.

My sister Nancy was only two by then, and my brother Skippy was five. Jeanie wasn't born yet.

We had an old summer kitchen down by the breezeway with lavender growing on both sides and that's where we used to play. There was an old black lady named Martha who lived in the tenant house. Her husband John would bet on horses and get drunk every weekend. She used to make the best homemade bread. Martha would chase John right across the hill with a hatchet and a shotgun.

One summer we were living at Culpeper and this guy came and wanted a job. Pop hired him and he stayed in the other tenant house. Martha and John lived in the one farthest away. All I can remember are the muscles he had! I watched him throw up bales of hay as high as we could stack them clear over the wagon. We were pretty impressed. We came to find out he'd just got out of prison.

Raymie and Larry were fighting all the time about girls. Larry was working and couldn't meet anyone and Raymie would bring girls out from school to the farm. I think they wanted the same girl. They got in a fist fight and this was the first time that Raymie beat Larry. It was terrible.

Raymie would climb that huge concrete silo, and there weren't any ladders. He shimmied around the little narrow top to tie the silo pipe up. There was a blower and when you stood up in the wagon it sucked the silage into the silo. Whenever Raymie had to get away fast, he would run up that sixty foot silo because Dad was afraid of height. Dad would stand at the bottom telling him to come down, and Raymie would sit up there at the top and tell him that if he would go away and leave him alone, He'd come down. Then Dad would say, "Boy you'd better get down here before I whip your behind."

We had a calf barn with a track for the manure carriage cart. Larry and I would clean out the stalls and the pens. I would get on and ride while Larry pushed. Larry would threaten that if I didn't do what he wanted he would spit on me! He made me stick my hand out and he'd just spit and, phew! I just about did everything but throw up. It made me so sick! I could have killed him for that! Phew! Phew! Nasty!

There was an old wooden silo before the hurricane took it down and blew it across the driveway. We would combine the wheat and bale the straw. I had shorts on and I was unloading. When I got through, my legs were solid blood raw because I wasn't wearing pants. I was only ten years old.

Jean took me to a birthday party. The girl lived across the inlet. She had a pony at Brandy Station. She got her foot caught in the stirrup and panicked and fell off her horse and was dragged all the way down that blacktop road.

Her whole scalp came off. They rushed her to the hospital. She went into surgery, and they said they had to skin her whole head off. It took forever to pick all that stuff out, and then put the scalp back with all her hair. She ended up fine. She had scars. I remember that party.

All I remember about Raymie was seeing him and Larry riding their horses out that long driveway in Culpeper into the sunset. As a child my brothers seemed so much bigger and older than me.

I got to ride Raymie's horse, Stardust, after he went into the Navy to watch over those cows in those two big back fields. She did a lot of tricks. All I would have to do is put a piece of baling twine onto her lower mouth and I could ride her all day long.

I married Margie Ford when I was twenty years old. We had gone to high school together. Her uncle owned a farm in back of us and she would meet the bus the same place that I did. Her mother and dad lived right up in Kenton, Delaware, and the school there only went to the eighth grade. I started dating Margie in eleventh grade. I was sixteen and it was 1960.

I had just gotten my first car. Pop helped me buy a '54 Chevrolet. I paid $325 for it. Dad signed the papers and I paid for it. He had given me a half of a cow and I was getting a little bit of money off of that. That's what I was buying my school clothes with.

Although now I think Dad used me, at the time I thought it was fair. I didn't know anything else. It really helped me grow. I learned how to work, although I think I was overworked. We were all cheated from our childhood and we all thought that. But those experiences gave us a great deal of strength and a lot of push. If it hadn't been for that work ethic, I don't know if we'd have survived.

Margie chased me and I finally gave in on Valentine's Day. I went and bought a box of candy or maybe it was flowers. She had been sick and had stayed home from school. I went to her house and I said, "I give up. When do you want to go out?"

She gave me a box of candy and a big kiss. She thought she had done something big. She finally got what she wanted. She didn't know what she had, but she finally thought she had something. From then on, I never dated anybody else. Ever. We dated the rest of the way through high school. I graduated in 1963 and she graduated in 1964 and we did everything together. I've never been the same since!

Dad and Jean didn't like the relationship. They didn't like Margie because she was part of the Downs Family. They didn't like him or her, Frances and Dottie. Every once in a while I'd ask Jean if I could invite Margie over for Sunday dinner and she'd let me do it but she didn't like it. We were kids. Margie would sit on my knee and man! That was a disgrace to them. That meant she was trash. She was a sexpot.

Why? Maybe it was their own guilt. They told me several times that she was trash. Jean went over and told her mom and dad, "You have raised a tramp.....a worthless tramp." I can't believe Marjorie Ford's mother let Jean get by with that.

Kids back then didn't even know that much about sex. And we didn't...her and me. Neither one of us did. I'd seen cows and all that, but...I didn't know anything about sex...nothing! She and I dated the rest of the way through high school.

We weren't supposed to get married until December. We moved it back to October and that's when Dad and Jean thought for sure Margie was pregnant. They swore up and down she was pregnant when we got married. The irony is that we didn't and weren't but they did and probably were.

Margie and I had some knock-down drag-outs. I was awfully jealous over her for a long time. I didn't want to see her talk to any other boys. She didn't know anything about jealousy. I was afraid of losing her and being alone. I didn't realize that then. I was possessive. I think we all were because we never had a home and a childhood and unconditional love.

We finally talked them into coming to the wedding, Dad and Jean and Pappy Shuster. We got married in Kenton at the Methodist Church.

Margie's folks were city people. They lived in the town of Kenton. That wasn't exactly a city, but they worked in a factory and they weren't farmers. They thought of me like their own son. Mom and Dad just tolerated us. They tried to talk me out of it. I paid no attention because all I knew was I was in love. I wasn't angry with them. I didn't care. I had what I wanted. I had someone that loved me and I loved her.

We bought a trailer and we moved it down where Larry had his trailer on Dad's property in Kenton. Then the same thing started all over again. Margie was no good. She was a tramp. This was over and over and Margie never did a thing to them. She went overboard to try to get along. It was the same syndrome.

I had my own six or eight cows. At the age of twenty, dairy farming was all I knew. I was scared of Dad, clear up till I was twenty-one years old. I was scared to death of the man. If he hollered, "Jump!" I'd say "How far?" We would watch Raymie tell him off and we loved it and wished we could do it. Larry never had the guts. I was the same way. Judy would tell Raymie to tell Dad something and he'd tell him anything. Then Dad would smack him and he'd get up and he'd smack him down again!

We'd made some friends that we went to school with, married couples. Dad didn't like my friends coming around. I think Dad was afraid that they'd pull me away from the farm. They didn't. I just got fed up with it. All the money I made was from my six cows, around $60 a week. Margie went to work right out of high school for a lawyer in Dover and she was making $50 or $60 a week. We made our trailer payment and a car payment, and we lived off of that.

I took another job and we moved. One day I finally realized that I was a man the same as Dad was. I just told him that I was fed up and couldn't take it anymore. I took my cows out and sold them. I was scared because I didn't know what he was going to do. He was really angry. He could have killed me. He said I was a gold digger. He wouldn't speak to me.

Our best friends had sold their farm with their cows and Richard and his wife had to move into town and they didn't have a garden. He had always had a big garden like we did. Dad didn't like them at all even though the boy was a farm boy.

I told him he could come out and share our acre garden and there was no problem with Pop. We sold enough out of that garden in one year for the four of us to go to Wildwood for the weekend. I left Dad's farm in the middle of the garden season. Richard went to Pop and asked him if he could have some of the stuff out of the garden. Pop told him he could have anything he wanted, but "Just don't tell Leslie I gave it to you."

I had gone back to get my pump out of the well. It was mine and I had paid for it. Larry gave it to me when he knew I was going to put a trailer in there. Pop wouldn't let me have it. We had another big confrontation.

I moved to Dover, Delaware in August. Margie's uncle worked for the state highway department and he gave me a job. We moved to her aunt's trailer park and we stayed there rent free. She was like a mother to Marjorie. I worked for the highway department driving the paint crew and painting the lines on the road. I didn't like it. Within six months I quit the highway job and went down to Larry's who was working for Mr. Hurt at the Bellaire farm in Culpeper, Virginia where we used to live. Mr. Hurt loved Larry. He was like a father to Larry. That's the reason why he stayed there so long.

Larry had come to visit us a couple of times with Maxine and she asked me if I wanted to get back into farming. Of course, I said yes. Here was the chance for me to be out on my own. Period. The farther away from Dad I was the better. I grabbed the opportunity of working with Larry, but Margie wasn't too crazy about it. She never had been away from home. Larry had built it all up and I went down there and of course I was young. I didn't have any experience with life, or marriage and we got so homesick for Kenton that neither one of us could hardly stand it. Margie and I thought an awful lot of her family.

Larry was managing the Hurt farm, and the dairy, and he said, "You can be the manager of the dairy. I'll let you take care of the dairy. You just handle it and run it."

Mr. Hurt didn't care, as long as it was done right. Larry knew that I knew enough about cows to do it, but he never did let me do it myself. Larry was still running everything. It didn't bother me a whole lot. Every chance we had we'd go back to Delaware to visit Margie's mom and dad. We stayed down there at the dairy for about three years.

Mr. Hurt was okay but I knew he was using Larry. I never thought Larry got out of it what he should have. He barely made a living. He was running three farms and a whole lot of tough men.

When we came back to Kenton, Delaware I had to find a job. I hadn't seen Dad in three years. We would only go back and see Margie's family. I was twenty-four years old. We rented a little house right in back of Margie's parents. I hated it because I was used to having a garden and a farm to run on.

I got a job driving a milk truck, delivering to houses and schools. I had to get up at two o'clock in the morning. My first stop was Mr. Donut. I always had a hot cup of coffee and fresh donuts right out of the grease.

Eventually I got sick of living in town even though it was just a little old town like Kenton. There was nothing to do. You got home and you'd sit down and watch T.V. Boring! I was miserable and of course I made Margie miserable.

Our anniversary came up and I told her that I'd take her out. I don't remember why, I'm sure she does, but we didn't go out. She was firing mad. She ran home to momma, which was right across the street. Her momma told her, "You married him... you go back and straighten it out."

When Margie grew up, her parents worked at the Playtex plant. Her dad worked day shift. Her mom worked second shift. They passed one another on the highway. She had it rough but she had everything she wanted. Since Margie was the oldest, her mom made her cook for her pop and her brother and sister and help keep house.

I wasn't satisfied driving a milk truck, so we moved to Marydel in Kent County. Marjorie and I bought our first house through the FHA. We paid $7,000 for it and the FHA loaned us $1,000 to put in a heating system. It was an acre and a half. We were on our own.

The first winter the wind would blow through the house, and the heater would run twenty-four hours a day. It wouldn't get above fifty-five degrees. Our neighbors, Mr. and Mrs. Wall, fell in love with us and we fell in love with them. I borrowed his tools and I helped him whenever he needed it. He loved our son, Chris, as if our boy was his grandson. He had two chicken houses and he'd take Chris with him every chance he had. Chris was just a little bitty thing and he would ride with him on the lawn mower. He knew Margie's mother and dad as grandmother and grandfather, but he didn't know my side. I wouldn't let him. This was his other grandpa... he called him Grandpa Walls.

I finally bought an old pot-bellied stove and stuck it in the kitchen. We were gonna get some heat one way or another. We were getting tired of freezing. I started that thing up and man! It turned cherry red. I didn't know anything about opening a draft. All I knew was that you were supposed to open it and start it! Man, she lit up! Years ago they had this Masonite that you used to put on the walls. Of course I didn't know you had to set the stove away from the wall. It scorched that whole wall.

I called Mr. Walls and he said," Calm down, just calm down. Just close your damper."

I closed the damper and it just went right down.

I changed jobs and went to I.L.C. Industries where they made space suits. That's when they were trying to get a man on the moon. This fascinated me. I loved the job, even though it was inside.

Margie was home with Chris. We were doing great. I was there when Tammy was born on Margie's mom's birthday!

I was making $3.50 an hour at International Playtex with all the benefits. That was big bucks. I thought, hey man! I'm going to town. Then they got a man on the moon and that project slacked up and they started laying people off. Mine was the only income we had. This was right in the beginning of the seventies. You couldn't find a job anywhere.

In the later part of 1971, I had to take a job that I hated in a chemical plant. There wasn't a choice. It was either that or starve. I worked there for six months as a night shift supervisor. I started to like it. It was the first time I got to be with other fellas and do things. I had never had any experience with drinking. I got it all when I worked there. I tried smoking but I never got anything out of it. I got to drinking a good bit.

There was another boy on my shift and we got to be real good friends. His wife and Margie and he and I would do things together. He had worked before at a collection agency. He had married a woman with seven kids.

The Vietnam War had just gotten started and they put me over in a different area to make barrier bags. They were rubber bags that went over the shells.

In Vietnam with all the dampness and humidity the shells were rusting and they wouldn't fire. We had big cars on a monorail and we dipped these bags in latex. It was the same idea as making rubber gloves. I was the shift leader and Eddie was on my shift talking about his seven kids, and that's when I started thinking about finding Clara.

My shoulder kept popping out of joint from pulling these big cars on the monorail. I had had surgery. Eddie had had a hernia operation. We were both in the hospital at the same time and we'd visit one another's rooms. That's when I decided to find my birth mother. Clara would have been around fifty-seven at the time.

Eddie said, "If you want to find her...when we get outta here, we'll find her. I can find anybody."

I couldn't go back to work. I had to go through therapy to keep my arm in its joint, and I was living on worker's compensation, $50 a week. Margie wasn't working.

Finally, I went to Philadelphia and saw Clara for the first time in twenty-five years.

We started by driving up the New Jersey Turnpike, and things started coming back to me. I saw the farm at Marlton. I went to the Coopers, and old Hog-Nose's son Malcolm came to the door. I asked if he could tell me anything about Mom and they kind of snickered and laughed.

"Are you the sons of a bitch that run off with the Shuster girl?"

"Hold it! No, I'm his son!"

"You look exactly like him."

"I'm no where's near as old as he is."

Then they calmed down and I told them what I wanted. Malcolm told me to give him an hour and they'd see if they could find her.

They knew exactly where she was. The only thing I could figure out was that somehow she had kept up with them, perhaps through Nellie who knew Mom's friend Joanie.

We drove around town. I was showing Eddie where I thought I was born. We got something to eat and came back in an hour. They rang Clara up on the telephone and I talked to her. This was around 10:30 at night, in 1970. Clara said to come and visit, and told me how to get there. Eddie went with me. We spent ... God! I don't know how many hours it was... just talking to Clara and George. We were hugging and kissing. After that I'd go up and visit on Thanksgiving or Christmas every year.

We weren't that far away. She was still in Philadelphia. Marjorie loved it. She finally had a mother-in-law who liked her. Clara loved Marjorie. She thought she was a good mom. Clara never would let me get that close.

I met Bonnie and Penny, her children with George, who were ten and a half and twelve. Now I had two more sisters and they liked me as well. They looked up to me like I was a big brother. I told them I hadn't seen Raymie in a long time.

Before we had moved away from Marydel we invited Clara down for Christmas. She wanted to know if she could bring Grandpa Williams and I got to meet him for the first time.

Of course I thought he was great. I didn't have a grandfather. Grandfather Williams loved Marjorie to death.

Margie cooked. She had always been a good cook. She made sweet potato pie and he said that that was the first time he had it in years. I think he ate half of it. He just thought the world of her and that's the only time I ever saw him. I'm glad I did.

I took Clara down to see Larry in 1971. Larry didn't know I was bringing Clara and he didn't like it. I did it anyway. Larry of course was the one who remembered her and knew her the best. Maxine didn't know what to think. That was the last time Larry saw Clara and he didn't want to see her again. Clara appreciated seeing Larry. I think he always carried with him the pain of rejection. Larry and Maxine had become close to Jean over the years, and they felt a conflict. Jean had also become very close with Larry and Maxine's children.

We'd go up and visit Clara in Philly and I'd call three or four times a year. I knew she was there and I knew she cared and that's really all I needed. We only saw her once after she moved to Florida in 1974.

After six months at Chesswood Chemicals, we sold our house in Marydel and I went to work at DuPont in Wilmington. There I met Phyllis DuPont Wyeth and her husband, Jamie Wyeth. It was about two weeks before Christmas when I went for the interview. She offered me the farm manager's job and invited us to a Christmas party. Phyllis gave Jamie toys and she had gifts for us when we arrived. Jamie had a whole display of things from the

Soviet Union. It was gorgeous. He had antique tanks all enclosed in a glass case on display.

We moved into a new house on their property.

They had a farm but all they were doing was taking hay off. In order to keep their farm status, they had to have a working farm, so they decided to get someone in there who could make it profitable.

Phyllis wore ankle braces and used crutches, but she was fairly paralyzed. She had been in a car accident. I started taking care of the grounds and the pool. The first year we had a big snow storm and I had already bought a tractor. I always thought a great deal of both of them.

I left the DuPont-Wyeth Farm because Pappy Shuster was going to sell his farm in Kenton, Delaware and I was going to rent it. I thought a lot of Pappy. I had a lease with the man that was buying the place. I had given Phyllis notice. When the deal fell through on the rental, I went to Phyllis and begged for my job back. She didn't want me to quit to begin with, and I had been living in her house. They were gracious and told me they were glad to have me back.

Larry had moved to Jefferson City, Tennessee by this time. He had owned the Stokely farm in Culpeper, a place that I always loved. It was a beautiful farm with a great big fieldstone house. Larry had just gotten it fixed up the way he wanted it. It was just the right size for him and his family. He had been there from the time he was thirty-four until he was thirty-nine. I could never figure out why he left that farm. He had a nice herd of cows and he had the farm laid out where one man could handle it without any problems. He had all the equipment he needed. It was a perfect place and everything he had dreamed about. He had it financed where he could handle it.

Larry had a stroke and an arthritis attack. Then he got where he couldn't even lift a bag of feed. His hands wouldn't hold the weight. I think when he had the stroke at such a young age he got scared and said he wasn't gonna fool with cows any more. He came out with enough to make a down payment on a house in Jefferson City. He was going to have a greenhouse. Larry has always been a worker and a dreamer. He's willing to try anything to make it work. He was going to have a greenhouse, but for a man with five kids, it costs money, and it was too much to save for. So, he got back to the thing he knew well which was cows. He had a nice home with only thirty five or forty acres. We visited while I was still working at DuPont, and we got to talking about dairy farming. Larry had built himself a small milking parlor with fifteen or twenty cows.

Larry didn't exactly talk me into coming down there. I was more than willing to do it. That weekend we went around looking for places to rent. Larry was going to keep his place and we were going to lease an additional farm together. I was going to manage it.

It didn't work out. We rented this farm that was nice but poor. The people that owned it had inherited it. There were five families living on it.

We got a big old house. The house wasn't in good condition. It had a coal furnace that heated it and a beautiful stream running right through the front. It was full of junk everywhere. We signed a lease.

We bought the cows and what little equipment there was.

One man was managing. He milked the cows and looked after the farm. It had a tobacco patch and he had pigs. The guy fed his own pigs and was starving the cows. They had these wild cows that were all black. They were skin and bones. The first week we lost something like eight heifers from starvation.

When Marjorie and I got down to Morristown, Tennessee part of the money that we borrowed to buy the cows and equipment with was used to make a payment on Larry's place in Jefferson City. Here I was dragging Margie away from her family and I had to do some talking to get her to move away. I mean I really had to do some talking. She did it for me.

We walked into this house and all the walls were solid smoke. The manager had left the door open and the rain had leaked in the back door and the floor was all rotted all out. The tub had fallen through the floor in the bathroom.

We had no heat and the house was filthy. Here we were with two little kids. We had to move in. We didn't have a choice. And that's how we started our life in late 1974 in Morristown, Tennessee. Margie sat down on the dirty floor and bawled.

I felt like killing Larry.

Years later, I was supposed to haul hay one day and I was asked by my church to come and work that day. I had been in serious communion with God. We were with a group of people who believed in self prayer, self belief, and self awareness.

Against my will and because of the storm that was coming and threatening to ruin my crop, I went out and hooked up the tractor and wagon and began to bail and haul the hay.

When it started thundering and lightening, lightning struck the load of hay and set it on fire at the very moment when I decided to pull the wagon over to the side of the road and go to church. I proceeded to unhook it and left it there, got dressed and went and helped my church. That solidified my spiritual calling to the ministry.

PART XIV

Larry 1956-1983

LARRY, MAXINE, AND LADDIE BALLINGER, 1963

Larry Ballinger

WHEN DAD SOLD OUT IN CULPEPER, he went down to Unionville in the fall of 1956 and looked at another farm. He had had Culpeper for sale for quite a while. It took him two years from the time Raymie went into the Navy until he sold out. He wanted to go back to Delaware so he bought in Kenton. While he was fixing the barn in Kenton, he left me in Culpeper and made an agreement with me to milk his cows.

I went down and saw the woman who owned Unionville. Her husband had had a heart attack and died and I made arrangements to buy the farm. I was twenty-one years old.

I had started writing to Maxine again. Morris and I drove down there one week-end on a Saturday night and came back on Sunday. Maxine was dating somebody else and was engaged. She was working in Kingsport, Tennessee. I waited for her to come home and we sat out in the car and talked for quite a while. When I came back home to Culpeper I called her and we started writing again, and she broke off with this other boy. I went back that Easter and we went over to the Smokey Mountains together.

I had the ring in the glove compartment and I asked her if she would marry me. I knew she was going to. I had that gut feeling. She said she would and I left that night to come back home. Finally I was going to get married! I had had to hire someone to come in and milk the cows and I had to pay them myself so that I could go down to Maxine's. That's when I had the wreck, on the way home.

A drunk down at Radford pulled out in front of me across the Interstate right there on Route 11. He had a whole carload of kids. To keep from hitting him, I had to hit the side of the road. There was a line of mailboxes by a trailer court and I hit all of those mailboxes and went down over the bank. I tore the whole front corner of my fender off. A state police car was about three or four cars behind me and had seen it all.

I was in a brown and white 1953 Chevrolet. I drove out of there and brought it to a service station and took a wrecking bar and pried the fender out and drove it home and put it in the shop to get it fixed. The next day I was ready to leave and go and get married.

Next, there was a state truck patching the road and warming the asphalt. I come around this curve and my tire rod broke. It threw me right up between the truck and the tar wagon. It's a wonder that the gas tank didn't go. I was thrown clear over into the side ditch. I guess that's what saved me.

I couldn't find another used car. I was supposed to have left that night to go back to Maxine's.

I had had enough of used cars, so the next day, I bought a 1957 Ford, brand new. I left that night. I had to tag the cows so that the man who was helping me knew which cow was which. I had begun my day at four o'clock that morning. I left at ten o'clock after working and it took me all night to drive down there. By the time I arrived I was too late. It was on a Wednesday and everything was closed. We had to wait until Thursday to get married. At long last, we got married at twelve o'clock on Thursday, May 3, 1957.

Leaving Tennessee at six o'clock that evening we drove back to Culpeper in time for the next morning shift. I had made arrangements with the woman who owned Unionville to close on the farm. I had bought her Jersey cows with the farm. I was milking the cows at Unionville the day after we were married. I had no way of getting in touch with the fella at Culpeper who was milking for me.

Dad signed a note at the Culpeper National Bank for the Jerseys that I bought. The woman that owned the farm had financed it herself. Dad gave me $2,000 for the ten cows that I had and the machinery I owned. The horses were supposed to be thrown in. I took the $2,000 and used it to make the down payment on the Unionville farm.

Dad sold the horses. He sold everything from our Culpepper farm. He sold my machinery and my cows. I kept my saddle and I sold it after I went to Unionville.

When I first got married I needed some more cows. Dad had four cows that weren't milking on his farm, so he sold them to me for $400 apiece. I didn't have the money to pay for them. I went to Mr. Miller and he drew up a note. Dad co-signed the note for me right in the Culpeper National Bank. Later he tried to say that I forged his name on that note.

I had my checking account and my farm loan through the bank. The note was set up for a year and it was to be renewed at the end of the year and put over in my name. When they called him about renewing it, he claimed that he had never signed the note. I didn't ask them to renew it. I paid it.

With the Unionville farm came a bed with one blanket on it and a sheet, and one pillow. There was no heat. We had an old cook stove in the kitchen. We didn't even have a table. We had stopped at Winston on the way home from Tennessee that night and bought an old frying pan with a bone handle, some forks and knives and a couple of dishes .The next day Maxine stayed and cleaned up the house and I went to Culpeper and bought some furniture. I had it delivered, a living room suite and a bedroom suite.

I had told Dad that I wouldn't go to Delaware, and that I was going to get married and buy a place of my own. Dad and Jean never gave me anything. They never even congratulated me. Not even a card.

Maxine and I had been married about a month when we went up to Kenton to see them. We might have gotten a "congratulations" then. Maxine was real shy and she didn't really want to go up there. She didn't want to face them because they were strangers.

Maxine was tickled to death with the new house and with being married to me. When I had said I was getting married and wouldn't go with Dad, he cut me off right then. We never had a relationship after that. He just wrote me off.

When I was gone there was a fellow who had worked with the old woman. He had done all the milking for her, an old black man. He made it possible for us to go home three or four times in the two years that we were in Unionville to see Maxine's mother who was sick.

The one time that Dad came down to see me he sat in the house and read my Hoard's Dairyman while I was milking. He came out after I finished and just looked across the fence at the cows and said, "Don't like the look of that cow that you bought from me. She doesn't look like she's milked out."

That was it! I took him for a little trip around the backside of the farm and he never said "hello" or "goodbye." He probably couldn't find anything else to criticize.

I finally sold Unionville and went back up to Delaware with Dad, and rented a farm near him. I didn't have any managing experience whatsoever, because Dad never let me do anything on my own. He just worked me worse than hired help. My first farm in Unionville was just a little more than I could handle, and when I had a chance to sell the farm I sold it. I was there with Maxine on my own for seventeen months and I was not really ready to be on my own. It was hard getting by, and I had lost a little money, about $500 or $600. Not bad for my first farm on my own.

I went back up to Delaware and I put some of my cows in there with Dad's which was the biggest mistake I ever made. I went up there that fall, bought some corn from his neighbor, and filled my silo with enough to feed my fifteen cows. I bought some hay from one of Dad's fox hunting buddies. In the meantime, Dad went to Greenberg and bought more cows. He had had twenty cows when I went there and I had my fifteen. Then he bought another ten and we were running out of feed.

He quit milking when I got there and I took over the milking. He started doing just like he did at Culpeper. That spring he put in more pasture. He blamed my cows for running out of feed but he was the one who put on the other cows that were cutting him short. He was weighing my milk and I was getting paid. He thought I should be paying him rent but I was doing the work instead which was the way the deal was supposed to have gone. I used my tractor and helped him get his grass sowed, and helped him plow all his bean grain. I had to do the work on my farm at night or on the weekends. I finally did get in a crop of late soybeans. He got mad because I worked on my land and wouldn't help him. That fall I cut it off right there.

Leslie was still living at home. He was supposed to have done some fencing. We got the fence up, but the cows hadn't been turned in and when he came back the cows were out in the corn field. They had got through an old rotten electric fence in the back. Dad came down to the house. I was in the bed asleep. He jumped all over Maxine and she told him off. She told him to get out and she told him just exactly what she thought of him and he blew up. I took my cows and sold them and then he really blew up.

I didn't have enough collateral, because I still owed money to Greenberg for the last cows that I had just bought. Dad had found a tractor, plow and cultivators for me to use on my farm for $500 and he had signed a note for me. When I left there, I left the tractor and he said he wanted to keep it. Then he came back and said that I owed him money and he wanted me to pay him for all the grass seed I used.

We had planted grass seed for pasture in March and I left in April. Dad still wanted me to pay for the grass seed and the oats and all the pasture he had put in that I had never even touched. I had planted it and he wanted me to pay for it because I had had my cows there. I had already given him the tractor to pay for that.

I went just across the county line to work for a fella over in Merrill and drove back and forth for a while. That was in the fall before combining season and Dad said I left him in a hole, just before silo filling time. Dad bought feed over in Merrill and saw me out in the field working. That really got to him.

It all had to do with his pride and not being able to give in and be fair. When he was angry he'd just reject you. Nonetheless, he always got the best from me.

I got tired of Dad's interference and I came back to Culpeper. That's when I went to Mr. Hurt to manage his Bellaire Farm. Of course Dad didn't like Mr. Hurt.

That really got to him. "You go down there with all them coloreds, that man will take you for everything you got." Dad came down to see me about money. He said, "I hate to come and see you because every time I see you, it seems like there's nothing but trouble. If you don't think no more of your family than that, we ought to just leave you, or forget about you."

I said "You might just as well because the only family I got is sitting right there in my house. As far as I'm concerned that's all the family I got. You just get out of here, and go right now."

Boy, his face just turned as red as a beet. He got in his car and left.

Dad had known Gordon Willis who had married Mr. Hurt's daughter. He told him that I was in Merrill, and Mr. Hurt called me to come down and talk to him. Maxine and I drove down one Sunday. He took us in and fed us ham and biscuits and homemade ice cream. That dinner was fit for a king. He had a huge old desk. He laid his record books out on the desk and said, "What do ye' think of em? Do you think you can manage that? I'm going to turn it over to you if you're interested. I've heard about you from Gordon and Polly and I know what you can do. You're capable and I'm going to give you the chance that you need."

That's the very words he told me. "I'm going to give you the chance that you need."

I went in there as manager over fourteen men, half of them colored. Some of them had been there thirty-two or thirty-three years and it didn't sit too well. I had my hands full and don't you think I didn't. He had two milking herds and two sixty cow barns. I took over all of the farm work for one of the main farms where I lived, a fourteen hundred acre farm, and managed it with fourteen men for six years.

We moved into an apartment in the big house. Mr. Hurt lived in the downstairs and we lived upstairs. He'd come up and get me at six o'clock in the morning.

"Larry, c'mon. By Jack! Let's go out and take a little ride."

We'd go out in his old Dodge coupe. We'd look at the cattle and we'd talk. Sometimes I'd go down and eat breakfast with him, or sometimes I'd go up to the apartment and eat with Maxine. I started taking over the records of the cows and then I took over the farm. He told the men, "This is the new man. He's in charge. You do whatever he says."

I had said when I started there was only one way this was going to work. I had thought very clearly about it. I took the job with a couple of conditions, one being that I've got to do the firing and hiring, and pay the men. That's the only way it'll work.

There were a couple of big young colored boys there - fourteen, fifteen, and sixteen years old. I mean big. One of their Daddies had been there since he was a little boy. He had been a kitchen boy. He cut wood and helped carry in water and stuff for Mrs. Hurt when he was a child.

I finished milking one morning and I had sent him and his dad and a couple of others to go and do some fencing. I went out there and they were fooling around the wagon. I wanted to get them started and get things going. He was on the opposite side of the wagon from me. His dad was in the shop getting some tools and stuff together.

He said, "You white so and so and so forth... I'm gonna kill you!"

I never stopped walking and never blinked an eye and I knew the post jabber was lying on the back of the wagon because I put it there. I just walked right around and I grabbed it like that and grabbed him by the shirt and said, "You son of a bitch. If you ever talk to me like that again ...I'll kill you!" I raised that thing right over his head.

"I didn't mean it. I didn't mean it!"

Right to this day I could go up there and he wouldn't do anything in the world to me. I gained his respect right then and I gained that of the rest of them and I never had any more trouble. When we went to the field they found out that I worked right along with them.

We had a bale loader, or kicker, to put hay on the wagon. We had three wagons. They got to the point where they put me on the baler. They said, "Mr. Larry, you bale and we'll unload the wheat." I started baling at ten o'clock in the morning and they wouldn't let me stop for lunch. They'd go to the house to Maxine, and tell her to fix my lunch, and they'd bring it out to me. I'd make deals with em'.

I'd say, "Now boys, we got thirty acres of hay to get down. When we get this field of hay in, you can have the rest of the week off."

Well, they were only making $15 to $18 a week anyway and you talk about working. Boy, they would work! Sometimes we'd be done by Thursday. We'd have put up 1,800 bales in one day, three of us, two colored boys and me, and put it in the barn. I'd sit lots of times with a milkshake or a jar of tea between my legs and a sandwich in my hands, driving the hay baler on that old International.

Mr. Hurt's dad was a preacher at Stevensburg, Virginia. He started out in high school working on a farm in the summer in Jonestown, Virginia while he was going to college. Hurt wanted to be a school teacher. He had been helping the Joneses for about ten years and a neighbor's farm came up for sale. He bought it.

The Joneses set him up in the dairy business with a farm, a team of mules and an old one horse plow, a hoe harrow, and a buggy.

Dr. Graves, our veterinarian, said he remembers seeing him up at the post office. His horse was tied up with baling wire and Hurt was in an old pair of bib overalls and arctic boots. Doc said that thirty years later you'd never think he was the same person. He started out with nothin' and built up to 1400 acres of land.

After the Depression, when the bank had foreclosed on the farmers, Hurt bought up a lot of small farms. He used to buy old cows and kill em' and dress em' out and sell the meat during the Depression to make a little extra money along with shipping milk. A couple of young colored fellas, they were just young boys, were working for him for fifty cents a day.

At dawn they had to have the horses and mules fed and harnessed up, ready to go to the field and they worked until sunset. It was long hard days back in the Depression. Mr. Hurt would say,

"If a man didn't break sweat, didn't have salt on his back where he broke sweat, he hadn't done a day's work." Lots of days he'd just work right along with them while they were cutting corn. If you were to see him now, you'd never know he wasn't always a businessman.

When I first met Mr. Hurt, he was in his sixties and a director of the Culpeper National Bank. He was also the president of the Southern States Co-Op in Culpeper and the Frozen Food Locker. He was head of the Baptist Home as well. Hurt had started the rock quarry in Culpeper with his son and his son-in-law. They also had a big dairy across the road from our place. They wound up with a cement plant in Culpeper. Then they went into the sand quarry business at Fredericksburg and wound up buying the rock quarry and now they own a cement plant in Fredericksburg as well.

He was a strong, strong man. Mr. Hurt walked like a southern gentleman. He had a well-used saying that I'll never forget. If I'd done something wrong, maybe tore something up, I'd call him.

"By Jack! By Jack, did you learn anything by it? By Jack?" he'd ask. That's all he would say.

"By Jack, if you learned something by it, it was worthwhile. If you didn't, then go back and do it again!"

I'd call him up maybe once a week or so and he'd call me early in the morning wanting to know how things were going.

The road went all the way around and in the morning he would pick up one of the colored ladies, the mother to one of the men that lived there on the farm. He'd come around the road and pick her up and take her to the house to work rather than come through the farm.

When he turned the farm over to me he wouldn't have a thing to do with it. We talked things over and discussed how we wanted to do things and he'd leave it up to me to do it. In other words, he trusted me, and allowed me to feel comfortable with it.

When he wasn't running a business, he dressed simply in a pair of khaki pants and a shirt. In the summertime he wore an old straw hat that must have been thirty years old because the brim was all folded over. He'd come down every once in a while. If we were in a tight spot he'd go and rake hay for us. That little old straw hat was just a-bouncing.

Once one of them hurricanes was coming through and we had the whole river bottom full of corn. That river bottom was badly flooded. He came down there and said. "Boy, By Jack. That hurricane's a-comin'. We gotta get that corn off that bottom. How long do you think it would take you to do it?"

"Mr. Hurt, it'll take quite a while to pick that field of corn."

"By Jack. I'll come down and help you! We'll get that field of corn cut!"

So I went down there and started choppin' and had them boys runnin'.

He went and got an old milk can with a little spigot at the bottom and filled that thing up full with lemonade. He set down there in the field all day long and fed them boys' lemonade and brought them their lunch while we cut silage. We worked from daylight to dark and we got it cut. Two days later that whole bottom was flooded. It would have taken all thirty acres of corn, the whole crop.

Mr. Hurt's voice was heavy, but smooth with Southern talking. He didn't smoke or chew tobacco. He had an old Dodge hatchback he drove right on the farm. Lots of mornings he'd come and get me out of the bed about six o'clock before I went to the barn and say, "By Jack, Larry! Let's go out and go for a ride! Look things over."

We'd get out and ride around all of the farms. We'd usually end up at his church.

He was a good man... he was just like a Daddy to me. I knew his wife and all of his five children.

Mrs. Hurt was awful tight. Stingy, I guess you could say, in a certain way. We were living in the apartment upstairs in the big house before she moved out, and she had flowers planted all around the yard. She bought a garden hose to water her flowers with. One of the colored boys came in to cut her grass and he cut her water hose up right in half and she said, "Oh Larry! What am I going to do? I've spent thirty years trying to save enough money to buy that water hose."

I said, "Mrs. hurt "What I can do is go get a splice and reconnect it."

"Oh! Can you do that?"

She was pleased so I went and fixed her water hose for her. I went to town and got a coupling to put it together, and that just tickled her to death because it saved her five dollars, and she couldn't afford to buy another one. I thought she was gonna hug my neck!

Hurt made all his money in dairy and beef cattle in the 1940's and 1950's.

The farm that he started out with, he sold that to Earl Hawkins who come up there from Abington and came to Culpeper as a milk tester. The farm was called Belle Meade. The farm that I ran for him was called Bellaire. Then he had another farm, Castle Thunder, and the Carr Place and the Culpeper farm and the Strewen farm.

Mr. Hurt started with one dairy and added a sixty cow stanchion barn that the Pruitt boys helped him with. He had his own saw mill. They sawed the lumber and he built the barn, all with farm help. He got it done a little bit at a time. He didn't do it all at once.

Now, what I'm getting at is not to put Dad down, but it's interesting how a man like that can go inch by inch and establish himself and make all that money and be so successful. Dad did just as much work but he ended up in a trailer on forty acres. What that means is that one of those men could manage a lot better than the other one, or maybe money was more important to Hurt. Mr. Hurt was the type of man that could manage. He didn't just manage money. He managed his help. He knew how to use people. He knew how to work people. He knew how to take care of people and how to treat people. He had men who were with him for years. I worked for him for eleven years.

He didn't have as much money as Dad did, startin' out. Dad was good at farming in his own way, but he wasn't the type of man that could handle a big operation. He couldn't take things and turn it over and increase them. He just made a living out of what he had.

Dad was the type of man that wanted to do things only his way. He couldn't accept change. He couldn't accept advice from other people. He couldn't adapt to something new. Everything had to be done his way and no other way. Even the people that worked for him had to do things his way. You know, there's different ways of doing things.

Mr. Hurt, he turned a man loose. If he could do a job, he'd let him do it.

Like he told me, "By Jack, if you do it and make a mistake and learn by it, that's for my benefit too."

Instead Dad usually fired the man or picked him up by the back of the neck or threw him out or yelled at him and that doesn't get you anywhere.

Dad wouldn't stay in one place, and moving around doesn't get you anywhere. Mr. Hurt started right there at Batna and he died right there eighty-two years later. Mr. Hurt cleared old land and created new acreage with farm help. In the wintertime we'd rebuild barns and we'd build houses. He rented them out or sold them. Hurt had five or six houses around Stevensburg. He kept his men busy year round. Lots of times we had more help than we really needed, but everybody stayed busy. He always had work for them to do.

Mr. Hurt had this young fellow, Charlie Tibbs. He'd milk with me at the home place, and did all the feeding. He went to see Mr. Hurt one day and said he was quitting. Mr. Hurt set him down on his front porch in a swing and brought him out a big bowl of ice cream. It wasn't about fifteen minutes later when he comes walking back to the barn and went to work. He set him down and talked to him and got him cooled off and then everything was fine. He could sit down and reason with people.

If I could have gone to Mr. Hurt's, before I went to Unionville, I would have still been at Unionville today. When I bought that farm I only paid $32,000 for it. It was sold ten years ago for $300,000. We were never taught how to manage and how to work with other people.

Dad could get along with a stranger a whole lot better than he could with us. When other young men came around they could sit down and talk to him for hours. Dad talked more to my friend Greg than he did to me. I also think that Dad didn't want the responsibility of a big place. He wanted to get out and do what he wanted to do. He wanted to be free to come and go, to fox hunt and to do whatever he wanted to whenever he wanted to. Of course, he couldn't see ahead enough that if he'd given us the opportunity to go in there as men, he would have had that freedom.

Culpeper was big enough and rich enough that it could have taken care of four or five families. Raymie didn't want to farm, but Leslie and I did. Dad was still young, in his early forties, and we could easily have picked up more land. He just didn't want to share with us or respect us as men.

After I left Leslie got married and he put his cows in with Dad and got treated the same way I did. Dad accused Leslie's wife Margie of coming in and out of that driveway too fast but nobody drove in or out of there faster than Jean did. Of course, they didn't like Margie either.

Leslie up and left Dad the same way I did, and came down with me to Culpeper to the Bellaire farm. He worked for me until he got an opportunity to go up to Delaware and manage the Wyeth farm.

I was there for eight years. Then I rented the home farm for a third on shares with Mr. Hurt for three years. After eleven years I bought a place up the road.

I never saw Dad in all that time. I didn't see him for ten years.

He never called. He never came around. I never heard a word from him and I started feeling guilty. I finally called and went up to see him and we started to communicate a little bit. They had left Kenton and were now living in Harbeson, Delaware. I went up to see him and to try to make amends.

We got there about dinnertime. It was the middle of the summer, 1969. Dad acted fairly friendly. I had called and talked to him the day before and he said, "C'mon." They acted decent and friendly. We stayed over. Dad was always doing something. He had to stay busy doing something.

Leslie was gone. Nancy was around seventeen and helping him milk. Ashley was about eight. Skippy was in Vietnam, and Jeannie was around thirteen. I think Marjorie was in New York at the time.

PART XV

Raymie 1956–1984

RAYMOND EVANS BALLINGER, 1962

Raymie, Raymond Evans Ballinger

WHEN I FIRST WENT INTO THE NAVY in 1956, I was stationed in Norfolk, Virginia, and waiting to be transferred to Africa. I choose to work in the kitchen with the cook. One morning we were making pancakes in big pot-like vats, that were about three feet high and had paddles the size of canoe paddles that we used to stir the batter.

The chef asked me to get him another sack of flour for the pancake mix. I lifted up the sack and started dumping it in while the cook was stirring the mixture. I didn't notice a hole in the side where a mouse had gotten in and all of a sudden a dead mouse fell into the batter.

I yelled "Oh my God! Let me take that damn thing out of there. You got a dead mouse in there!"

He said "That's alright. It'll make the batter a little bit thicker. Give the sailors some protein."

The cook just dumped the rest of the sack in and mixed everything up.

I didn't eat pancakes in the Navy for a long time. Years later I found out why my brother Larry didn't eat Campbell's soup.... because of a similar experience!!

I was stationed in Morocco for about a year and I loved it. I had a motorcycle and I'd go out in the desert and ride. There were hundreds of acres of woodland just covered with cork chips that were left from trees when they had cut off the bark. I had found some Arabian horses that I was able to ride in their cork forest. I'd take an Arabian stallion and I'd ride with just a bridle and no saddle. He was a beautiful horse and belonged to the stable owner and he let me exercise him. I'd go through that forest lunging through the woods. You couldn't hear the hoof beats. All you could hear was the horse's lungs, giving way to the beat. I liked being there and I loved horseback riding.

My time in the Navy ended with me behind bars in Germany, hospitalized for a nervous breakdown. They put me there because I had pulled an M-1 rifle on a guy who was fucking with my life. Would I have used it? I think I would have.

I was in Tangiers and the Texans were on our base and in my barracks. I had had a prior history with these two Texans. A young Mexican guy had taught me how to play pool. He was a pool shark and nobody else would play with him. Man this guy could shoot pool! He could take three or four balls and knock them off the table in one shot. He was so smooth. When he shot there was nothing left on the table. It was that simple. Nobody would even bet with him.

The Texans were the only other sharp players and they wouldn't play him. Instead they'd play this little game of putting the ball into the cushion and then shooting it into the side pocket. They had learned to do this really well and they kept repeating the same thing, over and over and over again. That was as far as they could go and they couldn't get any better than that. There were a lot of Texans that were really out of line. They continually tried to foster the image that anyone who went against them was going to be killed while they slept.

I was one of the youngest kids on the base and extremely naïve. It was tough on me because I was such a kid. Never having been out in the world, I had a hard time going along when they were out with whores every night and drinking. They tried to get me to go with a whore once and I wouldn't do it. I sat on her bed and begged her.

"Tell them I went with you. I'll give you the money, but I don't want them to know that I'm not sleeping with you." She sat there and talked to me and finally, she said,

"You're a nice boy. You're not like those guys. If you ever want to come and talk, you just come and talk to me." Then she went to the window, cranked it open and yelled out to the other sailors. "He's fantastic! Fantastic! Better than you bums."

The Texans had a habit of making jokes about switching guard duty. We'd have a calendar up on the bulletin board, and they would arbitrarily switch names with anyone they pleased.

I made some friends and I started doing quite well. My only trouble was getting along with those two rough, very insensitive and really nasty Texans. Finally they switched my name with theirs for guard duty one night. When I came back from town, they said, "Boy, you're in real trouble. You're on report, because you had guard tonight and you weren't there."

"Well that's a lie," I replied. "I wasn't on guard tonight. I was on guard for next Tuesday."

"Well, your name was up on there for today."

"Well, I'm not supposed to be on there," I said.

I looked at the thing, and you could see where they had erased their name and changed it. They joked about it. I reported to the petty officer and he told me, "This is only a warning. We're not going to put you on report."

They could have court-martialed me for not appearing.

"Next time you don't appear, we're gonna put you on report."

Things went along for about a month and nothing else happened. Then those bastards switched my name on that bulletin board thinking they were just messing with me. When the officers asked them whose duty it was to back me up, they lied right to the lieutenant and the C.P.O. and told them that it was my night to be on guard down at the main runway.

I just walked back to the lockers, got my M-1 rifle out, loaded it, and said, "Alright, you sons-of-bitches, you tell the Chief and the lieutenant the truth right now, or I'll blow your fucking brains out!"

I cocked that rifle right back with the pin out. That Texan looked at me like I was out of my mind.

"You're fucking crazy. What the hell is the matter with you? Goddamn it! We were just playing a joke, just making a joke!"

I yelled, "Tell him. What did you say? Tell him!"

I was ready to pull the trigger. The Texans finally told the officer that they had played a joke on me. Nonetheless, I was gonna be court-marshaled for not reporting.

The chief petty officer told me, "You had a right to be angry, and to go to court for it, but you had no right to pull that rifle on your own man."

"He's not my own man. He's a man who lied right to my face and he got me in trouble."

"Look, you're really too wild, and too intense, and you're too nervous. We can't have that, and we want you to take a break." The chief said.

They sent me to sick bay for observation and to see if I was going to have a breakdown. Afterwards I was sent to the base at Wiesbaden, Germany, where they gave me a psychological evaluation. Then they put me in an institution where these crazy people were and that damn near drove me crazy. It was frightening in there. They gave me tests, and I did well. A week later they gave me the okay, and said they were going send me back to my base in Morocco.

I didn't want to go back. I knew those two Texans were still going to be there.

The officers agreed and decided to send me to Nassau in the Bahamas. After two or three weeks in Nassau, they sent me back to the Air Depot in Philadelphia, where I was honorably discharged. When you join at seventeen years old you have the choice of a one or two year enlistment. It's called a kiddy cruise. I took the year because I had served my full term overseas.

They sent my father a letter and told him he could visit me, but with Larry gone he had no help, so he couldn't come to Philadelphia.

WHEN I WAS DISCHARGED at the Air Depot in Philadelphia I started looking for my mother, Clara. I was the first of her five children who found her on September 17, 1956.

The USO was holding their usual Friday night entertainment. I had met a girl and asked her to dance. At the end of the evening, she gave me her address. It was 651 Unruh Avenue, Rising Sun, Philadelphia, Pennsylvania. Of course, I didn't know at the time that my mother lived at 663 Unruh Avenue. I had been looking for her without success for two weeks and then I called my Uncle Bob, Ruth's husband, and he took me to see her.

It was a late afternoon in September, about three o'clock, and the sun was still up and shining brightly. Clara was pushing her new daughter Bonnie down the street in a baby stroller. Penny, her two- and-a- half year old daughter, was walking alongside of our mother, holding onto the handlebar of the coach.

Bob pointed at her. "That's your mother Clara, right there."

No sooner had he said it then I jumped from his slow moving car. My mother and I were no more than ninety feet apart. This was the closest that we had been in those eleven years from the day that she drove out the driveway of that rented farm in Barrington and the afternoon she visited for my seventh birthday.

When Clara recognized me, her son, getting out of the car, she stood there frozen.

I didn't know what to call her. Embarrassingly, I said, "Clara?"

"Raymie" she answered. "Is it really you?"

We ran toward each other with the sidewalk becoming a runway for flight. The flight was an illusion of the past. The present, for the first time, shone brighter and more real than ever. We embraced in a collision, hugging, kissing, and crying to make up for the lost years.

Bob had quickly stopped and parked his car. He had taken the children while my Mother and I embraced and we walked awkwardly toward her house across the street. She invited me into the living room, but all I could concentrate on was eleven years of longing and the need to know her once again, with her rounded smile and auburn hair. Her voice rose at a particular pitch as though it were reaching out for you, and she would smile invitingly.

I knew she was with me, in my life again, but who were these children, Bonnie and Penny? Who was her new husband, George? What was this house on Unruh Avenue? She belonged in the tall grasses, holding my hand and walking from our Pine Grove bungalow to the Homestead. That was the only way I could fix her in my mind. Those were the most intimate memories lodged at the end of my knowledge of her.

I could hear the voices in the room, but they were just noises. They meant nothing to me. I needed to focus in, to redefine a mother's look to her son, and a son's look to his mother.

I turned on the couch. Clara squeezed my hand, pulling me to her which started the tears all over again. We sat for what seemed like hours, talking and sharing our past. Finally Bob said that he had to go.

I thanked him graciously and hoped that I would see him again soon. That evening I had to return to the base while they prepared my discharge. I said goodbye to my long-lost mother like a sailor going out to sea even though I would be seeing her again very soon. After my discharge I came back and lived with her.

That's when I found out about Sandy, my youngest and the last sister, whom I had never known.

While living with Clara, I took a drive into Barrington. I had last lived there with my mother and dad in 1944 when I was six and here I was returning at eighteen. I parked my car, and went in and looked at the school house. Then I tried walking home from the school house, the way I used to as a little boy. I cut through what had once been cornfields totally oblivious to the reality that a whole town had been built where the farm once had been. I became feverish, as though I were etherized. I found myself walking through people's yards, tripping on their garbage cans, and pulling down their clothing lines.

I felt as though I were in a total hypnotic state, thrust back in time. I saw nothing but the cornfield. People were yelling at me from their houses,

"Hey, you! What the hell are you doing in my yard?"

I just kept walking. I became that six-year-old child again, walking home from school and feeling that my mother Clara would be there waiting.

After twenty minutes of cutting through yards, jumping over fences, with cars beeping at me on the avenues, I came to a clearing, a cul-de-sac. I just sat there on the curb. I had gotten dizzy from this time warp, so I just sat there for a moment. I looked up and a chill ran through my whole body. There was the old farmhouse and I could see my mother sitting on the glider on the front porch.

I stood up to take another look.

It was not my mother, and I was not six years old. The woman on the porch asked me if she could help me.

I said, "Yes, could I bother you for a glass of water, please. I'm a little dizzy."

She said, "Of course. Come up on the porch and sit down."

While she was in the house getting the water, I sat there trying to envision that long narrow driveway that went south for half a mile through our fields to the Black Horse Pike. We talked for a while on the porch while I drank the water. I tried to explain to her what had happened, and she asked me,

"Would you like to come inside and look around?"

With nervous excitement, I said "Yes." I had been too anxious to ask.

As I slowly walked through the halls and into the rooms, memories assailed me. I saw myself riding on the back of the pickup truck counting the telephone poles going by. Their wires became the thread, the connection of the distance that I was traveling.

I could hear my mother's voice in the kitchen. I could see my sister Judy sliding down the upstairs banister. It was all coming back. Each room was like a shattered star falling out of the sky with fervent memories.

I could hear my parents arguing in the good parlor where her crocheted lace curtains hung.

This strange woman was calling me into the next room and was telling me how she had changed the house. I could hardly hear her. My ears were ringing with echoes of the past.

We went back downstairs and I thanked her very graciously for allowing me to come in. I then asked her if she would mind if I took some pictures of the outside, and if I could write to her if I needed any further information.

"Yes," she replied. "I would be glad to answer." She wrote out her address on an old envelope and gave it to me. I never saw her again, although we exchanged Christmas cards for years.

I got a job in Philadelphia driving a flagstone truck. I don't know how many ton it was, but it was dangerous as hell. I drove and went to night school for a while, and then I switched and worked at night and went to day school and finally I went to a drama school to learn how to act. Clara supported me in that.

"You want to act? We'll find you a drama school."

It was the wrong drama school for me. I was only in Philadelphia with Clara for three or four months, and then we had some fights.

After a while it was obvious that Clara didn't really want me living with her. I was not her family. She had made a new family for herself.

I HAD TO THINK ABOUT MY PERCEPTIONS and the feelings I had for Clara while living with her in Philadelphia those three months. I was so hungry for love that I needed to step back before I had any reliable insight about the kind of woman she was. I was only eighteen years old and very lonely. My mother was then forty-two. I watched her every move.

Clara was vivacious, strong, and tenacious with a bit of devilment. She wasn't a classic beauty, but she was striking and sensual looking. She had incredible unused energy, like so many women of her time. Women liked her and admired and respected her for her courageous approach to life. Clara tried to live ahead of her time, in a world that my father couldn't understand. She smoked, danced, drank and loved life.

She was not formally well educated, but she always felt that she had to better herself in order to keep up. If she'd had different opportunities, she probably would have done very well. Because of her background and her family, she was limited to thinking that Mount Holly and a good marriage was all she could aspire to. She was a likeable woman, walking solidly on her heels, seeming to be in command of things. Her strong jawbone reached forward as though she knew where she was going, although the tightness in her mouth revealed a certain tension and uncertainty.

When my Dad first met Clara he was an impressionable naive twenty year old. He was attracted to her, but he also thought she was "damn common." Clara on the other hand had no aspirations toward being a farmer's wife. She decorated her house, and shelves with little doggies and porcelain cats, and had frills on her curtains. She knew how to care for a man and handle him as a woman, but she wasn't interested in caring for his house and children. She loved my Dad as a rodeo man and a shipyard worker, but never as a farmer.

Shortly after Clara left us, she married George Mahaffey, a railroad brakeman. They had two children eight years later. From the time she married

George in 1947, she began building a career. Her first job was as a sales clerk at Sears, the next as a bookkeeper for JC Penney's department store, and then as a bookkeeper for Tasty Cake. Later she worked as a buyer and inventory manager at the Confectionery Sugar plant off Rising Sun Avenue, not far from where she lived. She worked until the birth of her first child with George in 1955.

George acted on her command, and she was still spoiled. Many mornings George would put on an apron and brought Clara her breakfast in bed while feeding the baby and changing its diapers, all before going off to work. This was certainly a big contrast to her life with my Dad. This was how her parents treated her, and this was what seemed to make Clara happy.

I would observe her in the kitchen with an unfiltered Camel cigarette tucked in the corner of her mouth, reading the morning paper while I made my breakfast. Occasionally she would greet me and cook for me. She scanned through the 'Wanted' ads trying to find me a job, and recommended a school for acting, after I had chosen my new career.

She would wash and iron my clothes and cook the evening meals for George and the children and myself, and clean the house regularly. When she was in her late thirties, George taught her how to drive her new pink Pontiac convertible. She never showed any recognition of my passion to fill the emptiness I had felt from her abandonment those twelve years ago.

She did agree to co-sign loan papers for me to purchase a car. Within three months of my residing there, she requested that I pay rent and a small amount for my meals. This was very hard for me since I was working only part time, and going to school full time.

We were both uncomfortable and I wasn't getting what I wanted. I wanted a mother and a home and a family, but I wasn't going to get that from her. It was too late. Reluctantly, I met her demands. At the end of the third month the transmission went out on my 1952 Mercury. I had no way to get around, and no money to fix it. George offered to pay for the repairs. There was a huge dispute, and she refused to allow this. At that point, I felt more cared for and more wanted by George than by my own mother. I told her to keep the car, and that I was leaving. She told me I couldn't do that.

"Watch me," I said.

That evening I was packed and out of the house. I had moved in, in September of 1956 and I moved out on December 31of that same year. I took a room at the 'Y' on Walnut Street in Philadelphia for one night and then bought a Greyhound bus ticket to New York City on New Year's Day.

I went to New York City alone. I was a young farm boy, a discharged sailor boy, in New York City with nothing! I pawned my typewriter and the coat on my back in the middle of winter and rented a room. I put Jell-O and milk on the window sill. I had nothing. Not a pot to piss in. I started my new life with no family and no nothing.

Of course Dad told me, "You want to go see Clara? I don't want anything to do with you."

I couldn't win either way. Once again I didn't have a father or a mother. Did you ever get a piece of a puzzle that was the perfect shape but had the wrong picture on it? You kept trying to make it work. It fit but it never looks quite right. There are pieces that will fit in other spots, but they don't match the picture you're putting together. You can only keep the piece that was there and paint a new picture on top. Painting a new picture meant Dad divorcing and marrying Jean and never looking back. Thus Jean became our "mother" and Clara was eradicated.

I BEGAN MY LIFE IN NEW YORK CITY with nothing. After I left Clara in Philadelphia, I started living in New York City in a tiny eight by ten room at the top of the Woodrow Wilson Hotel. The room had a sink in the corner and a hot plate, and I was eating cans of stew, like a dog, every

night. I couldn't even afford a refrigerator so the meat and milk would go bad from the heat. It was incredibly hot at the top of that hotel. I was so lonely and sometimes I just lay in my bed and looked at the ceiling. I was going to school at nights to get my high school diploma and working at McGraw Hill Publishing in the daytime.

When I left Culpeper the agreement I had with Larry was that he would buy my cows. I sure as hell could have used some of that money from those cows I owned in Virginia. I never got any money from Dad or Larry for my horse, my four cows and four heifers or my chickens.

I knew a guy in the city who had a car, and he drove me down to Virginia to see Larry in Unionville. I asked Larry for the rest of my money so this guy and I could rent an apartment and I could get out of that little closet of a room. Larry told me he was real short and couldn't do it right then.

Dad had rejected me for having found and lived with my mother, and Larry was all I had, so I didn't get too hot about the money. I just turned around and went back to New York City, to live in my eight by ten room. When I got back to the city, I was hurt and bitter. I was hurt that they made me an outcast. I was bitter that Dad had told me I couldn't sell my cows and they had to stay on his place, and then he sold them with the farm. Dad said he had given the money to Larry to buy the farm in Unionville. Realistically, I owned over $2,500 worth of cows and was owed $400 for my horse and saddle. I needed that money to start my life living alone in New York City. I was angry about walking out of my life in Virginia with nothing. At the least Larry had a farm and a family.

I started studying acting with Kurt Conway, Kim Stanley's husband. I lived life as though it was one big stage. I was acting when I was out in the world and constantly trying to change myself and put a new public self forward. I would put forth my changing view of what I wanted life to be and how I should be perceived and who I wanted to give the impression of being.

People didn't buy it. They didn't respond to me. I didn't understand why they didn't like me but they didn't have a chance to know me, because I wasn't allowing it. I didn't have people sharing with me, because neither they nor I knew who I was. Only on stage could they share with me because there I was being the real me. I don't think that I ever dealt with my entire self. I didn't know who or where my real self was.

I was often angry about what I perceived to be my real self, and I didn't always like me, but it was all I had. You can neither negate nor totally remold yourself. You can understand, change, and finally learn to live with who you are.

The summer of 1959 I had a contract to work in Memphis, Tennessee, at the Front Street Theater. I was supposed to play Reverend Hale in *The Crucible*, Simon in *Hay Fever*, and the tutor in *Five Finger Exercise*. I had been doing *The View from the Bridge* at the Carnegie Theatre in New York City. Dick Cavitt's wife, Carrie Nye, was casting from New York. She had seen me in Miller's play and she came back stage and told me that she really liked my performance as Rodolfo. She asked if I would be interested in working at a theatre in Tennessee, and would I read a scene from *Five-Finger Exercise*? I read the scene with her perched up in a large armchair. I walked the floor and directed my lines to her as best I could. As soon as I finished, she asked if I would be willing to sign a contract for three plays at the Front Street Theatre in Memphis. This was a professional equity company. I agreed and flew out to Memphis a week later.

My only problem was that I had this Basset Hound, Lady Duchess of Jericho, and I couldn't take her with me. I had not seen Dad in almost three years. He agreed to keep the dog for the summer so I brought her to his new farm in Kenton, Delaware. After subletting my apartment on Jane Street, I arrived at the airport in Memphis one week later.

The producer, Barbara Carson, and the director, her ex-husband George Taliosi, met me at the airport. George took one look at me, and hated me on sight. I felt the same about him. Nevertheless, I loaded my luggage in his car and I was taken to the theatre to be introduced to the cast. The first play was to be *The Crucible*.

The following day we began rehearsal. After three days of grueling and agonizing effort, George and I overcame our dislike of one another. It was only temporary. In the middle of rehearsal on the third day he continued screaming at me. I stopped in the middle of rehearsal and said to him right in front of the cast, "You're never going to accept me or my work. Let's just call it quits. Give me my week's pay and my plane ticket and I'll return to New York."

He didn't mind the week's salary, but he absolutely did not want to pay for my plane ticket. Barbara felt terrible and told me that he was impossible. She said that he did that every year with one actor. Barbara bought my return ticket. She told me she was sorry, especially since Carrie had said that I was a wonderful actor.

Soon it dawned on me that I had sublet my apartment. Once I reached the airport I called Dad and asked if he could use help for the summer. He agreed but said he couldn't pay me very much. They were still struggling with the new farm in Kenton. I agreed that he would pay me what he could afford. I flew from LaGuardia to Wilmington.

Judy was staying in Kenton since her husband was away in the service. Judy was also heavily pregnant with Penny. The kids would push two year old Paula up and down that driveway a thousand times just to give Judy a break.

Leslie was fifteen. I had been away from the family for four years. Being back felt reassuring.

City life was harder and lonelier. I had a lot to reconcile. Working in New York City was demanding and had confirmed all those earlier difficulties. Taking a break and being back on the farm and working with Dad felt easier and more understandable this time.

Leslie and I were helping Dad clear a field and build a silo. We were also taking blackberry briars as high as your head and piling them up and burning them. We had made a fire and the fire got away from us. Les and I beat ourselves to death trying to put it out. Dad was mowing ahead of us in the swampy area, where we built the pond. Dad finally got off the tractor and helped us to get it out.

Judy and I told Leslie that summer that Jean wasn't his real mother. Judy told him about Clara and that she had left Dad and Leslie when he was one-and-a-half years old. I told him that he had two more half sisters and that they were blond like him and beautiful. Leslie didn't believe it at first, but we finally convinced him. Dad didn't tell him until two or three years later, just before his high school graduation, that Jean wasn't his mother. Four years later he went to find Clara.

While Jean and Dad lived in Kenton, Jean put her foot down and said she didn't want her son Skippy working out in the barns. Skippy liked my Dad and was a different kind of child. He would go to the barns of his own choice to help out.

Marjorie on the other hand was rigorously protected because she was Jean's first daughter and the first 'real' grand-daughter. Mrs. Shuster insisted that Jean not let Raymond get his hands on that girl and make her like the boys. Jean defended Marjorie defiantly and wouldn't let her fight for herself. She kept her in the house.

Nancy was strong and independent. She stood up to Dad and he respected her. When Jeanie came she was kept in the house. Jean tried to manage Jeanie's life and her world as she had Marjorie's.

Ashley was born much later. He became the first boy that Jean could direct. Jeanie finally escaped the house for the barn. Ashley was in danger of becoming like Jean's brother, Bud, who depended on his mother up until she died.

Toward the end of his childhood, Ashley turned around and went out to the barn to work with his father and then he went into the service following his sisters, Nancy and Jeanie.

The paradox is that my father was initially protected by his mother from his own father. She tried to keep him from working in the fields. She was afraid that his father would "break the boy." My father loved working in the fields and bragged that he was working alongside the men at twelve years old. Of course, that was in 1926.

My father encouraged Larry to quit school after the eighth grade. Larry didn't have a mother to protect him. Dad crippled Larry by not letting him make his own decisions. In turn, Larry farmed and idolized my father. He wanted to be just like him and have his own dairy but Dad never taught him how. Instead all he wanted to do was manage Larry.

WHEN I RETURNED TO NEW YORK CITY, I went to work for Lincoln Adair. He wanted me to narrate a manuscript that he'd written, and to go around to colleges and bookstores and act out the script. He would go on stages with rockets and time capsules to show how you could freeze your body so you could come back in time a hundred years later. I worked with him a little until I was cast in a major production. I was always fascinated by his concept, and almost wished that I had stayed with him. He was going on a lecture tour and wanted to take me as his assistant and thought I was the right person for the job.

At twenty-three, I had written a play called *The Imbecile*. I launched it myself without any apprehension of failure. I had heard of a theatre on Thirty-first and Madison, called the Seven Arts Center that was closed for four and a half months. I took the bus down there and met the custodian. I told him I wanted to use the theatre and asked him how to go about it. He laughed at me like I had just told him the funniest joke. But he did tell me that the owner of the theatre, Arthur Kennedy, was in Paris working on a film. I asked for the telephone number and followed him in.

I was now inside of the theatre. The seats, the smell and the feeling of something happening surrounded me. I was mesmerized by the atmosphere, and just knew this was going to happen. The custodian was still laughing at me as he handed me the number and told me I was even more foolish than he had originally thought. He let me use the phone in the office, and I called France.

I managed to reach Mr. Kennedy and told him I was at his theatre, and that I had admired him and his work. I had seen him play Biff in *Death of a Salesman*. I told him that I had played the same role at the Olney theatre in Washington, and that I needed a favor. Passionately I explained how I had written this play that meant my life to me, and that I was sure that a man with his understanding would appreciate that. Again, I invoked Curt Conway's name and how he had spoken of Kennedy's playing the role of John Proctor in *The Crucible*.

Mr. Kennedy started laughing and said he had no idea why, but he was going to let me do it. I would have to be responsible for the electric bill. Then he threatened to lock me out if there was any damage. He spoke to the custodian, and I walked away with a theatre and a key!!

The following Saturday I was ready to start production. The cover for my program was a prison cell made to look tall like a cathedral, with great bars on the gates opened wide. A man was standing alone on the inside, unsure about coming out into the world. Initially, I had felt compelled to write this play. I had gone full circle and came back to write *The Imbecile*. This was the first time I had any artistic control. I cast my future wife, Lee, as a Salvation Army woman. I was sure this play had a great power of its own.

The reviews included one critic's comment, "That young man, he's a strange young man, but he's very interesting and very unique. He frightened me a little bit on the stage, but he makes me think a great deal, and I'm not quite sure whether he's a genius or a madman."

Orestes, my first wife's father, taught me to assert myself. Without him I don't believe that I would have had the urgency to be the most of myself at every moment and expect it from everyone else that I worked with.

Dorothy Kilgallen was the head of all NBC's casting. While I was working in the printing department at MCA, I had the guts to go to her office and leave my showcase film on her desk. The following day she called.

"I want you here at 9:30 am Wednesday morning." She sat and played the film in front of me and asked me why I had picked this particular piece and would I be interested in working in the soap, "Another World"?

The following Thursday morning I went to Avenue M in Brooklyn to the NBC studio to work. Four and a half months later, I began playing Walter Thompson, the Matthews family attorney, and continued in the role for two and a half years.

I LEFT NEW YORK CITY for Johnstown, New York, also leaving behind a good agent and a budding career. I felt lost. By this time I was married and had two children.

I thought that I would grow in New York City but instead I was replanted in one of their pots and I grew uncomfortable with who I was becoming. I was growing in a direction different from the one I really wanted. I couldn't breathe. I needed a greater freedom. My choice for freedom was to leave and buy an abandoned farm in Johnstown that had barns like those at the Homestead. I think I was trying to relive the first seven years of my life. I wanted to have back what I thought I had lost. I wanted to come home to myself.

When I first went up in Johnstown I wanted to be part of their world of knitting mills and tanneries and hang out with the people in the hardware store and at the diner. I started working at the Lexington Training Center for the Handicapped.

I felt like one of the handicapped and I understood where they were coming from. The center's director told me, "You can't get involved emotionally. You can't see them as human beings. They're lames." That's the very word he used, lames. Then they joked about me. "Maybe we should put him in one of the workshops. Which workshop should we put Raymond in?"

I couldn't be dispassionate. They were not like our cattle and I couldn't herd them and make their decisions. They had souls.

My friend Ben came and worked in one of the workshops for a while. He made a leather hand for Jessie, a thalidomide baby who was blind and had no hands. Ben thought he could do things for them.

I built a film studio and tried making my own short films. That was my dream, to work and have an acting company, and make short films. I knew that I could do industrial documentaries until I could afford to be on my own. I would then take the money from the documentaries and make short films. I failed to do that, but I came close. I made my short films, won prizes for my photography, and worked at the Colonial Theatre in Johnstown.

When I came back to the city, in my forties, I started to come full circle with who I was as a person, bringing the child to meet the adult for the first time.

WHEN I HAD LIVED WITH CLARA I had asked her about Sandy, the child she was pregnant with when she left us. She told me that she had been adopted by her brother-in-law's brother and that she had watched her grow up through reports from her sister, Edith, and her husband Alex. Clara's youngest daughter, Bonnie, had visited me once in Johnstown. She was the only one who knew my telephone number. Bonnie was the one who called in 1981 to tell me that our mother, Clara had died, and that my full sister Sandy, who I had never seen in my life, would be meeting me at the Fort Myers, Florida airport.

Until we stood in the center of the airport terminal, I had no idea what she would look like or if she would know who I was. Out of those three hundred and some people we recognized each other immediately. She knew me and I knew her. We hugged and kissed. We sat in her car and talked for hours. We were like any brother and sister who had been away from each other for a long while.

She drove me to her house, where I met Will, her adoptive father. The next day we drove to the funeral, and afterwards I went to my mother's trailer home. I wanted to see where she had lived and died.

Dad's letters that he had sent to Clara from out West in Reno presented a contradiction for me. It appeared that she did not know that he was getting a divorce, yet he was asking her to sign papers. The letters were loving and promising. He missed his ten-year-old daughter, Sissy, and he would see her soon. He approved of Sandy's name. Why? When he told Clara that if she walked out of that farmhouse door she could never come back, he meant it. Whichever child she took it was the same for them. How could that man say such a thing about his daughter? I felt that what was said was said only in anger. It was a cover up for his pain, rejection and guilt.

I WAS FORTY-SIX YEARS OLD and I was in my prime time. That summer I had opened the Rhinebeck Summer Theatre with William Inge's *Picnic* taking actors from my classes in New York and fulfilling the enormous challenge of converting our farm's antiquated Dutch barns into a summer theatre. For the first time this integrated the feelings of paradise that I had on the Homestead and my passion for acting.

I had remarried in 1982. Babette was the partner that I had always wanted. Now there was nothing to keep me from succeeding at anything that I wanted to do. Both of my sons were now living with me. Babette was pregnant with our child. My sons were helping me build and stage manage. I felt surrounded by a loving family for the first time in my life.

My ex-wife Leonora had become a very compatible and good friend.

We thrived the first season with radio and television advertisements, grants and financial support from Rhinebeck locals and surrounding areas in Dutchess County. The season had to be a success, and it was. When I went back into the city in the fall I felt strong, and everything was working for me. I was teaching more classes, doing commercials and numerous small parts in major films.

Babette was working for and being exploited by another garment industry company, Oak Hill. She had not yet owned her own business. I encouraged her in that direction. We had traveled that winter in Europe, since she had some business with a knitting mill in Florence, Italy. We spent some time in Cairo, and traveled from Paris to Milan.

I was looking forward to the upcoming season. I had already chosen the plays, picked some of the directors, and was ready to start casting in March and April, confident that I could act in three of the plays and direct one out of the six.

The first one was *Equus*. I was playing Dysart, the psychiatrist, who was having a midlife crisis of his own. For me, going into this role was like falling into an abyss. In some ways it matched me too well. I had hired a professional manager for the theatre, and unbeknownst to me he had been an alcoholic. As soon as he was under pressure at our theatre he cracked and began drinking again, leaving me with managing, building, and playing the role of Dysart.

In the beginning rehearsals went well. We had begun them in New York at Lee Strasberg's Fifteenth Street Theatre and Film Institute. The director I had chosen had, like me, worked with Strasberg. We understood each other's language.

Except for music, sound, costumes, and choreographing the horses with their copper sculptured heads, the play was pretty well set after the first two weeks, so well that we did a limited performance for Strasberg's studio. This was received as being both powerful and riveting. Yet, despite all the preparation, when we arrived at the theatre the business demands shook me. I tried to get deeper into my creative role and ignored the problems surrounding me as we began to launch the second season of a business.

I was using my brother Larry as a parallel in the play for Alan Strang, the boy who had learned to worship horses instead of God and through his guilt had gouged the eyes out of six horses with a hoof pick. I reached in to my sensory imagination for Larry as a version of Alan, nurturing and giving Alan all the things that I could not give Larry. I was continually thinking of our Homestead and our teams of horses, their colorations, manes and tails, the way they wore a harness or a collar, and would pull as a married team.

All of this ignited a volcano in me. There was no room for anything else, neither managing nor caring about what was going on around me. Then suddenly, the play was supposed to open in four days, and I could see that the physical theatre wasn't ready and it was not going to happen and that the play would be destroyed along with the theatre I had worked so hard to build the previous two years.

We had been required to put in a new sewer system, and that was not completed. We could not legally open. The town engineers had made allowances for us the first year, but they would not waver an inch this season. My only choice was to cancel the play and go on to the next production, *Foxfire*, that was already in rehearsal. I had to take over the management for the rest of the season, servicing and watching other actors act and other directors direct. Each play became more difficult than the next. The sixth play, *The Dark at the Top of the Stairs* by William Inge, was the last of the season, so I was finally able to manage, direct, and act in this production.

Reuben Flood, the father and central figure in the play was my kind of role, a man who was lost in his past, and could not seem to find a space for himself in the present or future. As with Dysart, the people of his town did not want his antiquated values.

For Raymond the actor, as well as Dysart and Inge's Reuben, it had become a throw-away world. My frustration was so deep that it forced me to go back and confront my father for the first time in nine years. I had not seen him since 1975.

Just as I was closing the theatre for the winter, I received a phone call from Babette in New York City that we were going to lose our baby. Quickly driving back to the city, I attended to all the things that had to be done and then, without thinking, I packed my suitcase and told Babette that I was heading to Delaware to see my father. It took me about five hours to drive. It seemed like one of the longest trips I had ever taken.

I had to return to confront and rectify all of these things that I had been feeling.

I parked the car near the carriage barn that my father had built. You could recognize his buildings anywhere. They were overbuilt and painted red and you knew they would last through his and my lifetime.

"Hey there, boy," he said. "Well, it's about time."

Jean, my stepmother, came out of the side door, greeting me as well. She was heading out to the school where she was a teaching assistant in Georgetown. This meant that Dad and I would be alone.

I left my bags in the car, bringing out only a loaded tape recorder. Dad was still strong and straight, but surgery to remove a cyst had damaged a nerve which affected his mouth and his left eye, and he wore a pair of glasses with thick lenses that was so unlike him. Nevertheless, he walked with the same confidence and easy, solid long strides, knowing exactly where he was going.

He was still full of pain and anger about his sons, especially us first three, Larry, Leslie, and me. He felt that we had all done him such injustice and that he had failed to raise us properly with the kind of values he was raised with. I wanted him to tell me, "Was it all worth it? Was my life worth it? Was his life worth it? Was there another path we could have taken?"

Going backwards in time we shared and relived the way it was and also the way we wanted it to be until at last we had the father and son relationship we wanted.

Now we had a choice. That lifted a great weight for me and I think it took a great weight from him as well. Growing up we were so absorbed in getting through our lives that we didn't see that we had choices.

The scars and damage that Larry, Judy and I received were extremely detrimental to us for the rest of our lives. These wounds were inflicted because of human failings. Dad had his truth, but he also had his lies.

Clara took care of us. As a child I never felt that she hurt me, abused me, or that she didn't love me. When she left I did feel hurt, abused, and unloved. I couldn't understand why? What did I do that was so bad? What did I do wrong? Why did she abandon her favorite child?

Judy could never forgive her. Larry just buried it. Dad never discussed it.

I wanted the least of that to happen to my children, and to my family. But, I was divorced. Many of the things that I mentally accused Dad and Jean of doing, I did.

When Clara left, she sent Larry and me to be with our Dad. He gave us our heritage, the Ballinger past, the Homestead, and the farm life. In spite of all the tragedies and the pain, I choose that life over a city life. I would still take the farm.

I'm glad I am who I am. I've come full circle and am reconciled with the man I am. I got all that from Dad and from the farm.

Late in 1992, Dad seemed to be repeating himself, and I felt that the third act of his life was ending and the curtain was coming down. He would often say," I know I told you this before, but…."

When I called and discussed plans for the spring he said, "I think we better take it one day at a time son." During this period, Dad had also reconciled with many of his other children. It was as if he felt completed by his reconciliations and had come to terms with his life. That's what he wanted at the end of his life. I think he wanted this with all of his children and his wife.

For five nights in late December he had gone deep into the woods through snow and ice looking for two of his lost fox hounds and he developed walking pneumonia. He died of respiratory failure on January 23, 1993.

Judy called the house to tell me. Rebecca, my daughter who was six at the time, answered the phone. I was in shock. It was as though my engine had stopped. Rebecca held me and cried with me, and said, "I'm here for you, Daddy. Daddy, I'm here." It was the most touching thing. I could sense the continuity. She was going forward in life and my life was one-half to three-quarters over, and his was over.

When Larry stood at his coffin and looked at Dad , he wanted him to come back to life, just enough to tell him how he felt. He hadn't had that closure and he wanted it. Larry just crumbled.

We all were jealous of his love. We all wanted his love. We each wanted to be the one who was loved the most by him. The children who ended up the farthest away from him were the most angry that he was dead.

Judy said, "Thank God this is over with."

EPILOGUE

It was early fall, when the wind was like a whisper, and the sun was hazy, and the sky a little gray. The oats had been combined and the corn was shocked. The morning glories still grew and bloomed along the roadside.

All of these new buildings, these contraptions, these forts, these shopping malls. These contorted little shelters.

Commercial entities, Subaru. Dunkin Donuts. McDonald's. The China Queen. Rosco's Furniture. Yurkey's Appliances. Kowalski's Bikes. Rolls and Remnants. Pesticides, Petroleum, and of course the National Banks.

Where does the money come from? Where's the money going?

Hoops and hallways. Shim sides, and slides and windows and doors. Liquors and wines. Fences, No minds. Aluminum and Honda bikes. Rancocas Valley Cycle Centers. Tents. Shacks. Houses. Trailers. Dumps.

Buses to live in, cars to ride. Rancocas homes. Larchmont homes. Mobile homes. Jammed together for rental rates. Sadly enough they doom the apple orchards' fate.

Plazas and Marts. People with no smarts. Tavern Stock, Condominiums.

Who made those exquisite old brick houses? Evesham's best on Kings Highway, at Chews Landing and Haddonfield? Our old Homestead in Marlton built three hundred twenty-seven years ago? What makes them less exciting than Bradshaw Avenue?

Leaves were deserting the trees blowing across to Hutcherson Drive. At Chews Landing they were more yellow and amber, ready for Halloween. By the time I hit Barrington Avenue they were still green.

On to Clements Bridge and Haines. The leaves are still on the trees here, on Oak Avenue, Chestnut and High Street.

I'm at the Barrington School now, on Wilmont Avenue and Gloucester Pike. The school is the same, the anchor fence, the red maple on the school lawn. Standing on the corner at the end of the driveway by the hall there is a red oak. In the very corner of the school is a cedar tree with long needles.

Children are playing on the grounds. Anchor fences surround the bottom windows offering safety. Grey brick on the bottom and blue at the top with a white mortar inlay. There's a new addition on our school now, bright red brick. This is all going to be torn down, so the custodian tells me. Why? A new expressway is coming through all the way to Atlantic City.

The four corners bus stop is where we were picked up to take us to the farm or Haddonfield. We never knew which. I'd stand on the back porch of the school waiting out of the rain, wondering who was going to come and pick us up. I watched the corner lights blink from green, to yellow, then red.

On the left of the school, where the buses used to wait, there were some railroad ties with light switches, and the old Ed and Ben Service Center where I used to buy candy. The bench across the street from the bus stop is still there. Clements Bridge Road is the road from Haddon Heights into Barrington School. Wilmont Avenue leads down to the school grounds.

As I drive down Gloucester Avenue, our cornfields are now full of wall to wall bungalows. The first new avenue of our corn field is South Moor.

The leaves are turning brandy, orange, sienna red, and yellow, putting a curfew on our east cornfield.

Here is Thomas Avenue. To the left of me, going toward the farm, are more wall-to-wall little houses and bungalows, clear to Browning Road, and who knows what's on Browning Road? It may be our driveway, it may not be.

These were our fields that I played in, lush with yellow buttercups and large varieties of wild flowers. The red oak and the burning sumac are all gone.

Devon Drive, on Second Avenue, looking north, I think it is the old farm house now surrounded. Why are Spruce and Devon Avenue standing in the middle of our back meadow which winds around, over the creek?

Bracton. Everview. A man scowled at me, as if I didn't belong there. Glenview to Dead End Creek. Spruce Avenue to Brazen. Where does it go from Brazen? Is it still our Barrington meadow? There are a few trees left at the bottom down to Wilson Drive.

The old Scots pines down by the privy still stand, and I can hear the murmuring of highway traffic beyond the lower pastures. There looks to be the same two maples on the east side of the house, either the same maples, or more newly planted. There are some stumps and humps left keeping company with a wild cedar at the corner of our yard, and a new blue spruce, where the old chicken house stood.

The lilacs still bloom showing their old roots after forty years. The forsythia emanates from the same sunny spot, along with the purple flags and the iris, growing just between the chicken house and the old pigpens, which are no longer standing.

The red maple is down near the cherry orchard. I can still see three of the original cherry trees amongst the drooping trumpet flowers, down to where the Thruway, like a large elephant walk, destroys everything.

The old back porch was taken off. Now this funny brick veneer replaces it. The shed where Dad first kept his cans of milk in an old tub with ice has left only the memory.

A couple of locust trees stand where the back meadow once was with two left over cherry trees growing high and wild.

The highway seems about two hundred yards down the hill by a big old tree.

The ravine to the west side of the back of the house is still there even though there are buildings nearby. There is an old apple tree in the front yard, which matches the old spruce tree.

A frightened woman had come to the McDonald house. Her husband had died. Fifth Avenue dead ends into the old farm estate. You have to go around the block. In front of the house is Fourth Avenue and over the drive, down to the Gloucester Pike where our lane used to be is Thomas Avenue. Appropriate and ironic.

Thomas Avenue is our old lane. Fourth Avenue, Third Avenue, and Second Avenue are rows of houses on each side of our lane, all numbered. One, two, three, four on a block.

Gloucester Pike was one half mile from the end of our long lane and a mile to the school. I'm on Haines Drive. The Sycamores, thick as anywhere, seem to be on Reading Avenue, as are the maples and white oaks.

I'm now driving along Third Avenue, which is more than likely the avenue we walked our horses on after the auction, through the snowstorm and the seeming end of our lives, and the banishment from Barrington into Haddon Heights.

The stinging barbed wire that my father cut to break through into the town was not there to remind me of the pain, but the houses and people were. I'm now passing the same houses that I looked into after school, searching for answers of why I had no family, trying to recognize how a real family would live.

I also recognize the lighting and the texture of the trees in Haddon Heights where I occasionally walked with Mrs. Shuster as she did her shopping. The double walkway that was the main street is back there. This is not the school. This is a Methodist Church. That is Station Avenue with the shops where we shopped and there is the railroad track. I'll be damned.

I'm back on Seventh Avenue now. I was in town on the main street and went into the Five and Dime Store. I took a picture. I went to the old drugstore with the fans running where the fountain used to be, where Judy and I stole the shoe box full of accessories, barrettes, combs, and ribbons that I placed in a hole of a tree on the school grounds.

Where's the Harwin Movie House where we went to see our first picture with Gene Autry?

Visiting Barrington in 1984

ACKNOWLEDGEMENTS

———

I wish to acknowledge some of the people who so graciously shared with my husband and gave him interviews and family narratives, diaries, and prized pictures.

Many people helped with this long project. Rosalind Mazzawi was forever supportive. She worked on early drafts with my husband and helped him to solidify his ideas and always expressed her belief in the book. I am sure my late husband would also want to express his appreciation to Leonora Ballinger, who encouraged him over the course of many years.

In numerous discussions with my husband while he was alive, it is clear to me that he would wish to mention the following people by name who shared their personal stories with him. Over many hundreds of hours, they were all unfailingly generous with their memories and personal observations.

Aunts and uncles, Ruth Dickenson, Don and Lois Mikell and Virginia Davenport shared old family photographs as well as their recollections. Cousins Kenneth Ballinger, Grace Haines, Bertha May Mainwaring, Irene Trapnell and Marguerite Core were equally forthcoming. Janet, George, and Dave Ballinger took Raymond to see his father's Cousin Dave.

Both the Raymonds died before the book was completed, but this book reflects their love of a good story and their passion for family history. Larry Ballinger was a source of encouragement, love and support for my husband, as was their brother and his wife, Leslie and Marjorie Ballinger. Will Wilkins graciously contributed his rich story. Sandy Wilkins, Marjorie Fisher, Nancy

Goggin, Jean Elizabeth Baldwin and Ashley Ballinger openly spoke with their brother, Raymie.

In our home, our shared children, Thomas, Jason, and Rebecca not only endured hearing their father's stories multiple times, but proved to be terrific listeners. I can only hope that their father's passions will inspire them.

Most of all I would like to acknowledge Jean Shuster Ballinger who opened herself to her memories and shared her lifetime of experiences with her stepson, Raymie, and who managed through guts and determination to raise nine children who are outstanding individuals.

–Babette Ballinger

To everything there is a season, and a time to every purpose under the heaven:

A time to be born, and a time to die; a time to plant, and a time to harvest that which is planted;

A time to kill, and a time to heal; a time to break down, and a time to build up;

A time to weep, and a time to laugh; a time to mourn, and a time to dance;

A time to cast away stones, and a time to gather stones together; a time to embrace, and a time to refrain from embracing

A time to get, and a time to lose, a time to keep, and a time to cast away;

A time to rend and a time to sew, a time to keep silent, and a time to speak;

A time to love, and a time to hate; a time of war, and a time of peace.

God hath made everything beautiful in his time: and set the world in our heart. I know that there is good in all, and man must rejoice, and do good in his life. Every man should eat and drink, and enjoy the good of all his labor; it is the gift of life. I know that whatsoever God doeth, it shall be forever.

All go unto one place; all are of the dust, and all turn to dust again.

The spirit of man goes upward. I perceive that there is nothing better, than that a man should rejoice in his own works; for that is his portion.

From Ecclesiastics 3

HISTORICAL NOTES

Human Nature, being what it is, is nothing if not consistent.

The first colony on the east bank of the Delaware was established at or near Gloucester Point around 1623. The fort was destroyed by the Indians but repaired again and occupied by the Dutch in 1639. In 1643 the Swedes erected Fort Elsinborg four miles below Salem Creek and subsequently purchased vast tracts from the Indians and began to settle in clusters of farmsteads that were reliant on the river.

An English colony settled near Salem in 1641 (sixty people), and was driven away by the Swedes and Dutch.

Charles II, King of England, seized New York, New Jersey, and all the Dutch possessions in America and on March 12, 1664, King Charles II, in an act of nepotism, granted his brother, James, the Duke of York, a patent for title to property in North America including all the territory between the Connecticut River and the Delaware Bay.

On June 24, 1664, James granted the land to Lord John Berkeley and Sir George Carteret. The Duke owed a favor to Lord Berkeley and Sir Carteret for their loyalty in the war against Cromwell and for defending the Stuart line. Additionally he needed money, so he sold his grant for the sum of ten thousand pounds from each man. Geographically, there was water on almost all sides with rivers and potential harbors situated very close to the sea. Since Carteret had defended the island of Jersey off the French coast he was given the east half of New Jersey and Berkeley the west. It was divided into East and West Jersey by a line drawn from Little Egg Harbor to the mouth of the Lehigh River.

On March 18, 1674, Lord Berkeley sold his half share to two English Quakers, Edward Byllnge and John Fenwick. Byllnge (Byllinge) and Berkeley had obtained indirect access to ongoing merchant ships going to the New World. Fenwick and Byllnge had a dual motive in making such a large investment in a largely unknown and distant land. First and foremost was profit. Second, probably a distant second, was the goal of establishing a refuge for English Quakers. The territory they were buying was envisioned by them and their fellow Quaker brethren as a colony with cheap and plentiful land free of religious persecution and the morally corrupting influences encountered in England.

Edward Byllnge had envisioned all this without paying off old debts. Subsequently Edward provided most of the financial backing, but as he was in the midst of bankruptcy, he arranged for his friend and purser, John Fenwick, to front the transaction on his behalf.

Because of the bankruptcy, Byllnge was forced to allow the deeds to be made in Fenwick's name, and then (of course) Fenwick refused to transfer them back to Byllnge. At this point, William Penn was appointed to arbitrate the dispute. Fenwick received ten percent and the trustees established a safe haven for Quakers and sold the balance of the land as shares in the colony. Of the one hundred twenty purchasers in total, thirty-two individuals acquired one or more full shares. Real estate speculators outnumbered potential colonists. Only twenty-five percent of the purchasers actually settled in West Jersey. Most who bought shares in the colony were from the wealthiest stratum of the Society of Friends. The first settlers for West New Jersey arrived in the ship Griffith (Griffin) of London in 1675 and landed near Salem. The ship's passengers included John Fenwick. They were creditors of Byllinge and received as their pay some of the parts. The other eight commissioners came later on the *Kent*.

The initial purchasers of Byllnge's shares did not arrive in the province until August of 1677.

Among those who purchased land on the river were two companies of Friends, one from London and the other from Yorkshire. In the summer of 1677 they came on the *Kent* with two hundred thirty other immigrants and landed at the site of New Castle, Delaware, August 16. The settlers found temporary shelter at Raccoon Creek in huts erected by the Swedes and the commissioners proceeded to the site of New Beverley (Bridlington /Burlington) and purchased land from the Indians between the Assunpink and Oldman's Creek for a few guns, petticoats, hoes, etc.

The Yorkshire commissioners took the upper tract and the London commissioners the lower half but they joined in settling in Burlington for mutual defense. The main street running back from the river was made the dividing line, the Yorkshire men on the east and the Londoners on the west. The market house was located in the middle. Ten lots of nine acres each were laid out for the *Kent's* arrival.

The ship's passengers included William Clayton, Thomas Eves, Thomas Harding, Benjamin Hewling, and John Woolston. The first house was a frame built by John Woolston. The first Friends meeting was held there around 1678. When the Friends settled in Burlington there were Dutchmen who had been there first. The jurisdiction of the courts of Delaware was extended into West Jersey on the grounds that the sovereignty did not pass to Carteret and Berkley when they purchased the land from the Duke of York.

Other boats arrived. The fly boat *Martha* from Hull arrived October 15, 1677, with families who settled on the Yorkshire purchase. Among them were Thomas Wright, John Lyman, Thomas Schooley, Thomas Hooten, and the families of Robert Stacy and Samuel Odas.

The *Greyhound* landed at Swedes Church (Philadelphia) in October, 1777, and then added additional landings in Virginia. The *Willing Mind* or *Willing Maid* came in November 1677.

The *Shield* of Hull under Captain Charles Towes sailed from Stockton, England and arrived November tenth, 1678. The *Shield* was the first English vessel that traveled up the Delaware River as high as Burlington, New Jersey. A gale of wind brought her upriver and the ship had to tack back and forth because of the headwinds, and got tangled in overhanging trees at Coaquanock, the place that is now Philadelphia. They did not have permission to disembark there, so they went across the river and during the night the ship was blown to shore. Legend has it that it was so cold that overnight the river froze. The next morning the passengers walked ashore on the ice. The passengers settled at Burlington, Salem, and other points on the river. A few found their way into Bucks County. This included the families of John and Thomas Lambert, Thomas Revel, Mahon Stacy, Thomas Budd, Abraham Hewlings, William Hewlings, Thomas Kirby and others. Mahon Stacy built the first gristmill at Trenton. Burlington became the third largest port in the New Country. The group of Friends on the ship was in part from the Nottinghamshire Friends Society.

The *Success* made two voyages and also exchanged emigrants from Virginia to Salem. The *Willing Mind* returned and The *Content* sailed to the New Country.

By the end of 1678 it was estimated that William Penn had been the means of sending some eight hundred settlers to this country, mostly Friends.

English immigrants continued to arrive on the west bank of the Delaware. William Biles arrived from county Dorset. He was a man of influence and a leader, and Governor Evans sued him for slander for saying, "He is but a boy. He is not fit to be our governor. We'll kick him out." Governor Evans recovered three hundred pounds, but failed to collect them. He did however catch up with Biles in Philadelphia and imprisoned him for one month!! Governor Evans claimed that "Biles had very much been influenced by the debauchery of Bucks county, in which there is now scarce any one man of worth left."

By 1679, the English houses on the River were built of clapboard nailed onto a frame, but you could stick a finger through the boards. The best people plastered them with clay. The Swedes' homes were block-like log cabins. The Friends in Burlington were considered the most worldly of men in deportment and conversation.

The progenitor of the Ballinger family in America was Henry (Henri) Ballinger (De La Ballinger) born around 1660, of Nailsworth, Gloucestershire, England. He came to America in 1678 on the *Kent, Martha*, or the *Shield*, and settled in Evesham Township around Burlington, West Jersey. On November 4, 1684, he was married in a Friends ceremony to Mary Harding, the daughter of Thomas and Eleanor Harding who had arrived on the *Kent*. Henry died on April 10, 1733, at the age of 74.

Initially, the Ballingers were established in Poitou, Pommel, and Picardie, France and were ship builders and French Huguenots. There are early records of Ballingers in Gloucestershire since the middle of the sixteenth century.

The New Jersey Archives show the records of the New Jersey Assembly in 1697. Among them is listed John Callinger who is plainly Ballinger. The Archives also show an agreement by the Quaker members of the House of Representatives to uphold the King signed by forty Quakers including Henry Callinger (Ballinger). Henry Ballinger was also appointed special tax collector for Evesham in May, 1701.

Henry and Mary had ten children. Josiah and Joseph were given 1200 acres of land by their Father, but they still left and went to Maryland, and later to Frederick County, Virginia. Thomas and Amariah stayed in Salem County. Henry II was a wanderer who crossed into North Carolina. He and another Friend (Hunt) gave the ground on which the Old Meeting House was built and where Guilford College now stands. They later moved to Ohio because of their feelings against slavery.

When there is no definitive history, family tradition has a way of becoming history, and obscuring or replacing those facts that are unknown. With the onset of the internet and ancestry sites, it is very easy for supposition to become fact. There are many different undocumented scenarios for the origin of the Ballinger family prior to coming to America.

Joseph Ballinger during the Civil War tells that he met a southern soldier, a prisoner of war taken by the Federals, named Ballinger who stated that the original family name was De La Ballinger. He claimed that there were five brothers in France. One brother was burned at the stake, one was hanged, and three escaped during the religious persecution of the French Huguenots and they came to America by way of Holland and England, one to New Jersey, one to Pennsylvania, and one to Virginia.

Eves Bellangee was born around 1674, and it is said that he came from the province of Poitou-Poiters, Vienne, Poitou-Charentes, France. Emigrating first to Gloucestershire and then to America. I believe his father was Theophilus Bellangee who was born in Poiters, France, and who was shot during the dragonades of Louis XIV. Theophilus's wife and children fled to the caves and were able to escape to England. Possibly Henry and Eves were cousins. Eves, a weaver, and Christian de la Plaine, who was the daughter of Nicholas de la Plaine and his wife, Rachel Cresson, both French Huguenots of New York, were married at the Friends Meeting House in Philadelphia in 1697. The minutes state that they produced a certificate from Virginia. Eves Bellinger and his wife owned land in Salem County on Oldman's Creek in 1701, later selling it and settling in Little Egg Harbor. Eves died there in 1720.

Historical records state that there was a James Bellangee in 1696 who owned 262 acres of land in Evesham. This would be Eves' son.

Edmund Ballinger (Ballenger) was born in 1657 in Berkampsted, Suffolk, England. He died in 1708 on James Island, Charleston, South Carolina. Edmund married Sarah Cartwright on January 20, 1656 in Wolstanton, Staffordshire, England. Their children's names were Thomas, Elizabeth, Ann, William, Edmund, and Mary. I have not found a relationship, but these are the same names of Henry's children. There is a record of an Edmund Ballinger in Cheltenham, England living in the same area that Henry lived in and at the same time.

Many of the ships sailed first from Hull in Yorkshire to New Castle and Burlington and then went on to Virginia and South Carolina where free land had been promised to Lutherans and Quakers.

Joseph English testified that Henry Ballinger was a member of the Nailsworth Meeting, Gloucestershire, England, as were many of the Evesham Quakers.

–Babette Ballinger

Evesham History

Burlington County was first home to the native Lenni-Lenape peoples, and their ancestors who lived in the modern day states of Delaware, New Jersey, New York and Pennsylvania over a period of 12,000 years (to the present day). The native name for the Lenape homeland was Lenepehoking, meaning land of the Lenape.

The present settlement of Burlington City was founded around 1677 by Quaker colonists from Yorkshire and the "home counties" of England. The name Burlington was taken from Burlington Quay adjacent to Bridlington, Yorkshire. Many Burlington colonists sailed to the New World from Burlington Quay.

Evesham was named after Evesham, England. Originally, Evesham included the present day township of Hainesport, Mount Laurel, Shamong, Lumberton and Washington. In 1692, it was incorporated as a township. The town is also known as Marlton, since the beginning of the 19th century.

The Homestead

William Evans I (1641-1688) was the direct progenitor of the Evesham Evans Family and a carpenter by trade. He was born in South Newton, Oxfordshire, England and lived in Oxon, Oxfordshire and immigrated to this country, probably on the vessel *Kent* in 1677. He later returned with his sons, Thomas I and William II and his wife Jane Hodges (1643-1697) around 1682. They landed at the town of Burlington and settled in the area now known as Willingboro on the Rancocas Creek.

William's son, William Evans II (1660-1728), married Elizabeth Hanke (1670-1745) and in 1688 he purchased a tract of land on the mount at Mount Laurel where his family had initially lived in a cave during the winter while they were building their first home. On August 2, 1701, William Evans II purchased a 1,000 acre tract about two miles east of Marlton in Evesham Township for the sum of 120 pounds from Margaret Cooke. This was one of the original land parcels sold by Edward Byllinge. The friendly Lenni-Lenape Indians were living on a portion of the tract at the time of the purchase. William negotiated a deed with the resident chief, King Himeson. The deed is signed by the chief and two other Indians using their peculiar markings and symbols. Later that year on December 1, 1701 he purchased an additional 50 acres from Joshua Humphries making his total holdings 1,050 acres.

In 1702 William II sold 100 acres to William Troth. On October 8, 1703 he gave the remaining 950 acres to his son, Thomas Evans II (1693-1783) as a "love" gift. Thomas II was the first Evans generation born in America. Thomas subdivided the land and gave his sons the following: William Evans 200 acres, and Isaac Evans 180 acres, Jacob Evans 250 acres, Nathan Evans, 230 acres, and Caleb Evans, 241 acres.

Thomas II married Esther Haines in 1715, and they made their home at the location of the Evans house on the present Indian Springs Golf Course. Thomas and Esther had twelve children, two dying in infancy. The plantation was eventually divided among his five sons with William Evans III (1716-1761) his eldest son married to Sarah Roberts (1720-1784), receiving 200 acres as a "love" gift, while the other sons purchased their tracts at a later date.

The section given to William III corresponds to a portion of the Bowker/Koppenhaver farm, the Ben Roberts Farm, and the dairy later owned by Joseph Evans. The older part of the Bower/Koppenhaver house was a part of the first house built for William III around 1739.

William III's brother, Jacob Evans (1725-1791), married Rachel Eldridge (1725-1799), and purchased the homestead and all of the acreage of the present Indian Springs Golf Club known as the Evans-Ballinger Homestead on June 30, 1763.

Jacob's son, Thomas Evans III (1752-1813) changed the spelling of the name from Evans to Evens, and married Mary Eves (1755-1834), the daughter of Joseph and Rebecca Haines Eves. They added their initials (T and E to the main chimney and built most of the "updated" Homestead house designed by Thomas Evans and Thomas Ballinger where the Ballingers lived in 1785.

Mary Eves and Lettice Eves were sisters. Thomas Evens/Evans III, Mary's husband and Joseph Evans, Lettice's husband, were first cousins. Joseph Evans was read out of Friends Meeting because he bought his daughter an organ. Thomas was so upset and disgraced by his cousin that he changed the spelling of his name to Evens from Evans (so goes the story).

The original part of the structure was made of sandstone and was built around 1710. The brick addition was made around 1785 by Thomas and Mary. Thomas Evans was the architect and builder who with Thomas Ballinger III (1743-1820) built seven brick homes in the area, among them the Homestead and the Thomas Ballinger Farm (T and S for Thomas Ballinger and Susannah Dudley) which is now the Beagle Club.

Thomas III and Mary had five children, Thomas IV (1752-1813), Elizabeth, Sarah, Martha and Mary. Thomas III's will left the farm and the Homestead to his son and namesake, Thomas IV (1772-1869) with the provision that his wife, Mary Eves Evans, should have full use of certain rooms in the house for herself and her daughters. At some time Mary decided that it would be best for her to move back to her family home (the Joseph Eves estate across the road) that was awarded to her when her father died. Mary died April 3, 1835 and left the Eves farm to her three daughters who had never married. The fourth daughter, Sarah, married Samuel Roberts.

Thomas Evans/Evens IV (1772-1869) married Sarah Burrough (1784-1858), Sally B's Grandmother. When Thomas IV died he left the Homestead to his son and namesake, Thomas Evans V, (1819-1898) who married Abigal Roberts, (1825-1886). They had several children, among them Rachel Evans who married Levi T. Ballinger.

Sally Evans (Evens) Burroughs married David Thomas Ballinger December 18, 1876. Shortly thereafter David T and Sally B purchased the Homestead from her uncle, Thomas Evans V and aunt, Abigal Roberts Evans when they decided to quit farming and move to town.

David Thomas (David T) Ballinger sold the Homestead to his youngest son, Raymond Lippincott Ballinger (Pop) around 1917.

Raymond Evans Ballinger Sr. (Dad), his only son, purchased the Homestead around 1948.

Raymond Ballinger sold the Homestead to the Jaggards in 1952.

The Homestead is currently the Evesham Township Cultural Center on the Indian Springs Golf Course on Elmwood Road. The barns built by David T were allowed to deteriorate and then were demolished.

Copy of the Indenture

This Indenture made ye six day of ye eighth month in the year of our Lord one thousand seven hundred and one between Himeson being an Indian King of ye one part and William Evans of ye county of Burlington and province of West Jersey of ye other part.

Witnesseth that the said Himeson for and in consideration of five pounds of currant pay within the province of West Jersey aforesaid to him in hand paid before ye sealing and delivering of these presents, ye receipt thereof he said Indian doth hereby acknowledge and acquit and release ye said William Evans, his heirs and assigns fore ever by these presents hath granted, bargained, sold, aliened, enfoeffed and confirmed and these presents (etc.) unto the said William Evans, his heirs and assigns forever all that tract of land situated in West Jersey upon ye branches of Ancokus Creek which was surveyed unto Walter Newberry, it being one thousand acres TO HAVE AND TO HOLD ye said thousand acres of land and promises with all the grass and trees for ever there growing unto said William Evans, his heirs and assigns forevermore.

Witness whereof ye said Indian first above named to this present Indenture hath you put his hand and seal ye day and year first above written.

REFERENCES

Many of the works cited below are out of print and available in facsimile, on-demand editions. Others were privately printed and are available in a limited number of research libraries.

Bell, James P., *The Lives of Our English Ancestors*

Boyer, Carl, *Ship Passenger Lists: NY and NJ (1600-1825)*, Heritage Books, Westminster, MD

Fernow, Berthold, *Calendar of Wills*, Genealogical Publishing Company, Inc., Baltimore, 1976.

Harvey, Lanson B, *The Ballinger Family 1660-1900*

Hinshaw, William Hade, *Encyclopedia of American Quaker Genealogy Volume I*

Genealogical Publishing Company, Baltimore, 1991.

Hinshaw, William Hade and Marshall, Thomas Worth, *Encyclopedia of American Quaker Genealogy, Volume II*. Containing every item of genealogical value found in all records and minutes (known to be in existence) of four of the oldest monthly meetings which ever belonged to the Philadelphia Yearly Meeting. Edwards Brothers Inc., Ann Arbor MI, 1940.

Historical Society of Moorestown, Moorestown *and Her Neighbors, 1973*

Hull, William, William *Penn and the Dutch Quaker Migration*, Keesinger Publishers, 2011 (On demand facsimile edition)

Koehler, Albert F., *The Huguenots or Early French in New Jersey*. Clearfield Publishing, Bloomfield, New Jersey, 2007 (On-demand, facsimile edition)

Myers, Albert C., Quaker *Arrivals at Philadelphia*, Bentley Enterprises. 2012. (On-demand, facsimile edition)

Reeves, Emma Barrett, *Three Centuries of Ballingers in America* Texian Press, San Antonio, TX, 1977

Schermerhorn, William E., *The History of Burlington, New Jersey From The Early European Arrivals in the Delaware to the Quarter Millennial Anniversary, in 1927, of the Settlement by English Quakers in 1677*, Enterprise Publishing, Burlington, NJ 1927

Smith, Frank, The *Encyclopedia of Quakers in America*-two volumes

Sheppard, Walter Lee Jr. *Passengers and Ships Prior to 1684*. Volume I of Penn's Colony: Genealogical and Historical Materials Relating to the Settlement of Pennsylvania Heritage Books Inc., Berwyn Heights, MD., 2006

Tepper, Michael *Immigrants to the Middle Colonies:* A Consolidation of Ship Passenger Lists and Associated Data from the New York Genealogical and Biographical Record

Genealogical Pub Co, Baltimore, Maryland, 1979.

Virkus, Frederick Adams, editor, *Immigrant Ancestors*. A List of 2,500 Immigrants to America Before 1750, Genealogical Publishing Co, Baltimore, 1965, revised edition, 1976.

ABOUT THE AUTHORS

RAYMOND EVANS BALLINGER was born in Mount Holly, New Jersey and grew up in Marlton, New Jersey and Culpeper, Virginia. He worked in New York City as an actor, director, and teacher. He built and was the creative director for the Rhinebeck Summer Theatre in Rhinebeck, New York. He moved to Yorktown Heights, New York where he taught acting and wrote *Earthbound*. Ballinger died in July of 2005 at the age of sixty-seven.

BABETTE BALLINGER was born in New York City and grew up in Memphis, Tennessee. She graduated from Washington University in St. Louis with a degree in Fine Arts. She worked as a fashion designer in New York City, where she owned a knitwear company. Babette was married to actor-writer Raymond Ballinger for twenty-three years. She felt that *Earthbound* was such an important story of an American Family and pertinent to today's changing environment that she was compelled to complete the work of her late husband. She currently lives with her three dogs in Yorktown Heights, New York.

Made in the USA
Charleston, SC
14 October 2013